How to Pass
Business Practice

THIS LEVEL

How to Pass
Business Practice

THIRD LEVEL

Stephen Jakubowski
MSc (Econ) BEd (Hons) Cert Ed

London Chamber of Commerce and Industry Examinations Board
Athena House
112 Station Road
Sidcup
Kent DA15 7BJ
United Kingdom

First published 1999

Reprinted with corrections 2000

© LCCI CET 1999

British Library Cataloguing-in-Publication Data
Jakubowski, Stephen
 How to pass business practice, third level
 1. Business – Examinations – Study guides
 1. Title
 650

ISBN 1 86247 080 4

All rights reserved; no part of this publication may be reproduced, stored in a retrieval system, or transmitted in any form or by any means, electronic, mechanical, photocopying, recording, or otherwise without the prior written permission of the Publisher. This book may not be lent, resold, hired out, or otherwise disposed of by way of trade in any form of binding or cover, other than that in which it is published, without the prior consent of the Publisher.

This is the only book endorsed by LCCIEB for use by students of this LCCIEB examination subject at this level. No other book is endorsed by LCCIEB for this subject at this level.

10 9 8 7 6 5 4 3 2

Typeset by Regent Typesetting, London
Printed in Great Britain by Henry Ling Ltd,
at the Dorset Press, Dorchester, Dorset.

Contents

	Page
Lists of figures and tables	*vii*
About the author	*ix*
Acknowledgements	*ix*
Introduction	1

Part 1: Influences on business activity — 3
1. An introduction to the business environment — 5
2. The influence of the marketplace — 25
3. The influence of the business environment on the size of firms — 39
4. The influence of financial services — 57
5. The influence of the government on the business environment — 77

Part 2: The functions and organization of the business — 101
6. The internal organization of the business — 103
7. The main groups involved in business activities — 126

Part 3: Business management — 143
8. Business planning — 145
9. Business finance — 162

Part 4: Personal contribution to business effectiveness — 183
10. Strategies for improving business performance — 185
11. Individuals, teams and business performance — 204

Part 5: Business values and culture — 219
12. Business culture — 221
13. Quality systems — 235

Contents

Part 6: Communication in business — 249

14 Business communication — 251

15 Communication systems and business performance — 271

16 Information technology in the business environment — 292

Appendix 1: Examination Questions and Model Answers — *311*

Appendix 2: Advice for students taking LCCIEB examinations — *339*

Index — *342*

Figures and tables

Figures
		Page
1.1	A simple trading cycle	16
2.1	The demand schedule	27
2.2	Shifts in the demand schedule	27
2.3	The supply schedule	29
2.4	The equilibrium price	30
2.5	Changes in market conditions	30
5.1	Relationship between economic growth, national income and the standard of living	89
5.2	Relationship between inflation, international trade and unemployment	90
6.1	Simplified version of the production process	104
6.2	The production process and the trading cycle	105
6.3	Simple organization chart of Teletech Ltd	115
6.4	Detailed organization chart of Teletech Ltd	115
6.5	Organization of the Finance Department of Teletech Ltd	116
6.6	The relationship between the main functional areas, specialization and internal economies of scale	117
8.1	The main components of a business plan	154
9.1	Fixed costs	174
9.2	Variable costs	175
9.3	Total costs	175
9.4	Total revenue	175
9.5	Break-even chart	176
14.1	Vertical and horizontal communication routes	257
15.1	The product life cycle	281
16.1	Processing a sales order	297

Tables
3.1	The advantages associated with internal economies of scale	43
3.2	Total costs and output	44
5.1	The impact of inflation on key groups within the economy	81
5.2	Comparison of national income between 2 countries	82
5.3	Comparison of the per capita national income between 2 countries	82
5.4	Characteristics of the different types of unemployment	84
8.1	Key planning areas	148
8.2	The relationship between the strategic plan, the operational plan and the administrative plan	156

Figures and tables

		Page
9.1	Profit and loss account showing how expenses reduce the gross profit	169
9.2	Profit and loss account showing how profits are apportioned	169
10.1	Rights, duties and responsibilities of the employee and the employer	206
10.2	Advantages of staff appraisal	207
12.1	Creating a corporate image/corporate identity	226
12.2	Management theories and their practical implications	228
14.1	Costs of producing a business report	262
14.2	Purchasing communication equipment	263
15.1	Range of information requirements of the main functional areas	274
15.2	Planning the introduction of e-mail	285
16.1	Summary of the main software applications	294
16.2	The impact and benefits of a new computer network	303

About the author

Stephen Jakubowski has held both Senior and Principal Lectureships in Business Studies and was a Head of Business and Secretarial Studies Department for 6 years.

He is currently Head of Faculty of Business and Service Industry Studies at Enfield College, North London.

His work for the LCCIEB encompasses External Verification duties for Training and Development and the Assessors and Verifiers Awards, which followed on from his previous appointment as a Regional Verifier for the Business Administration VQ awards.

He has been a Chief Examiner with the LCCIEB for 10 years and has worked closely on the development of the Business Practice examinations at Second, Third, and Fourth Levels. His other examination duties involve moderating a component of the LCCIEB's Executive Diploma in Business Accounting.

He has spent time in The Netherlands, Denmark, Spain, and Italy working with educationalists engaged in curriculum development projects and associated training initiatives.

Acknowledgements

My thanks are due to:

Debbie Lewis for her help in the production of this text.

Barry Mort, LCCIEB Moderator, for his help and guidance in reading the draft copy of the text.

Those business organizations that have been referred to in the text, including the Merseyside Police, the *Observer*, Vega plc, Heal's of London, British Telecommunications plc, cafédirect ltd, the *Guardian*, and the European Union Jobrotation programme.

Finally to my wife, Sylvia, and our family, for their enduring patience whilst the book was being written.

Introduction

The purpose of this book is to provide candidates of the LCCIEB's Third Level Business Practice examination with the necessary knowledge, understanding and skills to enable them to complete their programme of study successfully.

The book is divided into six sections, each of which follows the syllabus for the Third Level Business Practice examination:

1. influences on business activity
2. the functions and organization of business
3. business management
4. personal contribution to business effectiveness
5. business values and culture
6. communications in business.

Each section contains:

- a series of chapters which identify the specific areas covered by the syllabus;
- a number of activities which provide the opportunity for the student to apply knowledge of Business Practice in practical settings;
- research activities which show how the principles of Business Practice are applied in the business environment;
- a series of short questions to test factual recall of key elements of each chapter;
- revision exercises which allow the student to consider in more detail the main points developed in each chapter.

In the Appendix to the book there are model answers based upon actual examination questions which will show the approach which should be adopted when preparing for the final examination.

Part 1
Influences on business activity

1

An introduction to the business environment

> **After carefully studying this chapter, you should be able to:**
>
> 1 *identify the purpose of business organizations;*
>
> 2 *distinguish between the purposes of the public and private sectors;*
>
> 3 *describe the nature of business activity and the importance of opportunity cost.*

> **Extended Syllabus references**
>
> 1.1 Identify the purposes of business organizations:
>   - 1.1.1 profit
>   - 1.1.2 growth
>   - 1.1.3 innovation
>   - 1.1.4 recognition
>   - 1.1.5 satisfaction of consumer/market demand
>   - 1.1.6 production
>   - 1.1.7 combining resources to meet market demand
> 1.2 Describe the differences between the public and private sectors
> 1.3 Describe what is meant by business activity and the importance of opportunity cost

The purpose of this chapter is to provide an overview of the functions and activities which are undertaken by business organizations operating in the business environment. The chapter will be a useful introduction to the rest of our study of Business Practice since it will introduce a number of important business terms referred to throughout the book and provide the basis upon which further reading and research activities can be undertaken.

The purpose of business organizations and their common features

One of the distinguishing features of a developed society is the existence of organizations. We have only to consider the range of activities with which we are involved in our own lives to see how much we are influenced by organizations. Schools, colleges, universities, hospitals, libraries and sports clubs are just a few of the organizations with which we may come into contact on a day-to-day basis. In this book we are going to consider a range of organizations which come under a broad category referred to as business organizations.

All organizations exhibit a number of common features which include:

- a defined structure within which activity takes place;
- a group of people who collectively engage in activity which contributes to the stated goals of the organization;
- specialized roles and functions performed by members of the organization;
- a set of rules within which the organization operates;
- an organizational culture which incorporates the values and ethos of the organization;
- communication channels and networks which enable decisions to be taken;
- channels of communication which link the organization to other organizations and individuals.

Activity

Choose an organization with which you are familiar, perhaps your school, college or workplace, and give examples which show some of the common features of organizations.

Our study of business organizations will include all these features in order to build up a comprehensive picture of the business environment.

The public and private sectors

In most developed countries, we can distinguish two parts or *sectors* of the economy. In the *public sector,* the *government* directs economic activity and is responsible for the production of goods and services on behalf of the public. In the *private sector*, on the other hand, goods and services are produced by *private individuals* or *companies*.

Most countries have both public and private sectors, but in some countries the government owns most of the businesses and directs their activities, while in other countries most of the businesses are privately owned and directed.

In many countries over the last decade a number of government or state-controlled organizations have passed into the hands of private individuals or institutions. This policy of privatization is discussed in more detail in Chapter 2, but for now we may note that, in most countries, both the size and importance of the private sector have increased.

We can now move on to describe the main kinds of organization involved in economic activity in each sector.

The private sector

For the purpose of our study, we will consider *three* business organizations within the private sector – *sole traders, partnerships* and *limited companies*. We shall look at each business organization in turn to discover their essential characteristics in terms of their ownership, finance, legal status, and the distribution of profits or the responsibility for losses.

Sole traders

Sole traders, or *sole proprietors* as they are sometimes called, are the simplest form of business unit found within the private sector of the economy. As the name implies, the sole trader is owned and controlled by *one* person who provides the capital, takes responsibility for the risks inherent in the private sector and, as a result, benefits from receiving all the profits generated as a result of business activity. However, it should also be noted that the owners of such organizations are also responsible for any losses which may result from business activities.

It is this last point which is particularly significant for the sole trader since, in legal terms, the owner of the business is personally responsible for all the debts of the business – a legal principle known as *unlimited liability*. In essence this means that sole traders can lose their personal possessions which may have to be sold in order to pay off business debts.

This being said, many people choose to accept this risk and attempt to start their own business. There are many examples of well-known companies, some with international reputations, whose roots can be found in humble beginnings as small sole traders.

Given the simple nature of this type of business organization, there are relatively few legal formalities to consider and, in general terms, finance is likely to be raised directly from the owner's own financial resources. Additional finance can also be obtained from commercial banks or, indirectly, from the trading activities in which the business is engaged. Friends and relatives may also be willing to assist those who are seeking to start their own businesses.

Influences on business activity

There is no doubt that there are a number of advantages which accrue to the sole trader:

- independence and being your own boss;
- easy to set up;
- decisions can be made quickly and are straightforward to administer;
- the business can react quickly to changes in market conditions;
- the owner is likely to have personal contact with the customers, clients, and suppliers;
- the successful sole trader can look forward to receiving all the profits generated by the business;
- depending on the type of business activity in which the business is engaged, it may not require much capital to set up the business.

Given these advantages, it is not surprising to find many examples of this type of business organization in the *service sector* of the economy, including such activities as hairdressing, small retail outlets, newsagents, and market traders.

Although there are a number of benefits which may be experienced by the sole trader, we should also note the *disadvantages* associated with the sole trader as a form of business organization:

- unlimited liability;
- the owner may have to work long hours, which may be unsociable and disruptive;
- the business may experience difficulties in obtaining additional funds to finance expansion;
- the owner may have to be a 'jack of all trades' and take responsibility for all aspects of business activity;
- the business may not be able to benefit from the advantages usually associated with bigger organizations such as discounts for bulk purchases and the employment of specialist staff.

Partnerships

The logical development for the sole trader seeking to obtain additional finance is to engage with other people who are willing to join in a partnership for the benefit of all concerned. As the result of establishing a partnership, more resources may become available to finance development, and expansion. Additionally, the partners may bring with them a range of specialized skills, interests, experience, and qualifications which can be utilized by the business organization. One partner, for example, may concentrate on marketing, another may specialize in financial matters, whilst a further partner may take a special interest in designing new products.

Inevitably, the more complex nature of partnerships requires more legal formalities. In the UK, 2 Acts of Parliament determine the legal status of partnerships – the *Partnership Act, 1890,* and the *Partnership Act, 1907*.

The 1890 Partnership Act lays down that the maximum number of partners is limited to 20 people. This number can be exceeded in solicitors' and accountants' practices, but in banking the number of partners is restricted to 10 people. Normally, all partners accept unlimited liability for the debts of the partnership. This can have serious implications, since the activities of any one of the partners are legally binding upon all other partners. It follows, therefore, that communications and business relationships between all the partners must be very good if the partnership is to be successful. In essence, the element of trust in a partnership is of paramount importance.

To an extent, the partners can reduce some of the risks of forming a partnership by drawing up a *deed of partnership*. Although it is not a legal requirement, the deed of partnership will establish the formal relationship between the partners. For example, the partners may agree within the deed of partnership that profits will be distributed to each partner on the basis of the amount of capital each has contributed to the business – the higher the proportion of capital contributed, the bigger the share of the profits. Such an agreement is a useful document if disputes occur amongst the partners.

Additional legal protection is available under the 1907 Partnership Act, which allows for some partners to be identified as enjoying *limited liability*. This is a significant advantage, since the partners with limited liability can invest capital in the business, but, if financial difficulties are experienced by the partnership, their liability is limited to the amount of capital they have invested. Unlike ordinary members of the partnership, partners who enjoy limited liability will not have to sell off their personal possessions in the event of business failure. It should be noted, however, that under the 1907 Partnership Act at least one of the partners must accept unlimited liability, and also that those partners who enjoy limited liability cannot take an active role in the day-to-day management of the partnership. If it is found that partners with limited liability are engaging in such activities they are liable to lose the protection afforded to them as limited partners.

The advantages of partnerships as a form of business organization can therefore be broadly summarized as follows:

- opportunity to get more funds for the business;
- opportunity for partners to specialize in certain aspects of business functions and activities;
- partners can share the burden of responsibility in operating the business, thus allowing themselves more time for social and recreational activities;
- relatively easy to establish;
- the drawing up of a deed of partnership can help to avoid disputes between partners;
- some partners may be able to benefit from limited liability.

On the other hand, we need to be aware of the disadvantages of this form of business organization:

- existence of unlimited liability;
- capital for future expansion may be limited by the number of partners engaged in the business;
- disputes may arise amongst the partners;

- the partnership ceases to exist upon the death of one of the partners, the resignation of one of the partners, or if one of the partners is declared bankrupt.

Limited companies

Although sole traders and partnerships may be the most numerous forms of business organization in the private sector of the UK economy, by far the most important and influential of all business organizations are *joint stock companies* or, as they are more commonly called, *limited companies*.

There are a number of features of limited companies which distinguish them from other forms of business organization:

- Limited companies are owned by *shareholders*. These shareholders provide capital to the company but do not necessarily take an active part in the day-to-day management of the organization.

- Shareholders will receive a share of the profits distributed by the limited company on the basis of the number of shares they have purchased – the greater the number of shares held, the larger the proportion of the profits received by an individual shareholder.

- All shareholders in a limited company enjoy *limited liability* which means that, in the event of business failure, they will only lose the amount of money they have invested in the company. Thus, although purchasing shares in a company can be viewed as a risk, the risk does not include the shareholder's personal possessions.

- A limited company is viewed, in legal terms, as an entity in its own right which can sue or be sued. This also confers benefits on the owners of the company, since they will not be liable personally in the event of legal action which may be taken by the company's employees, customers, clients or suppliers.

- It follows from the previous point that the limited company will continue to exist even if shareholders die or sell their shares to a third party.

- A limited company must, by law, include the word 'Limited' or 'Ltd' in its official name in order to inform its customers, clients, and suppliers that the owners enjoy limited liability. If the company failed, the company's creditors (those individuals or other companies who are owed money by the company) might not receive all that is owed to them, since there might be insufficient financial reserves to cover all the business debts.

- The board of directors may appoint specialized managers (who need not be shareholders or directors themselves) to run the company from day to day.

- The responsibility for the overall direction of the business organization rests with the board of directors, which is elected by the shareholders.

Limited companies in the UK must, by law, submit certain documents to the Registrar of Joint Stock Companies. The most important of these documents are the

Memorandum of Association and the *Articles of Association*. The Memorandum of Association provides details such as the name of the company, the address of its head office, a statement to the effect that the company enjoys the benefits of limited liability, the amount of share capital and how this is divided up (for example, £500,000 divided into 500,000 £1 ordinary shares), and the 'objects' of the company, in other words, a broad description of the company's main business activities. The Articles of Association, on the other hand, are, in effect, the *internal rules* of the company. This document will detail the rights of the shareholders, the powers and responsibilities of company directors, and the conduct of meetings.

The above documents must be submitted to the Registrar of Joint Stock Companies before a limited company can begin trading. Once the Registrar's office considers that the company has met the legal requirements, a *Certificate of Incorporation* will be issued. The company may then commence its operations.

Activity

Choose 2 companies which are engaged in different types of trading activities and are quoted on one of the international stock exchanges (London, New York, Hong Kong, etc). For example, you might decide to choose a bank and a manufacturing company.

Over the period of your study of Business Practice, monitor the prices of the shares of both companies. At the same time, monitor the overall changes in your chosen stock exchange's share index. Identify reasons why the value of the shares you have chosen may fluctuate over time, and identify any relationship which you see being established between the value of your chosen shares and the overall stock exchange index.

The term 'limited company' covers two main types of business organization – the *private limited company* and the *public limited company*. (This is sometimes confusing for students of business practice, since a *public* limited company is actually located in the *private* sector of the economy.)

The difference between the 2 is governed by company law. In general terms, private limited companies are usually smaller than public limited companies (PLCs) and, unlike PLCs, private limited companies cannot sell shares directly to the general public. Additionally, the sale or transfer of shares in a private limited company may be limited to new members who are 'approved' by the existing shareholders. This is not the case with PLCs, whose shares can be freely bought and sold on a stock exchange by anyone who can afford them. Thus, they are appropriately termed public limited companies, since the *public* has the opportunity to invest in them.

Influences on business activity

> **Activity**
>
> Read through the advantages and disadvantages of sole traders and partnerships listed earlier in the chapter.
>
> Now draw up your own list of what you consider to be the main advantages and disadvantages of limited companies.

The public sector

The public sector includes all activities involving the production of goods and the provision of services which are financed and controlled by central government and its agencies. Additionally, local government plays an important role in the public sector, since it is responsible for the provision of many important local public services. In the next chapter we will consider the influence of the government on the business environment and how the activities of both central and local government can influence the business organization and the environment in which it operates. In this section, however, we will concentrate upon the most important organization in the public sector, the *public corporation*, more commonly referred to as a *nationalized industry*.

As with those business organizations we described in the private sector, our description of public corporations will concentrate upon their ownership, finance, control, and the distribution of any surpluses which may be generated as a result of their trading activities.

Public corporations

Public corporations are set up by Acts of Parliament. This may involve the government taking over the whole of an industry which was previously in the private sector and owned by private shareholders. In the UK immediately after the Second World War, a number of key industries were taken over by the government, including railways, coal, steel, water, gas, and electricity. The nature of these industries provides an insight into one of the main motives underlying a policy of so-called 'nationalization'. Such industries and *public utilities*, it is argued, are too important to be left in the hands of private shareholders whose prime objective is to make a profit. It is better instead for them to be managed and controlled by the government, which is better placed to take account of the needs of all the community – even if their business activity does not result in profits or surpluses and, indeed, in some instances may actually result in a loss.

This principle of meeting the needs of all the community also applies to the funding of the public corporations. Funding is obtained from the government, which uses taxpayers' money in order to provide the public corporations with grants, subsidies or direct investment. If the public corporations generate any surpluses as a result of their trading activities, this must be used to invest in the industry, to reduce prices to the consumer, or, in some instances, to increase the salaries and wages of those employed within the industry.

The accounts of public corporations are open to public scrutiny and are monitored by Members of Parliament, who have the power to question those government ministers who have direct responsibility for specific public corporations. The ministers excercise their responsibility mainly by appointing the senior managers, who are, in turn, responsible for ensuring that the overall operations of the industry meet government plans and associated targets.

In many advanced industrialized societies, perhaps the most important change to the business environment in the last decade has been the return of a number of public corporations to the private sector of the economy, a government policy referred to as *privatization*.

Activity

Draw up a table showing the differences between public limited companies and public corporations using the following headings:

- ownership and control
- management
- finance
- distribution of profits/surpluses.

The nature of business activity and the importance of opportunity cost

So far, we have identified the features of organizations and described the main business organizations in the public and private sectors. Now we will consider the main purpose of these organizations and introduce some important terms and concepts which will set the scene for the rest of our study of Business Practice.

What is 'business activity'?

The main purpose of business organizations is to produce goods or provide a service for their customers and clients. What does the business organization need if it is to fulfil this purpose? For the purpose of our study we will highlight 4 essential

Influences on business activity

requirements of the business organization – *people, raw materials, capital,* and the *organizational skills* necessary to combine these resources together in order to produce goods and services.

Let us briefly consider each of these 4 requirements in order to appreciate the contribution they make to the activities of the business organization.

People

It seems obvious that the business organization will require people to engage in producing goods or providing the services. For the purpose of our study we need to appreciate that these people – employees, staff, managers and the like – need to possess the necessary skills, knowledge and aptitudes to enable them to make a positive contribution to the organization. The need for well-trained, qualified staff with the required specialized skills will therefore have an important influence on the success of the business organization.

Raw materials

Raw materials and other *physical resources* are also required by the business organization. For the business organization engaged in the production of goods – cars, washing machines, TVs, and the like – the importance of raw materials is easy to understand. The organization may require, amongst other things, metals, paint, wood, and plastics, which will be used in the production process. However, even those business organizations which are not engaged in the direct production of goods, and which choose instead to concentrate on the provision of services, will still require physical resources in order to enable them to meet the needs of their customers. The office environment provides a good example of such physical resources, including computer networks, fax machines, photocopiers, telephone systems, and even filing cabinets, which collectively enable the organization to provide a specific service to clients and customers. Equally, administrative staff are keenly aware of the importance of good-quality office resources if the level of administrative services is to meet quality standards.

Capital

In the business world, the term 'capital' has a number of different meanings. In this book we will consider capital to be either *physical machinery, equipment and plant* (the unit within which the production process is housed), or *financial resources* which are used by the organization to purchase new plant, machinery and equipment.

Organizational skills

In essence, a successful business organization will combine people, raw materials or physical resources and capital in such a way as to enable them to meet the needs of their customers and clients. Behind this process, however, will be those people who have specialized organizational skills and, above all else, the ideas and vision to turn their business dreams into a reality. The term 'entrepreneur' is used in business to describe the people who have these special skills, and they are central to the process we will refer to as *business activity*.

In essence, business activity is the process by which the factors described above are combined to produce goods and services, thereby satisfying consumer demand. Business activity can be contrasted with the *business environment,* which concerns the prevailing conditions within which business activity takes place.

> **Activity**
>
> Choose an organization with which you are familiar and complete the following table giving examples of each of the resources described in the previous section.
>
> | *Resources* | *Examples* |
> | --- | --- |
> | People | |
> | Capital | |
> | Raw materials and equipment | |
> | Organizational skills | |

Before we move on to look in more detail at the influences which are to be found within the business environment, we need to consider 3 other important concepts which are applied in the business world:

- the trading cycle
- specialization
- opportunity cost.

These 3 elements are vital components which are at the heart of the business activities undertaken by all those business organizations described in this chapter. Let us take each one in turn in order to discover its influence on the business environment.

Influences on business activity

The trading cycle

There are a number of specific activities which are undertaken by business organizations:

- ordering raw materials
- making payments
- producing goods
- making a profit
- receiving cash and other payments
- selling goods.

The trading cycle enables us to understand that all these activities are in fact *interrelated*, in that they show the cyclical nature of business activity. Figure 1.1 shows the essential features of a simple trading cycle which incorporates purchasing, producing, selling, and the creation of profits.

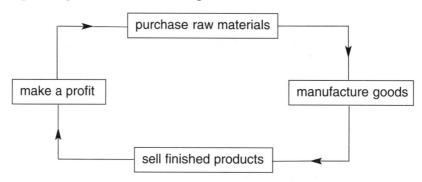

Figure 1.1 A simple trading cycle

What does the trading cycle tell us about the nature of business activity that is undertaken by business organizations? The following points should be noted:

- business activities are interrelated – the *purchase* of raw materials by one organization represents the *sale* of raw materials by another organization;
- business activity tends to be *market-driven* – business organizations will manufacture those goods which they are confident will create sales and accompanying profits;
- business activity tends to involve organizations *specializing* in different parts of the trading cycle.

> **Activity**
>
> Illustrate the trading cycle of a business organization with which you are familiar showing the specialized functions which are undertaken in each part of the trading cycle.

Introduction to the business environment

Specialization in the business environment

The trading cycle identifies the importance of specialization within the business environment. In fact, in a modern economy, specialization touches every aspect of our lives in terms of:

- the specialization of *job roles*
- the specialization of *business organizations*
- the specialization of *regions within a country*
- the specialization of *countries*
- the specialization of *institutions*.

Why has specialization become such a defining characteristic of a modern economy? In truth, the answer lies in our everyday work roles. Most of us will specialize in, or concentrate on, a particular aspect of the business – administrators, computer programmers, secretaries, supervisors, operatives, invoice clerks, managers, and the like. When staff concentrate on specific functions, a number of benefits accrue to the business organization:

- we become more skilled at our jobs;
- we make fewer mistakes as we become more experienced in our job role;
- we can concentrate upon those tasks which are more suited to our skills, interests and aptitudes;
- job satisfaction may increase;
- specialist jobs can be broken down into simpler functions as a result of specialization;
- if complex tasks are broken down into simpler functions, it can allow the introduction of machinery, which results in *a bigger output from a given set of resources*.

It is this last point which is particularly relevant to our study of Business Practice. We have already noted that the productive factors – people, raw materials, equipment and capital – are in short supply. The advantage of specialization for the business organization, and indeed for whole countries, is that more goods and services will be produced from the same input of productive factors, leading to an *increase in productivity* and to *efficiency gains*. In other words, specialization is the essential ingredient if we are to produce more goods and services, thereby satisfying more consumer needs.

Activity

Choose 6 countries and identify the individual products, services or produce in which they specialize.

Choose one of these countries and identify the various regions within it which specialize in certain types of goods or services.

The individual business organization seeking to participate in the trading cycle is therefore faced with certain critical decisions which hinge around 2 questions:

- What aspect of the trading cycle should they concentrate upon – sales? production? services?
- How should they organise their business in such a way as to gain the maximum benefits from specialization?

We shall constantly return to these two questions throughout our study of Business Practice, but before we look in more detail at the influences which will guide the business organization's decisions, we need to consider the third component which impacts on business activity – *opportunity cost*.

Opportunity cost

Combining people, materials and capital in the production process involves costs, so-called *costs of production*. These costs of production will have a monetary value related to the country where the production has taken place. People in the UK will be paid in UK pounds, those in America in US dollars, those in Malaysia in Malaysian ringgits, and so on. Similarly, financial resources are required to purchase raw materials and capital equipment.

We need to understand, however, that costs can also be viewed from a different perspective, that is, in terms of other products which could have been produced with the same raw materials, people and capital. If limited resources are available, the cost of a school may be counted as the hospital which cannot now be built. For the business organization, this way of looking at costs is particularly important, since, once they have been committed to a particular project or product line, funds cannot be duplicated to produce other products or services. Again, the office environment provides us with a relevant example. The business which has to choose between installing either a new computer network or a new telephone system needs to understand that the cost of choosing one of these competing alternatives is not simply a monetary consideration, since it has to take account of the forgone alternative. It is this principle which is referred to as *opportunity cost*.

The business environment – the importance of decision-making

An understanding of the concept of opportunity cost provides an important key to an understanding of the business environment, and with it, the activities and practices associated with business organizations. Every aspect of business, from the initial thoughts, ideas and concepts of an original business innovation through to its eventual production, involves *making decisions*. Throughout our study we will constantly refer to this basic idea, and we will concentrate upon a number of factors which must be taken into account when business decisions are made.

In a conventional sense, these decisions centre upon 3 key questions and associated decisions:

- What to produce?
- How to produce it?
- Who to produce it for?

For the purpose of our study we will consider these questions and the associated decision-making process from 2 main perspectives. Firstly, we will look at them from the perspective of the *specific activities undertaken by the business organization* and, secondly, we will attempt to understand how the *activities of individuals* within the business organization can have a direct impact on the success or otherwise of the decisions made by that organization.

The importance of the decision-making process and its impact on those people associated with it should not be underestimated. Business organizations will involve people in the capacity of employees, managers, shareholders and suppliers. It is not difficult to understand the impact of a decision which leads to a reduction in profits or, worse still, business failure. This would not only affect the owners in their capacities of sole traders, partners or shareholders, but employees might lose their jobs and livelihoods and suppliers might not be paid the money which is owed to them, thus resulting in a knock-on effect to their own businesses.

What is perhaps more difficult to understand are those decisions which do not necessarily lead to a reduction in profits or business failure but, nevertheless, are questionable on the basis that the *opportunity cost* is high – in other words, taking a different approach or making a different decision could have resulted in bigger profits or greater efficiency.

This provides us with an insight into the business environment since, if the main activity involved in business practice is making decisions, we need to understand that such decisions involve *risks*. Indeed, it can be argued that successful business organizations are those which are skilled in assessing the nature of risk and make their decisions accordingly.

We can now begin to see relationships starting to be developed within our study of the business environment. In essence, business activity which takes place in the business environment can be viewed as a *trading cycle* made up of *specialized functions* which involve decisions having to be made on the basis of *opportunity cost*.

Before we leave this aspect of our study we need to understand that the decisions undertaken by the business organization do not only affect those directly involved with the business. In recent times the concept of people as *stakeholders* has arisen. The idea behind this concept is that we all have a *stake* or *interest* in the consequences of many business decisions, – even those of us who are not directly involved either as owners, managers or employees.

The impact of the business organization on the wider community is an increasingly important element in any study of Business Practice and we shall show in later chapters how business organizations have attempted to respond to the concept of the *stakeholding society*.

Influences on business activity

> *There now follow some quick questions and revision exercises. They relate specifically to the chapter you have just studied. You are advised to attempt the questions without reference to the text, and then compare your answers and solutions with those on pages 22–3.*

Introduction to the business environment

QUESTIONS

1. Describe **4** features which are common to **business organizations**.
2. Name **2 sectors of the economy**.
3. Describe a **sole trader**.
4. What is the **main disadvantage** of being a **sole trader**?
5. List **4 advantages** of being a **sole trader**.
6. Describe a **partnership**.
7. Describe **4** advantages of a **partnership**.
8. Describe **4** disadvantages of a **partnership**.
9. What is another name for a **limited company**?
10. What is meant by the term **limited liability**?
11. Name **2** types of **limited company**.
12. What is another name for a **nationalized industry**?

EXERCISES

1. Describe in your own words the term *business activity*, showing clearly the role played by raw materials, capital, and organizational skills.
2. Describe the relationship between the trading cycle, specialization, and opportunity cost.
3. 'An understanding of the concept of opportunity cost is vital to an understanding of the decision-making process.' Discuss this statement in relation to the decision-making process.

Influences on business activity

ANSWERS TO QUESTIONS

1.
   - A defined structure within which activity takes place.
   - A group of people who collectively engage in activity which contributes to a common goal.
   - A set of rules within which the organization operates.
   - Channels of communication which enable decisions to be taken.

2.
   - Private sector
   - Public sector.

3. A sole trader is a type of business organization which is owned and controlled by one person, who provides the capital, takes responsibility for the risks inherent in business activity and, as a result, either benefits from receiving all the profits generated by the business or takes the responsibility for paying any losses.

4. Unlimited liability.

5.
   - Easy to set up.
   - Independence.
   - May not require substantial capital to establish the business.
   - Can provide a personal service to customers.

6. A business organization which, in the UK, is defined as a group of between 2 and 20 partners who are collectively responsible for providing the capital, taking the risks, receiving the profits and sharing the losses.

7.
   - Opportunity to obtain more capital.
   - Partners can specialize in certain aspects of the business.
   - Relatively easy to establish.
   - Some of the partners can benefit from limited liability.

8.
   - Unlimited liability for some or all of the partners.
   - Disputes may arise between the partners.
   - Opportunities for future expansion are limited to the number of partners engaged in the business.
   - Partnership ceases to exist upon the death of one of the partners, or the resignation of one of the partners.

9. Joint stock company.

10. In the event of business failure, the owners' liability for company debts is limited to the amount of capital they have contributed to the company.

11.
    - Public limited company.
    - Private limited company.

12. Public corporation.

Introduction to the business environment

SOLUTIONS TO EXERCISES

1. Business activity is the process by which productive factors are combined together in order to produce goods and services. These productive factors include skilled labour, capital equipment, and raw materials, along with those people with the organizational abilities, skills, ideas, and vision to ensure that the process of combining the productive factors results in the production of goods and services which satisfy consumer demand.

2. The trading cycle describes the relationship between business activities and identifies, in particular, the cyclical nature of business activity. An organization will need to purchase raw materials in order to manufacture goods which can then be sold in order to generate the profits which enables it to purchase more raw materials in order to manufacture goods, and so on. Business organizations tend to specialize in particular aspects of the trading cycle. For example, one business may choose to specialize in providing raw materials or components, another may concentrate on selling the finished product, whilst others may provide specialized services such as banking and insurance to businesses.

   Business organizations will have to make decisions about which part of the trading cycle they will specialize in and how their business will be organized in order to meet market requirements. These decisions will involve an understanding of the principle of opportunity cost which, in simple terms, identifies the cost of a particular decision on the basis of forgone alternatives.

3. At the simplest level, business activity involves taking risks, since combining together the productive factors in order to satisfy consumer needs may result in financial losses. Consumer wants and market requirements may change over time, an important business contract may be lost to a competitor, or a company's major international market may suffer an economic crisis resulting in fall in demand for imports. Effective decision-making in business is therefore critical in order to minimize such financial risks.

   The concept of opportunity cost considers the decision-making process from a different perspective, and highlights the cost of a decision in terms of the forgone alternatives. For example, the decision to install a new computer network will have a direct financial cost but will also mean that the business is then not able to purchase other equipment from its limited resources. Decision-makers in business must therefore have a clear understanding of both financial costs *and* opportunity costs if their decisions are to be effective.

POINTS TO REMEMBER

- Business Practice is concerned with the study of business organizations and how they operate within the business environment.

- The economy can be divided into the public sector and the private sector, each of which can be classified on the basis of ownership and control of the productive factors.

- The main types of business organizations in the private sector are the sole trader, partnerships, and limited companies.

- The main type of business organization in the public sector is the public corporation, also known as a nationalized industry.

- Privatization is a government policy which seeks to return previously nationalized industries back to the private sector.

- Limited liability is a legal term which means that, in the event of bankruptcy, owners of a limited company will only be liable to the amount they have invested in the company. As such, the company's creditors cannot call upon the personal possessions of the owners.

- Limited companies must submit Memorandum and Articles of Association to the Registrar of Joint Stock Companies.

- The business organization requires people, raw materials, capital and organizational skills if it is to successfully engage in business activity.

- Business activity involves the process of combining together productive factors in order to produce goods and services which satisfy wants.

- The trading cycle enables us to understand that the various activities undertaken by business organizations are interrelated.

- The business environment is characterized by specialization which involves people, organizations, regions, countries, and institutions concentrating on specific aspects of business activity within the trading cycle.

- Specialization leads to a bigger output from a given set of resources.

- Decision-making is a key activity within the business organization.

- Opportunity cost is the principle of considering a business decision on the basis of forgone alternatives.

2

The influence of the marketplace

> After carefully studying this chapter, you should be able to describe how the pattern of consumer spending influences the business environment.

> **Extended Syllabus reference**
>
> 1.4 Explain how the pattern of consumer spending influences business activity

The purpose of this chapter is to introduce the importance of the marketplace in determining the price of goods and services. The chapter will concentrate on how demand and supply, through the operation of the price mechanism, influence the activities of the business organization.

The business environment and the importance of the marketplace

Chapter 1 highlighted the importance of decision-making as a central activity within the business organization. However, we need to understand that the decisions made by the business organization must take into account a number of factors which may not necessarily be under the direct control of the organization.

Just as we are influenced by our own environment, so also a business organization is subject to a number of influences within the environment in which it operates. It is important, therefore, to understand some of these influences and the effect they have upon the business organization and the decision-making process.

One of the most important concepts to understand is the relationship which exists between the business environment and the *marketplace*. All of us are familiar with a marketplace in which stallholders sell their products and in many respects this kind of marketplace provides us with an insight into the operation of the business

Influences on business activity

environment. If we were to consider the basic organization of our marketplace we would probably arrive at the following features:

- it consists of stallholders and customers;
- the stallholders aim to sell their products to the consumer;
- the customers are likely to be attracted by low prices;
- the stallholders try to compete against each other in order to attract customers;
- customers' tastes and preferences are likely to change over time, and these changes will be reflected in the range and types of products, which will change in response to consumer preferences;
- new products will appear on the market at regular intervals;
- surplus stock is likely to be the subject of price discounting as the stallholders try to replace it with new stock.

In many respects this simple market structure mirrors the more complex notions of the marketplace to which we will refer to throughout our study of Business Practice. Whether we talk in terms of local, regional, national or international markets the basic idea is still the same – that any market consists of buyers and sellers. It therefore follows that a *competitive market* is one where individual sellers compete against each other in order to sell their products to the consumer.

The existence of competitive markets is one of the most important influences on the business organization, since the forces of *demand* (how much consumers are willing to purchase of a particular product) and *supply* (how much producers are willing to supply at a particular price) are constantly changing in response to changes in market conditions. The following analysis provides a brief overview to show how the forces of demand and supply serve to influence the activities of business organizations.

Demand

For our purposes we will assume that there is an *indirect relationship* between price and demand. In other words, if price falls then demand will increase, whereas if price increases, then demand will fall. This relationship can be shown in the form of a graph.

We can see quite clearly from Figure 2.1 (opposite) that the lower the price, the bigger the demand and vice versa. But is price the only determinant of the level of demand? Are there any instances in which the consumer may be willing to purchase a bigger quantity of a particular product even though price remains the same and, conversely, are there examples which show that, in certain market conditions, consumer demand will fall even though price remains the same?

The influence of the marketplace

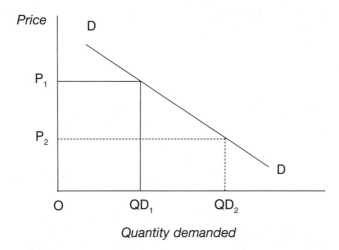

Figure 2.1 The demand schedule

In the business environment there are indeed numerous examples of consumers being influenced by factors other than price when deciding whether to purchase a particular product. In such circumstances what will happen to the demand schedule we have plotted in the above graph? This will become easier to understand if we make reference to specific examples. Firstly, let us take a situation in which, as a result of a successful advertising campaign, demand for a particular product increases at all price levels. In this case, the demand schedule will shift to the *right* of the existing demand schedule, from Di to D, as shown in Figure 2.2.

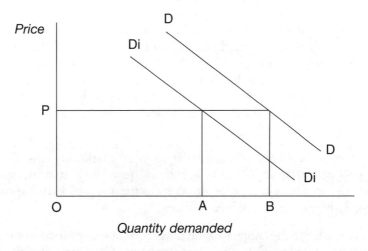

Figure 2.2 Shifts in the demand schedule

In the above example, although price has remained the same, demand has increased from OA to OB.

The same analysis can be applied in reverse if we consider a situation in which market conditions change to the extent that demand for a product falls even though the price remains the same. We only have to consider the impact of a 'food scare' to see how consumers' preferences can quickly bring about changes in market conditions. This was the case in the UK in the mid-1990s when a link was established between infected beef and a degenerative brain condition which affected humans. In more recent times a link was established in Hong Kong between chickens and a particularly serious form of influenza. In both instances, the markets saw a reduction in demand which was not connected to a change in price. In Figure 2.2 this would be shown by the original level of demand being OB and the new, reduced level of demand being OA.

Now complete the following activity in order to gain a better insight into the influence of consumer spending patterns.

Activity

Draw a series of demand schedules to show the effect on demand of the following circumstances:

- an increase in consumer income;
- a report which identifies the beneficial effect on health of a particular product;
- denim jeans are no longer fashionable amongst young people;
- the impact of a fall in the price of computers on the demand for software;
- a report which highlights the detrimental effect on the environment of using a particular product.

What does this tell us about the influence of the consumer on business activity? If nothing else, it shows us that the consumer is one of the most important factors which determine changes in the level of business activity. However, above all, it makes us realise that the business organization ignores the wishes of the consumer at its peril. Without doubt, successful businesses will be those which put consumer needs at the heart of their operations and are flexible enough to respond to changes in market conditions.

As we shall see when we consider the role of marketing and its associated functions, business organizations are also keenly aware of how they themselves can influence consumer demand and perceptions by activities which incorporate, amongst other things, advertising and public relations.

Before we leave the subject of the marketplace we must consider the second element which we can identify as a basic component of business activity – supplying products to the market.

Supply

In theory at least, we can assume that suppliers will react to high prices by seeking to supply more goods to the marketplace. By doing so they will hope to increase their profit levels. We can therefore conclude that there is a direct relationship between price and the quantity of a product supplied to a particular market. In other words if prices increase, more goods will be supplied. This relationship is identified in the supply schedule shown in Figure 2.3 in which an increase in price from OP_1 to OP_2, will result in an increase in supply from OQD_1 to OQD_2.

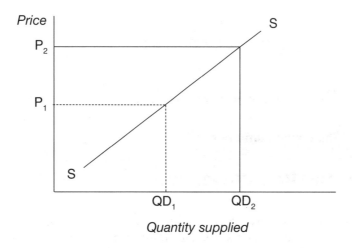

Figure 2.3   The supply schedule

Market price

It should be clear from the previous analysis that, in a *competitive market*, prices are determined by the forces of demand and supply which work together to determine *market price*. In effect, the market price of a product is the price at which the quantity demanded of a particular product is equal to the quantity supplied.

Our own experience confirms these conclusions. In the simplest of markets with which we are familiar, if a number of stallholders are selling identical or similar goods, we are likely to find that prices are broadly the same amongst all the stallholders. In other instances we can recognize situations in which some firms are able to benefit from short-term 'excess' profits until such time as new firms are attracted into the market resulting in competition, an increase in supply and a reduction in price.

In other words, in a competitive market, demand and supply will work together to produce an *equilibrium price,* ie *the price at which the level of demand equals the amount supplied to the market*. It therefore follows that in circumstances where demand is greater than supply, consumers will, in effect, 'bid up' the price of the product until such time as a price is reached at which demand equals supply. Should the price be higher than this equilibrium price, suppliers may have excess, unsold stock which can only be disposed of if prices fall.

The operation of demand and supply in a competitive market to produce an equilibrium price is shown in Figure 2.4 (overleaf). The only price at which demand will equal supply is Pe, the *equilibrium price*, since at this price what is demanded will be sold and stock cleared from the market.

Influences on business activity

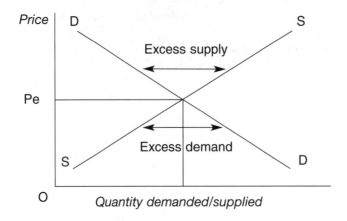

Figure 2.4 The equilibrium price

Changes in market conditions

Are there any circumstances where business organizations may increase or decrease the supply of goods to the market even though prices may remain the same? Let us consider the following circumstances:

- the workers employed within a particular industry negotiate a substantial increase in pay;
- an increase in the price of raw materials used in the production process.

The impact in both of these circumstances is that business organizations will be faced with increased costs of production. This increase in costs will reduce the amount of profit being made by the firms and they will therefore seek to remedy the situation by reducing the amount of the product that they supply to the market. Indeed, some firms may leave the market altogether and seek more profitable markets. In any event there will be a reduction in supply which will result in the market price of the product increasing which, in turn, will allow profit levels to rise.

Figure 2.5 illustrates the previous analysis by the use of demand and supply schedules.

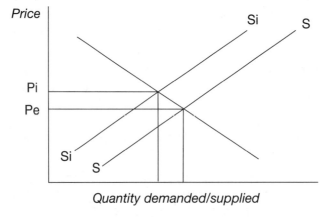

Figure 2.5 **Changes in market conditions**

30

The influence of the marketplace

In Figure 2.5 the original supply function, SS, has shifted to the *left at all price levels* thus resulting in a new supply function, SiSi, which, in turn, has resulted in an increase in price from Pe to Pi.

Now let us consider a different set of circumstances:

- the introduction of a computer-operated production line;
- the development of a new, low-cost material which replaces traditional, more expensive materials used on the production line.

In both the circumstances described above, costs of production are likely to fall, leading to an increase in profit levels. In order to benefit from these increased profit levels, the existing firms in the industry will increase the supply of the product to the market whilst, at the same time, other firms will enter the industry in order to benefit from the increased profit levels. The increase in supply resulting from the actions of firms will result in lower prices which will have the effect of reducing any 'excess' profits which may have been made by firms in the short term.

> **Activity**
>
> Draw a diagram which shows the impact of a reduction in costs of production on the price of a product in a competitive market.

What does this analysis tell us about the business environment and the actions of the business organizations which operate within it? We can draw together the following broad conclusions:

- market prices are determined by the forces of demand and supply;
- profits are one of the main driving forces of business activity;
- business organizations will seek to produce in those markets where they can maximize their profits;
- business organizations will strive to increase their profits by reducing their costs.

> **Activity**
>
> Read through the business sections of the quality press and identify 3 examples which show the operation of demand and supply in competitive markets.
>
> From your research try to identify the following factors:
>
> - the reasons for changes in demand and supply
> - the impact of these changes on prices
> - the responses of individual firms to changes in demand and supply.

Influences on business activity

Monopolies

It is interesting to note that in our analysis of the competitive market, firms can only make excess profits in the short term. In those situations in which demand exceeds supply, prices will rise, generating excess profits which, in turn, will attract other firms into the industry who will seek to benefit from these excess profits. The increase in supply which results from the increase in the number of firms will cause prices to fall along with profit levels, until such time as the equilibrium price is reached, when firms will make normal profits as opposed to excess profits.

Is this always the case or can we identify any circumstances in which the competitive market will not operate? In the business environment we are likely to find a number of instances where markets do not necessarily operate in the way we have suggested. Indeed we are drawn to the conclusion that most markets for goods and services are not so 'perfect' as we have indicated.

Our analysis so far assumes that it is easy for firms to enter new markets in order to benefit from excess profits. In other words, it assumes that firms can easily switch from producing one type of product to another, although, in practice, this may not be possible in the short term. Equally, our analysis assumes that firms will have all the knowledge at their fingertips to allow them to make decisions regarding the markets and associated prices for all products. Again in the business world this is highly unlikely.

Markets are therefore more likely to be 'imperfect' in that, although they are likely to exhibit the characteristics which we have described in terms of demand and supply, there may be instances in which some firms are able to make excess profits over the long term because it is difficult for new firms to enter the industry.

One market condition in which a firm can make long-term excess profits occurs if there is only *one* firm which supplies all the goods to the market in a particular industry. Such a *monopoly* can effectively control the supply or fix the price, since it does not have to face the possibility of other firms entering the industry. Monopolies are therefore powerful business units which are able to manipulate the market to generate excess 'monopoly profits'.

This is the most extreme form of *imperfect competition,* and in the 'real world' we are unlikely to find many examples of real monopolies. Instead, we are more likely to discover from our studies, or simply our own life experiences, that the demand and supply for individual products is made up of a variety of *market formations* each of which will exhibit its own individual characteristics regarding the number of buyers and sellers.

The influence of the marketplace

Activity

Complete the following table by identifying the number of buyers and producers, using the following criteria:

- few
- many.

Product	No of producers	No of buyers
Cars		
Petrol		
Gas		
Electricity		
Computers		
Clothes		
CD Players		
Specialist scientific equipment		

There now follow some quick questions and revision exercises. They relate specifically to the chapter you have just studied. You are advised to attempt the questions without reference to the text, and then compare your answers and solutions with those on pages 35–7.

Influences on business activity

QUESTIONS

1. Describe **5** main features of a **market**.
2. What is the main feature of a **competitive market**?
3. Draw a simple demand schedule and explain the relationship between **price** and the **quantity demanded**.
4. Draw a simple supply schedule and explain the relationship between **price** and the **quantity supplied**.
5. What is meant by the term **market price**?
6. Draw a diagram to show how **demand** and **supply** determine the **market price** of a particular good or service.
7. What is a **monopoly**?
8. What are the disadvantages for the consumer of a **monopoly**?
9. What is an **imperfect market**?
10. Describe **2** reasons why the **market** for a particular good may be **imperfect**.

EXERCISES

1. Describe how the workings of a competitive market assist the decision-making function of the business organization.
2. 'The consumer is the most important influence in a market economy.' Explain this statement with reference to the workings of the price mechanism.
3. Describe how prices are determined in a competitive market.

While attempting to answer the questions and exercises on this page, you are strongly advised not to read on and to cover the answers on the following page with a sheet of paper.

The influence of the marketplace

ANSWERS TO QUESTIONS

1.
   - Consists of buyers and sellers.
   - Sellers will compete against each other in order to attract customers.
   - Similar or identical goods will be sold.
   - Price will be an important influence on the level of consumer demand for a particular product.
   - Consumer preferences will change over time which may result in surplus stock or shortages.

2. Large numbers of buyers and sellers in which the sellers compete against each other in order to sell their products to the consumer.

3. A demand schedule

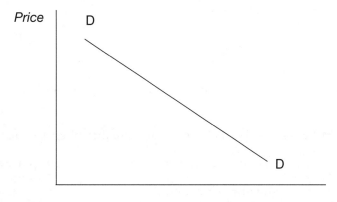

The demand schedule shows that there is an indirect relationship between price and quantity demanded. In other words, consumers will demand more of a product at a lower price than they will at higher prices. Put simply, if the price of a product rises, demand will fall, and vice versa.

4. Supply schedule

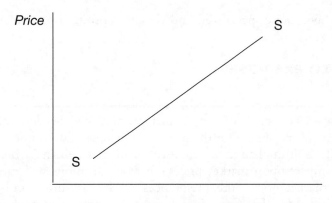

35

Influences on business activity

The supply schedule shows that there is a direct relationship between price and the quantity of a particular good supplied to the market. In other words, sellers will supply more goods if the price is high but will contract supply if prices are lowered.

5   The market price of a product is the price at which the quantity demanded of a particular product is equal to the quantity supplied.

6   Determination of market price

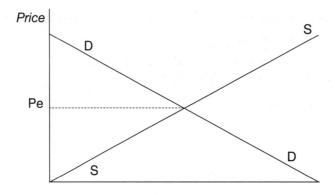

Quantity demanded and supplied

7   A market in which there is only one supplier of a particular product or service.

8   Supplier can manipulate the market in order to make excess profits.

- Less choice for the consumer.
- No competition.
- May result in higher prices.

9   A market in which it may be difficult for new firms to enter an industry, resulting in a reduction in the level of competition and the opportunity for firms within the industry to benefit from excess profits.

10
- Start-up costs to enter a particular industry may be high.
- May require specialized knowledge to produce particular products.

SOLUTIONS TO EXERCISES

1   The market price of a particular product will be determined by the level of demand and supply for the product. Changes in consumer tastes and preferences will result in changes in the level of market demand which, in turn, will have an impact upon market prices. Business decisions will therefore be influenced by market prices, the preferences of the consumer and the actions of their competitors. In some instances, a business may seek to reduce or cease

production of some products in order to move into more profitable areas of production. The level and trends in market prices will be an important factor when such decisions are being made.

2. In a competitive market, goods will be produced only if there is a demand from the consumer. If consumers are willing to purchase products, then business organizations will engage in business activity which satisfies consumer requirements, resulting in the generation of profits for the business. Conversely, if the demand for a particular product falls as a result of a change in consumer tastes and preferences, then business organizations will reduce or cease production of the product and switch production to new product lines which are experiencing an increase in demand.

3. In a competitive market, prices are determined by demand and supply. A competitive market has many buyers and sellers, with the sellers competing against each other in order to sell their products to the consumer. In circumstances in which demand is greater than supply, consumers will be willing to pay more for the product and will effectively 'bid up' the market price of the product. However, if sellers attempt to sell their products at a price greater than that at which the consumers are willing to purchase them, then the sellers will be left with excess stock which can be sold only if prices are reduced. In effect, this will result in the establishment of an equilibrium market price at which market demand exactly equals market supply.

In a market economy, changes in price and the impact on profit levels which follow such changes, will have a direct influence on business decisions relating to which products to produce and which markets to enter.

Influences on business activity

POINTS TO REMEMBER

- A market consists of buyers and sellers.
- A competitive market is one in which individual sellers compete against each other in order to sell their products to the consumer.
- In a competitive market, the price of a product is determined by the forces of demand and supply.
- The level of demand and supply are both influenced by the prevailing market conditions.
- Changes in market conditions result in physical shifts in the demand/supply schedule which, in turn, will have an influence on market price.
- The market price of a product is the price at which the quantity demanded is equal to the quantity supplied.
- In a competitive market, demand and supply will work together to produce an equilibrium price at which the level of demand equals the amount supplied to the market.
- Business organizations will be attracted to produce those products which have a high market price, since, by producing these goods, profits will increase in the short term.
- A competitive market assumes that business organizations are free to enter the market in order to produce goods and services for the consumer.
- A monopoly is a business organization which is able to control the supply of goods to the market, thereby essentially fixing the market price.
- A monopoly market is characterized by the existence of only one supplier and is an example of imperfect competition.

3

The influence of the business environment on the size of firms

> **After carefully studying this chapter, you should be able to:**
> 1 *describe the reasons for differences in the size of firms;*
> 2 *explain why small firms are important.*

> **Extended Syllabus references**
> 1.5 Describe how the following affects the size and organization of firms:
>   1.5.1   mergers
>   1.5.2   take-overs
>   1.5.3   different types of integration
>   1.5.4   internal economies and diseconomies of scale
>   1.5.5   external economies of scale
> 1.6 Explain why small firms are important

In this chapter we will show how the business organization is influenced by a range of factors which affect the size of its operations. In particular we will focus on the reasons for differences in the size of firms, the importance of small firms, and the dynamics of organizational growth including mergers, takeovers and integration. Finally, we will consider the importance of internal economies of scale and diseconomies of scale in influencing the size of business organizations.

Identifying differences in the size of firms

So far, we have identified a number of features of the business environment, including:

- the existence of the public and private sectors
- different types of business organizations, in terms of ownership and legal status
- the competitive market economy.

However, by far the most striking feature of the business environment concerns the marked differences in the size of business organizations. Such differences can be identified with reference to some of the following criteria:

- number of people employed
- physical size of the plant
- range of products produced
- range of products sold
- ownership: number of shareholders
- scope of operations: local, regional, national, international
- sales volume
- profit levels
- turnover
- market share.

From this list we can classify the differences in the size of firms into 3 specific areas:

- the number of productive factors employed
- the physical features of the organization
- financial performance.

Let us now look at these aspects in more detail.

The number of productive factors employed

Productive factors relate not only to the number of people employed but also to the degree of specialization in the form of the division of labour. Large firms tend to use a greater degree of specialization in all aspects of the business, ranging from the organization of the workforce through to the organizational structure of the business unit.

Large firms, particularly those engaged in the production of manufactured goods – such as motor cars, defence equipment, and consumer durables such as washing machines, TVs and dishwashers – require large amounts of capital equipment in the form of machinery. Additionally, these firms will use large quantities of raw materials and associated inputs into the production process. This aspect of a firm's activity is referred to as the amount of 'capital employed', which simply means the value of the capital equipment used in the production process.

The physical features of the organization

Typically, large firms are likely to be involved in large-scale production activities or services to the consumer or the business community. Examples of these organizations can be found both in the manufacturing and in the service sectors of the economy. For example, motor car giants such as Ford, General Motors, Nissan and Toyota, and large retail outlets such as Marks and Spencer, Tesco, and Safeway.

Indeed, so great is the scope of some organizations that their production and sales units are located in more than one country. These so-called *multi-national corporations* (MNCs) because of the nature of their activities, dominate the global marketplace and include many famous household names such as Coca Cola, Kodak, Ford Motor Company, and McDonalds. It follows that these large firms will enjoy a bigger market share than their smaller competitors. A common feature of these large firms is that they are likely to be public limited companies, owned, as we have previously described, by shareholders. The size of their operations also makes it easier for large firms to produce, or sell, a range of different goods or services. In this respect, we say that firms are more able to *diversify* their operations. Finally, the actual number of products sold, the so-called *sales volume*, can also be used to differentiate one firm from another.

Financial performance

For the purposes of this chapter we will identify 2 financial performance indicators which are likely to distinguish a large firm from a smaller business organization.

At the most basic level, a large firm is likely to generate bigger profit levels than a small firm. Given that the large firm is likely to sell a bigger volume of goods than its smaller counterpart, we are also likely to see it generate a bigger *sales turnover*, calculated by multiplying the number of sales by the price of the product.

At this stage, it is advisable to add a cautionary note to our analysis by adding that profit levels and sales turnover alone do not signify business success or the continued existence of the firm. A study of Business Practice will inevitably need to consider business performance with reference to a greater range of financial performance indicators, and Chapter 9 will cover this aspect of *business finance* in more detail.

Our discussion so far has centred upon the way in which we can distinguish a large firm from a smaller business organization. We have also made assumptions which would lead us to the conclusion that a large firm has a number of distinct advantages over the small firm – greater market share and higher profit levels being 2 of the most important. In the next section we will look at how these advantages may arise for the large firm.

Influences on business activity

> **Activity**
>
> Obtain the annual report of a large public limited company and identify the main features of its operations in terms of:
>
> - the number of productive factors employed
> - the physical features of the organization
> - financial performance.

Internal economies of scale

Internal economies of scale is the term used to describe the *advantages of large-scale production*. For the purpose of our study we need to consider these advantages in greater depth in order to discover:

- how the business can generate internal economies of scale;
- how the business can benefit from economies of scale.

How the actions of the business organizations can generate internal economies of scale

Internal economies of scale can be identified in a number of areas of business activities and organization. In this section we will look at 5 types of internal economy of scale:

- marketing economies of scale
- purchasing economies of scale
- technical economies of scale
- risk-bearing economies of scale
- financial economies of scale.

Table 3.1 provides an overview of the types of advantages available to the large firm with reference to each type of economy of scale.

The influence of the business environment

Table 3.1 The advantages associated with internal economies of scale

Type	Activity	Example
Marketing economies of scale	• selling and advertising	• large firm can utilize its sales force more effectively by forming sales teams for specific geographical areas • large firm can make use of its own transport fleet for distribution
Purchasing economies of scale	• bulk-buying of raw materials	• large firm can negotiate discounts
Technical economies of scale	• large-scale production	• large firm can use up-to-date and expensive machinery 24 hours a day • large firm can introduce the division of labour into the production process • large firm can engage in research and development activities • large firm can afford to pay high wages in order to attract specialist staff including good managers
Risk-bearing economies of scale	• diversification of product range	• large firm does not have to rely on the sales of *one* product • large firm does not have to rely on one supplier, so reducing the risk of shortages
Financial economies of scale	• obtaining loans • issuing shares	• large firm may negotiate preferential interest rates • large firm can gain access to additional sources of finance

Although Table 3.1 clearly shows how large firms can benefit from internal economies of scale, 2 factors must be stressed:

- Internal economies of scale do not arise automatically. The managers of the company must still plan business activity, growth and development in such a way as to maximize the benefits of growth in the form of internal economies of scale.

Influences on business activity

- Internal economies of scale are directly related to specialization which, as we have shown previously, leads to a bigger output from a given set of resources. As such, internal economies of scale are directly related to *efficiency savings*.

It is this aspect of efficiency savings which we will now consider in more detail in order to show the direct financial benefits of internal economies of scale to the large firm.

How the business can benefit from economies of scale

The previous section provides a clue as to how the business can benefit from internal economies of scale. In essence, internal economies lead to production being carried out *more efficiently*. Consider the information provided in Table 3.2 which shows how total cost varies with output.

Table 3.2   Total costs and output

Output	Total cost (£)
100	10,000
200	18,000
300	24,000
400	28,000
500	30,000

What does the table tell us? The first conclusion we can draw is that increasing output will result in an increase in total costs. This follows since an increase in output will involve the employment of more productive factors – people, raw materials, and the like – which need to be paid for. However, the business is not simply concerned with its total costs, since a better understanding of its efficiency is gained by calculating how much *on average* it costs to produce *one unit* of output.

Unit costs, also known as *average costs*, are calculated by dividing total costs (TC) by output, ie

> TOTAL COSTS ÷ OUTPUT = UNIT OR AVERAGE COSTS

For example, from Table 3.2, at an output of 100 the unit or average, cost would be:

$$£10,000 \div 100 = £100$$

In other words, producing 100 units would cost, on average, £100 for each unit. Now complete the following activity:

The influence of the business environment

Activity

Complete the following table and construct a graph showing how unit costs vary with output.

Output	Total cost (£)	Unit cost (£)
100	10,000	
200	18,000	
300	24,000	
400	28,000	
500	30,000	
600	42,000	
700	56,000	
800	72,000	
900	90,000	
1,000	120,000	

What does the graph you have drawn in the activity tell us about the impact of internal economies of scale on unit costs? Quite simply, economies of scale result in *lower unit costs of production*. It therefore follows that, since unit costs are one measure of efficiency, internal economies of scale result in *efficiency savings for the large firm*.

However, the graph you have drawn also identifies another feature of large-scale production – that, after a certain level of output is reached, unit costs start to rise. It is to the factors which lead to a rise in unit costs that we now turn.

Internal diseconomies of scale

Internal *diseconomies of scale* are the *disadvantages* which arise if a firm becomes too large. At the onset of such diseconomies, unit costs of production will begin to rise, resulting in inefficiencies within business operations.

In effect, after a certain level of output is reached, the firm becomes too big to manage effectively. Problems may start to arise associated with:

- communications between staff;
- coordinating the business activities;
- decision-making becomes more time consuming;

Influences on business activity

- wasted raw materials because of a lack of strict controls;
- possible strains in management relations with staff.

Given the range and scope of these disadvantages, it is not surprising if we see an upward pressure on unit costs.

Planning business growth

What does this analysis tell us about the business organization which is seeking to expand its activities?

In essence, a company which is embarking on a strategy of growth must ensure that the process is *planned* and *monitored* in such a way that the company can benefit from internal economies of scale, maximize efficiency savings (in the form of lower unit costs) and minimize the risk of generating internal diseconomies of scale.

Let us now consider the possible strategies which can be considered by the organization which is seeking to expand its business activities.

How do firms promote growth?

In general terms, firms can grow in one of 2 ways:

- internal growth
- amalgamation.

Internal growth

Internal growth involves using the company's own resources to increase the scope and range of its activities – for example, opening up a new factory or a new retail outlet, employing more people, extending the product range, or expanding the company's market share.

If a firm seeks to expand in this way, it will need to have access to financial resources and will need to engage in detailed planning which will enable it to identify the various stages in its development plan. There are a number of sources of finance available to the business but, with regard to our current discussion, we will concentrate on two possible strategies which will almost certainly be involved in planning for growth:

- ploughing profits back into the company
- borrowing funds from a financial institution.

These 2 strategies provide us with the opportunity to show the range of decisions and choices in which the firm must engage. For example:

- What proportion of profits should be ploughed back into the firm?
- How much should be borrowed, from whom, and over what period of time?
- What are the likely costs and risks of borrowing over a long period of time?
- How will the firm convince shareholders of the need for growth and expansion?

Since internal growth involves addressing these critical issues, it is important that the business engages in a detailed planning exercise to identify:

- the costs of growth
- the benefits of growth
- timescales
- possible pitfalls to be avoided.

Inevitably, internal growth can be slow, but there is no doubt that it can bring significant advantages to the business organization.

Amalgamation

Amalgamation involves the business joining together with another firm or firms. Unlike the process of internal growth, amalgamation will lead to an immediate increase in the scope and range of the business unit. However, as with internal growth, amalgamation involves a range of decisions and choices which must be made by the business organization which is seeking to join with another company:

- Which company?
- What type of company?
- How do we convince the shareholders of the need for amalgamation?
- What will be the effect of amalgamation on our current business practices?
- Will new systems need to be established within the newly amalgamated company?
- What will be the impact on the workforce?

In effect, as with internal growth, the process of amalgamation needs to be carefully planned in order to distinguish the likely costs and benefits of the proposed strategy. This aspect of planning is of critical importance since rumours of a possible amalgamation can have a disruptive influence on current working practices. Both managers and employees tend to view any proposals for amalgamation with concern since those business organizations who follow this course of action have a tendency to engage in *rationalization* and *restructuring*.

Rationalization will involve the organization taking an in-depth look at the newly established business unit. Less-efficient factories and branches may be closed or re-located, and the production of certain product lines may cease.

At the same time, the newly amalgamated firm will want to consider the way in which the various activities of the organization are structured and managed. This restructuring will involve looking at the number of managers required in the key areas of business activity and may result in a more streamlined management team.

Influences on business activity

In effect, no amalgamation will take place unless there are distinct advantages to the firm which can be quantified in relation to such factors as:

- increased profitability
- lower costs
- greater efficiency
- higher productivity
- bigger market share.

Types of amalgamation

Amalgamation between firms can take 2 forms:

- mergers
- takeovers.

A *merger* involves 2 or more independent firms engaging in discussions to identify the benefits which would accrue to the parties involved if they were to combine their business activities by forming a new business organization.

A *takeover* on the other hand, involves one company seeking to gain control of another business without necessarily gaining the consent of the other organization. This process is normally undertaken in public limited companies since the existence of shares can provide the opportunity for one business to purchase the shares of another organization in order to gain a 'controlling interest'.

Shares are bought and sold openly on stock exchanges, so we are likely to see an increase in the price of a company's shares if it is subject to a takeover. The price of its shares will rise as a result of the increase in demand caused by the firm that wants to take it over.

Activity

With reference to the financial press and other sources of business news, find examples of companies whose share prices are increasing as a result of a possible takeover by another firm.

The direction of business growth

We have identified that amalgamation will require the firm to address a number of important decisions and choices. Let us return to these decisions and choices, and look at those which are concerned with the *direction* of growth – in other words, those decisions and choices which seek to identify the *type* of firm with which to amalgamate.

In the study of Business Practice we use a special term when considering the direction of business growth – *integration* – and it is generally accepted that there are 3 directions in which a firm may seek to join, or integrate, with other firms in order to increase the scope of its business operations:

- vertical integration
- horizontal integration
- lateral integration.

In this section, we will consider each type of integration in turn in order to show the range of advantages which can arise for the business organization.

Vertical integration

This involves the joining together of firms at different stages of the production process. Vertical integration can either be *backwards* towards the raw materials or *forwards* towards the final retail sales. For example, a brewery might integrate with a chain of restaurants (forward integration) or an oil refinery might integrate with an oil exploration company (backward integration).

There are a number of reasons for this type of integration:

- to secure supplies of raw materials (backward integration);
- to secure retail outlets (forward integration);
- to monitor and ensure the quality of raw materials (backward integration);
- to increase market share (forward integration);
- to increase the profile of the company (forward integration).

Horizontal integration

The distinguishing feature of horizontal integration is that the firms who are joining together will usually be involved in producing the same type of goods or services. Common examples of this type of integration include:

- car manufacturers
- aircraft manufacturers
- banks
- insurance companies
- pharmaceutical companies.

Horizontal integration has resulted in some of the largest business organizations, sometimes on an international scale. For example, the integration of Midland Bank, a major UK bank, with the Hongkong and Shanghai Banking Corporation (HSBC) established a major international financial corporation.

Influences on business activity

The motives for horizontal integration centre upon the size of the resulting business organization. The business will be able to enjoy *internal economies of scale,* which may involve purchasing economies (bulk buying), technical economies (linked processes of production), marketing economies (access to a wider market) and other economies associated with staffing and research and development opportunities. In essence, such economies will result in greater efficiencies as output is increased and unit costs of production are lowered.

However, horizontal integration can also lead to *monopolistic tendencies* as the number of independent firms in the market is reduced. Since monopolies can have an adverse impact on the consumer, many countries have established government-controlled bodies to investigate any mergers which may reduce the level of competition in the market.

Lateral integration

Lateral integration involves the joining together of firms which are engaged in the production and supply of *different* types of goods. In such instances, lateral integration may result in the establishment of giant, multi-national *conglomerates* whose main distinguishing feature is the level of *diversification* within the business organization.

There are many examples of this type of integration – Cadbury-Schweppes, for example, is involved in the production of a wide range of diverse food and drink products.

Since lateral integration involves diversification, it can protect the large organization against changes in consumer tastes and preferences which may affect one of their core products or services, which means that firms are able to spread the risk of production over different product ranges. Lateral integration can also enable a company to develop its interests in markets which are less competitive and reduce its interest in a product which is reaching the end of its *product life cycle.*

> **Activity**
>
> Undertake research activities to find examples of business organizations which exhibit characteristics associated with
>
> - vertical integration
> - horizontal integration
> - lateral integration.

The importance and influence of small firms in the business environment

The advantages of internal economies of scale, along with mergers, takeovers and the drive for efficiency savings in the form of lower unit costs might lead us to the conclusion that all firms have an overwhelming desire to achieve growth. Although there may be an element of truth in this, the fact remains that there continues to be a large number of small firms in the economy.

There are a number of reasons for the existence of small firms:

- some small firms may be in the process of getting bigger;
- small firms may not wish to see power, influence and ownership dispersed into the hands of a large number of shareholders;
- the size of the market may limit expansion;
- small firms can more easily cater for the needs of the consumer, particularly in the service sector of the economy;
- small firms may wish to expand but lack the funds to do so;
- small firms are better able to respond to changes in market demand;
- small firms may fear the onset of diseconomies of scale if they expand their business activities;
- decision-making in small firms is easier and less bureaucratic.

However, by far the most important reason for the existence of small firms is *external economies of scale*.

External economies of scale

External economies of scale are the advantages which are gained by *all* the firms in an industry, regardless of their size. Such advantages arise as a result of the expansion of the industry as a whole. There are many examples of such external economies of scale, but they are generally associated with *geographic or regional specialization*. For example, in a region which has a high volume of car manufacturing, the local economy will be geared towards providing a range of ancillary services – courses at a local college, for example, will promote the supply of skilled labour. Additionally, the growth of the industry will stimulate the development of smaller firms which specialize in providing components and services to the main industry. As a result, the local *infrastructure* will be developed to meet the needs of the main industry. All these developments serve to benefit all firms in the region, both large and small.

However, the importance and influence of small firms extends beyond their providing components and specialized services to larger business organizations into a number of other aspects of the business environment:

- small firms provide a good foundation for training the managers of the future;

Influences on business activity

- there are a number of examples of business innovation which have their roots in the research undertaken by small firms;
- the history of even the biggest multinational corporation is likely to be able to be traced back to its humbler origins as a small firm.

Activity

Undertake research to find out the origins of 3 multinational organizations. In particular try to find out:

- their original country of origin
- their original product
- a brief history of key dates in their growth and development
- any examples of different types of integration in which the company has engaged.

There now follow some quick questions and revision exercises. They relate specifically to the chapter you have just studied. You are advised to attempt the questions without reference to the text, and then compare your answers and solutions with those on pages 54–5.

The influence of the business environment

QUESTIONS

1. List **5** ways which can be used to determine the size of a business organization.
2. Define the term **internal economies of scale**.
3. List **3** types of **internal economies of scale**.
4. Define the term **unit cost**.
5. What is the relationship between **internal economies of scale** and **unit costs**?
6. Define the term **diseconomies of scale**.
7. Give **2** examples of **diseconomies of scale**.
8. What is the relationship between **diseconomies of scale** and **unit costs**?
9. What is the difference between a **merger** and a **takeover**?
10. List the **3** main types of **integration**.
11. What is meant by the term **external economies of scale**?

EXERCISES

1. 'If there are so many advantages to be gained by business expansion, why are there so many small firms?' Discuss.
2. Describe the relationship between internal economies of scale and the integration of firms.

Influences on business activity

ANSWERS TO QUESTIONS

1.
   - Number of people employed
   - Market share
   - Profit levels
   - Physical size of plant
   - Sales volume.
2. The advantages of large-scale production.
3.
   - Marketing economies of scale
   - Purchasing economies of scale
   - Financial economies of scale.
4. The cost of producing one unit of output.
5. Internal economies of scale result in lower unit costs of production.
6. The disadvantages of large-scale production.
7.
   - Raw materials may be wasted owing to a lack of strict controls.
   - Decision-making becomes more protracted and time-consuming.
8. Diseconomies of scale result in increased unit costs of production.
9. A merger involves 2 or more independent firms engaging in discussions to identify the mutual benefits which would be gained if their business activities were combined together. A takeover involves one company seeking to gain control of another business without necessarily gaining the consent of the other organisation.
10.
    - Vertical integration
    - Horizontal integration
    - Lateral integration.
11. The advantages which are gained by all firms within an industry, regardless of size, as the industry grows and develops.

SOLUTIONS TO EXERCISES

1. Although it is generally accepted that there are significant advantages to be gained as a result of business growth and expansion (primarily as a result of internal economies of scale), even the most developed economies are likely to be identified as having a large number of small firms. There are a number of reasons for the existence of small firms:
   - small firms may lack the capital to finance expansion;
   - the size of the market may not be sufficient to warrant large-scale production;
   - some firms are in the process of getting bigger;
   - some small firms offer specialized personal services;

The influence of the business environment

- small firms are more flexible and can make business decisions quickly and effectively;
- some small firms are traditional family businesses who do not wish to see the ownership of the business shared with other people;
- the existence of external economies of scale means that small firms can benefit from the growth of the industry as a whole and take on specialized functions which serve the interests of the larger business organizations. At the same time, small firms can benefit from developments in the local infrastructure which inevitably follow on from the growth and development of a particular industry.

2 Internal economies of scale are the advantages which a firm can seek to obtain as a result of expanding the size, scope and range of its operations. There are a number of strategies which a business may seek to employ in order to expand. For example, it may choose to use its own resources by using its profits for expansion. It may also obtain financial assistance from one of the commercial banks or other financial institutions, and, if it is a public limited company, it can offer shares for sale to the general public.

Another strategy is to promote growth by joining together with other firms, a process referred to as business integration. Integration can involve joining with firms producing similar products (horizontal integration), or with firms engaged with different stages in the production of a particular product (vertical integration). In some instances firms may also wish to diversify their operations and will seek to join together with a business which produces a different type or range of products (lateral integration).

In all these cases, one of the primary objectives of the business will be to ensure that internal economies of scale are generated in such areas as marketing and production. If this can be completed successfully, the process of integration will result in internal economies of scale which, in turn, will lead to lower unit costs of production.

Influences on business activity

POINTS TO REMEMBER

- There are marked differences in the size of firms in relation to the number of productive factors they employ, the scope of their operations and their financial performance.
- The advantages of large-scale production are referred to as internal economies of scale.
- Internal economies of scale lead to production being carried out more efficiently resulting in lower unit/average costs of production.
- As a firm grows in size it is able to benefit from a greater degree of specialization in its activities and functions.
- The disadvantages of large-scale production are referred to as internal diseconomies of scale.
- Internal diseconomies of scale lead to unit/average costs.
- Firms can seek to grow either by using their own resources or by joining together with other organizations.
- Amalgamation involves the business joining together, or integrating, with another firm, or firms.
- Amalgamation may result in rationalization and restructuring.
- A merger involves two or more independent firms joining together to obtain mutual benefits.
- A takeover involves one company seeking to gain control of another business without necessarily gaining the consent of the other organization.
- Vertical integration involves the joining together of firms at different stages in the production process.
- Horizontal integration involves firms joining together at the same stage in the production process
- Lateral integration involves the joining together of firms who are engaged in the production and supply of different types of goods.
- External economies of scale are the advantages which are gained by all the firms in an industry, regardless of their size.
- The existence of external economies of scale is an important factor which encourages the growth in numbers of small firms within the economy.

4

The influence of financial services

> **After carefully studying this chapter, you should be able to:**
>
> 1 *describe the role and importance of the financial sector to business organizations;*
>
> 2 *explain the different types of insurance which the business organization can take out;*
>
> 3 *describe the role and functions of Chambers of Commerce and business networks.*

> **Extended Syllabus references**
>
> 1.7 Describe the role and importance of the financial sector to business organizations and how they influence bank activity:
>   - 1.7.1   commercial banks
>   - 1.7.2   merchant banks
>   - 1.7.3   insurance companies
> 1.8 Explain different types of insurance which business organizations can take out:
>   - 1.8.1   business interruption
>   - 1.8.2   liability insurances
>   - 1.8.3   key person insurance
> 1.9 Describe the role and functions of Chambers of Commerce and business networks

In this chapter we shall describe a range of activities undertaken by specialist organizations which aim to meet the needs of the business community. The focus of our discussions will be the role of specialist financial organizations and how they influence the business environment.

Influences on business activity

The business environment and risk

Chapter 2 highlighted one of the most important influences on the business environment – the operation of the forces of demand and supply in a competitive market. However, this is not the only factor which influences the business organization and the environment within which it operates.

Previous chapters have highlighted the choices which have to be made by the business organization if it is going to operate successfully. But what if the owners or managers of the business make the wrong choice or take the wrong decisions?

Let us take as an example the development of a new product which the business is convinced will be successful and result in significant profits. It is likely that additional costs will be incurred in such areas as:

- research and development
- new machinery
- staff training
- marketing
- advertising.

If the new product is not successful, the investment involved in its development and production will be lost. The failure of one new product can have a significant impact on the business:

- the reputation of the business could suffer;
- shareholders might lose confidence in the management team;
- there might be insufficient funds available to repay loans;
- jobs might be lost;
- it may result in business failure.

This simple example provides an insight into another essential element which is to be found in the business environment – the element of *risk*. Indeed, it could be argued that profit is the reward received as a result of taking risks, and that, the greater the risk involved in a business venture, the greater will be the expected profits.

There are a number of other risks which can be identified when business activity takes place. The following list provides an insight into the scope and nature of such risks:

- employees of the business may be injured on company premises;
- members of the public may be injured as a result of the activities of the business organization;
- business premises may be damaged, resulting in a loss of stock and equipment;
- business property may be stolen;
- companies and private individuals who owe money to the business may no longer have the ability to re-pay the money.

If we consider each of the above examples in more detail we will find that the common feature in all these cases is that they lead to *additional costs to the business*.

The employee injured on company premises may take legal action against the business which could result in the business being fined and also having to pay compensation to the employee. The same applies if a member of the public is injured as a result of the activities of a business organization. Damage or loss to business premises will have to be paid for, whilst 'bad debts' will result in lost income.

In other words, business activity which takes place in the business environment involves risks which collectively can have an impact on costs and hence profit levels. Indeed, such is the nature of business risks that sometimes the very existence of a business organization can be put at risk.

What is the response of the business organization likely to be to such risks? The following section describes the influence of one service offered to the business community, which serves to reduce the level of risk inherent in business activity.

Business insurance

Insurance companies are financial organizations which specialize in the management of risk. Private individuals and business organizations, upon payment of a sum of money, *the insurance premium*, can transfer all or part of their risks to an insurance company. In the event of the risk materializing, the insurance company is then contractually obliged to pay for financial losses incurred by the individual or business organization.

The actual amount of money which will be paid out by the insurance company will be governed by the legal contract which exists between the insurance company and the insured organization. This contract is known as the *insurance policy*, a legally binding agreement which contains a number of separate clauses each dealing with specific parts of the contract. Thus the policy document will contain information on the following:

- name of the person or business being insured and their address;
- specific details of what is being insured;
- the circumstances in which the insurance company will pay out money to the insured;
- any risks, events or circumstances in which the insurance company will not pay out money to the insured;
- the previous insurance history of the insured;
- a statement signed by the insured to the effect that the details they have provided to the insurance company are truthful and correct and that all relevant facts have been disclosed to the insurance company.

It is this last point which is particularly significant. An individual or business seeking to take out an insurance policy must, in the first instance, complete a *proposal form*. In effect, this is a questionnaire which aims to elicit information regarding the nature of the insurance required by the person seeking the insurance, referred to at this stage as the *proposer*. The information contained within the proposal form will form the basis of the insurance policy, and, since this policy is a legally binding agreement, the proposer must complete the proposal form truthfully, disclosing any information which might influence the insurance company's decision as to whether or not to accept the risk. If the proposer does not disclose all the relevant information then, in the event of a claim by the insured, the insurance company could be within its rights to refuse to pay out any money to the policyholder.

Another important principle which governs the relationship between the insured and the insurance company concerns the total amount of money which will be paid out by the insurance company to the policyholder. The policyholder is not allowed to make a 'profit' when making an insurance claim. In other words, the policyholder is allowed only to be *compensated* so that, in the event of a claim, the amount of money received from the insurance company will be equal to the value of the financial loss incurred.

This principle is extended further if we consider the nature of risks which can be insured. Firstly the person seeking the insurance must have a financial interest in that which is being insured. The business organization which wishes to take out insurance on its business premises must be the legal owner of those premises. If the premises were simply rented from a property company, then (in the event of a successful insurance claim) the business would make a profit since it has suffered no financial loss. (The financial loss would in fact have been experienced by the legal owners of the business premises, the property company.)

Finally, the principle that the policyholder may not make a profit from an insurance claim extends to the legal ownership of goods which have been the subject of a successful insurance claim. The insurance company will become the legal owner of the goods and may seek to sell them in order to offset the costs of the claim. Thus, once a claim has been settled, the policyholder has no claim on the property. (If they did, they too might be able to sell the item, which would lead to their being in a better financial position than before the loss occurred – in effect they would have made a profit.)

All the circumstances described above are denoted by legal terms, the most important of which are:

- *utmost good faith* – the person seeking the insurance must disclose all relevant facts when completing the proposal form;
- *material facts* – any piece of information which affects the insurance premium or the decision of the insurance company to accept the transfer of the risk to them;
- *insurable interest* – the proposer must have a legal or financial interest in whatever is insured;
- *subrogation* – the transfer of property rights from the policyholder to the insurance company.

One final point must be stressed if we are to understand the basic principles of insurance – the relationship between the level of risk and the premium paid. Put simply there is a direct relationship between the level of risk and the insurance premium – in other words, *the higher the risk, the higher the premium*. Indeed there may be circumstances in which the level of risk is so high that the insurance company may decline the proposal. No insurance company is obliged to accept a risk just because insurance is applied for.

What types of risks could be the subject of an insurance policy? For the purposes of our study we will concentrate upon the following aspects of insurance:

- property insurance
- financial insurance
- liability insurance
- life insurance.

Property insurance

The business organization is likely to own a significant number of assets including:

- business premises
- stock
- vehicles
- machinery
- computers.

Each of these assets may represent a considerable investment on behalf of the business, and loss or damage to any of them could result in financial difficulties, particularly if they have to be replaced. Insurance companies provide a range of policies for such risks.

- *fire insurance* – provides protection in the event of damage by fire;
- *motor insurance* – covers damage to company vehicles as well as damage caused by company vehicles to property belonging to others;
- *business interruption insurance* – in effect a combination of different business insurance policies which provide protection in the event of disruption to the business owing to such events as fire or flooding. Unlike the standard fire policy which simply covers damage to company premises, this type of insurance will aim to allow the business to continue with its operations whilst the damage is repaired and until such time as normal business operations can be resumed. These policies are likely to include such elements as payment for temporary accommodation, protection against loss of net profits, the payment of wages and salaries to key staff and the payment of loans and other business commitments that require continued regular payments.

Financial insurance

A business which sells goods on credit is taking a risk, since there is a possibility that the 'purchasers' of the goods or service will not be able to pay for them. An individual customer might become unemployed and experience a fall in income which results in financial difficulties, or a business customer might suffer a fall in profits which reduces that business's ability to pay its debts. Both these examples lead to *'bad debts'* and a high level of bad debts can cause potential difficulties for a business organization whose financial planning will have been based on the notion that the goods sold should result in sales income.

Similar financial difficulties can arise in cases where individual employees of the business steal money or embezzle funds which belong to the business.

For such instances, 2 business insurances are offered by the insurance companies:

- *credit insurance* – provides protection for the business organization which has sold goods on credit. Outstanding bad debts will be paid by the insurance company as detailed in the policy.
- *fidelity guarantee insurance* – protects the business against the activities of dishonest staff who steal company funds.

Liability insurance

There are likely to be instances where the activities of the business organization result in injury to individuals or damage to their property. Where it can be proved that the business was at fault, and was therefore *negligent* in the way it conducted its duties, a legal claim may be made against the business. If the claim succeeds, the business may have to pay out large sums of money to any injured parties. What makes this type of risk even greater is that, in law, there will be instances in which the business has responsibility for the actions taken by its employees. Three main types of responsibility can be identified with regard to the business:

- to provide a safe working environment for employees;
- to ensure that the activities of the business do not injure members of the public or their property;
- to ensure that any products which the business manufactures are safe.

Insurance policies have been developed to protect the business organization in the event that these responsibilities are not met.

- *Employer's liability insurance* – protects the business against claims following injury to an employee carrying out work on behalf of the business. In many countries, including the UK, this type of insurance is required by law.
- *Public liability insurance* – protects the business against claims made against it by members of the public who have been injured or whose personal property has been damaged.

- *Product liability insurance* – protects the business if a claim is made against it as a result of a faulty product causing personal injury or damage to personal property.

Life insurance

In some business organizations, the contributions of one or 2 key people make a significant contribution towards the continued success of its operations, for instance:

- a research scientist engaged in developing new forms of raw materials;
- a talented and respected fashion designer;
- an engineer working on new production processes which will significantly reduce costs.

In the event of the death of one of these key people, the business may suffer financial consequences which have a direct impact on profit levels. Partnerships also have a significant problem if one of the partners dies. Once again the insurance industry is on hand with a suitable range of policies:

- *Life insurance* – provides for the payment of a lump sum in the event of the death of the insured. There are 3 main types of life insurance:

    – *term insurance* lasts for a defined period or term and provides for the payment of a lump sum in the event of the death of the insured during the policy term;

    – *endowment insurance* lasts for a defined period or term and provides for a lump sum to be paid either on the death of the insured or upon their survival at the end of the policy term;

    – *whole life insurance* involves paying premiums until the death of the insured, at which time a lump sum will be paid to the policyholder's beneficiaries.

- *Key person insurance* – a special type of life insurance which pays out a sum of money to the business in the event of a named 'key person' dying.

Insurance and the business environment

In later chapters we will see how the investment activities of the insurance companies have a direct impact on business activity, but for the purpose of our current discussion we need to stress the influence of the insurance sector on the business environment.

In essence, the existence of the insurance sector indirectly promotes the development of business organizations, since people who wish to start their own business can at least organize the activities of the business with the security of knowing that a number of major business risks can be transferred to the insurance companies.

Without the 'safety net' of insurance, even large firms would be worse off since the value of the risks they are able to transfer to the insurance companies enables them to engage in investment and development activities with a greater degree of confidence.

The business environment and business finance

Chapter 9 will be devoted to *business finance* but here we need to consider this topic as an influence on the *business organization* when it engages in *business activity* within the *business environment*.

Although we have previously described business activity as the process whereby people, raw materials, and capital are organized together in such a way as to produce goods and services required by the consumer, in a developed economy, *money* plays a vital role in ensuring that such activity can be organized as effectively as possible.

We can show the importance of money with reference to the production process:

- people need to be paid wages and salaries;
- raw materials need to be purchased;
- equipment needs to be purchased and maintained;
- the business may need to borrow money to engage in business activity;
- sales need to be made and profits monitored;
- consumers need money to purchase the finished product.

Money is therefore used to finance expansion, to pay for the factors which have been engaged in the production process, to reward the owners of the business for taking risks, to monitor the financial success or otherwise of the business, and to record and monitor the level of business activity which has taken place.

These activities are all aspects of *business finance,* and the following sections highlight the influence of an important sector in the business environment that provides a range of specialized financial services to the business organization.

Commercial banks

Commercial banks, also known as *joint stock banks*, are the familiar 'High-Street banks' which include some well-known names in the business world – Barclays, Lloyds/TSB, National Westminster and the Hongkong and Shanghai Banking Corporation (HSBC). Such is the importance of these organizations that some of them have an international reputation, since their operations are based in countries throughout the world.

The commercial banks are located in the private sector of the economy and are traditionally, although not in every case, public limited companies. In other words, they exhibit the characteristics of all limited companies:

- they enjoy limited liability;
- they aim to generate a profit from their business activities;
- they are owned by shareholders.

For the purpose of our study we need to identify 3 main aspects of the activities of the commercial banks:

- How do they generate profits?
- What services do they provide to business organizations?
- How do they influence the business environment?

How do the commercial banks generate profits?

In order to understand how commercial banks make a profit, we need to refer to an important concept in the world of business finance – the *rate of interest*.

The rate of interest can be defined in two main ways:

- a reward for saving
- a cost of borrowing.

If people save money with a financial organization, they will expect to receive a 'reward' in the form of a rate of interest. Similarly, if people borrow money they will be aware that they will normally have to pay back more than they have borrowed, the difference being calculated according to the prevailing rate of interest.

Since 2 of the commercial banks' primary functions are to accept deposits and loan out funds to borrowers we can now identify how they make a profit from their business activities. Put simply, the rate of interest they pay to savers is less than the interest charged to borrowers, the difference between the 2 being equivalent to the profit which will accrue to the commercial bank.

Services provided by the commercial banks

Two of the main functions of the commercial banks have already been mentioned:

- to accept deposits
- to provide loans.

We now need to add a third:

- to provide a range of related financial services to their customers.

In this section we will consider each of these functions in turn.

Accepting deposits

The traditional function of banks from the earliest times was to accept the safekeeping of valuables. Cash, gold, jewellery, and the like were deposited with the goldsmiths, the forerunners of the modern commercial banks. The commercial banks of today still regard this as one of their primary functions. In order to provide this service the banks have designed a range of bank accounts which allow their customers to deposit money directly into their individual accounts.

Current accounts provide customers with a cheque book which allows them to purchase goods and services without the need to pay in cash. The cheque and the associated *cheque guarantee card* confirms to the seller that funds will be made available from the customer's current account to pay for the goods.

Savings accounts provide customers with the opportunity to receive a rate of interest on their savings. In today's competitive market for savings deposits, banks offer a range of such accounts which cater for the needs of individual savers.

Providing loans

Commercial banks' lending activities can be broadly classified into 2 main types:

- bank loans
- bank overdrafts.

The main difference between the 2 can be summarized as follows:

Bank loans – an agreed amount of money for a fixed period of time:

- usually a fixed rate of interest for the period of the loan
- usually repaid by fixed monthly repayments
- some banks may be willing to approve loans to those people who are not account-holders with the bank

Bank overdrafts – an agreement between the account holder and the bank to allow the account holder to 'overdraw' on their current account up to an agreed limit:

- rates of interest may vary during the period of the overdraft
- no set time to repay the overdraft
- no fixed monthly payments

Providing a range of related financial services

Modern banking is a highly competitive marketplace, with each bank striving to attract a bigger share of customer deposits and seeking to promote its own loan facilities. This competition has been brought about by a number of factors:

The influence of financial services

- in the UK, building societies have been allowed to offer services which were traditionally associated with the commercial banks. This increase in competition has become more marked as other large organizations also begin to offer financial services – insurance companies and some of the major UK supermarkets now offer traditional banking services;

- business finance, and the associated banking services, is an international market;

- the development of new technology and international communications systems enables funds to be invested in financial markets throughout the world.

For these reasons, commercial banks have been keen to promote a range of ancillary services which seek to meet the financial needs of their private and business customers. Such services will include some or all of the following:

- credit cards;
- advice on investments;
- share dealing service;
- insurance services;
- 24-hour telephone banking;
- access to individual accounts through the customer's own personal computer;
- advice to business on overseas markets;
- bank references provided to business customers;
- will-writing service, including executor and trustee services;
- specialist services for new business start-ups, which may include dedicated small business advisers and, in some cases, free banking in the first year of the business's operations;
- payroll services on for business customers.

Activity

Obtain information from a number of commercial banks on the range of services they provide to private individuals and to the business community.

Compare and contrast the services provided by each of the banks in the following areas:

- range of accounts provided and their different rates of interest
- the rate of interest charged on bank loans by each of the banks
- the range of services they each offer to the small business.

Present your findings as a table.

How do commercial banks influence the business environment?

The previous section provides an insight into how the commercial banks can influence the business environment. In the first instance, the services of the commercial banks can be of direct assistance to the business organization. Like the private individual, the business organization can deposit money into its business bank account and negotiate loans to finance future developments and overdrafts to cover short-term cash-flow problems.

We should not underestimate the importance of these services since they have a direct impact on the level of business activity which takes place within the business environment.

- *Loans and overdrafts*
    - provide funds for expansion;
    - provide the necessary funds to purchase necessary stocks and raw materials;
    - promote business activity through investment in new plant and machinery;
    - promote the creation of job opportunities;
    - stimulate the development of small firms;
    - promote research and development into new products and production techniques.
- *Payment services*
    - current accounts, credit cards, and the like, allow customers to purchase goods and services without the need for cash;
    - loans and overdrafts to private customers stimulate demand for goods and services;
    - increased sales and profit levels.
- *Ancillary services*
    - payroll services allow a business to concentrate on its 'core activity';
    - business advisers promote the needs of small firms;
    - international trading divisions can assist firms seeking to export to overseas markets;
    - share-dealing services promote investment into public limited companies thereby increasing the flow of funds into the private sector of industry which can be used for investment purposes.

Later on in our study we will look in more detail at how the activities of the commercial banks can be regulated by the government to influence business activity. However, at this stage it is sufficient to understand that commercial banks are a key influence on the business environment.

Like the insurance companies, the commercial banks are important financial institutions which exert a large degree of influence on the business organizations which make up the business community. However, it should be noted that the commercial banks and insurance companies are just 2 of a number of organizations which influence the business environment. In many cases, these organizations provide specialized services to the business – market research companies, management consultants, and advertising agencies will all at some stage be referred to in our study of Business Practice.

In this final section of the chapter we will consider another kind of organization which specializes in providing financial services to the business organization.

Merchant banks

We saw in Chapter 1 that one of the common features of a developed economy is that of *specialization*. In the financial sector of the economy, an example of specialization is to be found in the role performed by the merchant banks. As their name implies, these banks have a long history of providing services to the business community. The fact that they are called *merchant* banks provides us with a clue to their origin, which is to be found in the early development of international trade.

The traditional role of the merchant banks is the service that they provide to those businesses whose trading activities involve the buying and selling of goods and services in international markets. A firm that wished to engage in overseas trading activities would want the assurance that the goods sold to businesses in other countries would be paid for since it was likely that the people who had ordered such goods would not pay for them until they had actually sold them in their own market. In order to overcome this difficulty, *bills of exchange* were developed. The bills of exchange were drawn up by the exporter and signed by the overseas trader as an acknowledgement that the goods received were subject to payment at a later date. It became common practice for the exporter to sell these bills of exchange to a third party for an amount less than that owed by the overseas trader.

As a result of this process of *discounting bills of exchange:*

- the exporter would have immediate access to cash funds;
- the purchaser of the bill of exchange would receive the full value of the money owed by the overseas trader, the difference being the equivalent of the purchaser's profit.

What was the role of the merchant banks in this process? Quite simply, they provided, in effect, an 'insurance' that, in the event of the overseas trader defaulting on the debt, they would provide the necessary funds to the purchaser of the bill of exchange. This was confirmed by the merchant bank signing the back of the bill of exchange, a process known as *acceptance*. Because the merchant banks still perform this function of *accepting bills of exchange* they are also referred to as *acceptance houses*.

The functions of modern-day merchant banks now extend well beyond their traditional service of accepting bills of exchange. Modern day merchant banks now offer a range of additional services which can usefully be classified in 2 main areas:

- advice to businesses
- issue of new shares on behalf of the business organization.

Let us now look at each of these areas in turn.

Advice to businesses

We saw that the commercial banks provide a range of services to the business community. The merchant banks offer broadly similar services but specialize in providing these services to large corporate clients. These services can involve the following:

- advice on organizational structure
- management advice
- specialized financial advice
- advice on mergers and takeovers
- advice on new markets
- investment services for corporate clients, for example, insurance companies and pension funds, who engage in large-scale share dealings and investments
- safekeeping of corporate legal documents.

Issue of new shares

We saw in Chapter 1 that large public limited companies can obtain funds for expansion by issuing shares. Issuing new shares involves complicated procedures many of which involve company law. The merchant bank will be able to offer a comprehensive service which ensures that all regulations are met, the administrative procedures are put into place, the advertisements are placed in the relevant press and the applications for shares are processed. This service is particularly valuable for those companies which are issuing shares for the first time. Potential purchasers of shares, who may not be familiar with the company, may be more willing to purchase the shares if they can see that the share offer is being coordinated by a well-known merchant bank.

Competition in the financial services sector

The 1980s saw a dramatic transformation in the financial services sector. In the UK, the driving force behind these changes was a government committed to introducing more competition into the financial services market. Competition, it was argued, would promote efficiency and provide more choice for the consumer. We noted earlier how building societies, insurance companies and even supermarkets have all entered the marketplace traditionally served by the banks. It should now be noted that, although we have identified the merchant banks as *'specialist'* banks, in truth, most of the commercial banks have also developed specialist divisions, some of which have functions similar to those performed by the merchant banks. Once again we see how the dynamics of the marketplace influence business decisions, structures and practice.

Chambers of Commerce and business networks

As we have seen, the financial services sector aims to provide a range of services which directly assist business organizations. At the same time, the business community itself has developed a number of formal organizations and informal networks which both assist individual business organizations and, at the same time, extend their own influence in the wider community which they serve.

Chambers of Commerce are examples of voluntary associations comprising representatives of prominent people engaged in the business community. In the UK they are found in most large towns and, although they are independent associations, they work together through membership of the Association of British Chambers of Commerce.

Chambers of Commerce provide 2 main services for the business community:

- they make representations to central and local government on concerns and issues which affect the business community;
- they offer specialized services to members.

The *representative function* may involve such aspects as the adequacy or otherwise of training schemes in a local area, the impact of government policies on specific areas of business, the provision of local services and the specific requirements of small firms with regards to finance, grants, the tax system and government regulations.

With regard to *services to business*, by far the most important is concerned with the promotion of international trading activities. In this respect the Chambers are able to provide specialist information on international markets, trade regulations, and opportunities for exporting to overseas markets. They are also able to arrange exhibitions and organize business trade missions.

Additional services are provided by an extensive network of libraries and research facilities. Such facilities enable those engaged in specialized areas of business to access up-to-date information on tax matters, health and safety issues and employment legislation. The Chambers can also organize training programmes which cover key aspects of business operations including management training. These training courses are available to all sections of the business community but member organizations are likely to benefit from lower charges for them.

In the UK, the most important Chamber of Commerce is the London Chamber of Commerce and Industry (LCCI). In addition to the services described above, the LCCI has a dedicated Examinations Board whose roots go back to the 1880s when

Influences on business activity

the Chamber established a Commercial Education Committee. The modern-day Examinations Board is responsible for developing a series of examinations and associated educational programmes which meet the needs of the international business community. In this respect, the LCCIEB has established an international reputation for its business examinations, and successful graduates from its programmes are to be found in many important sections of business throughout the international business community.

Business networks are to be found throughout the business community, and many of them are representative organizations from specific sectors of business and commerce. Whereas Chambers of Commerce represent all sectors of the business community, these business networks comprise organizations which seek to represent the views and common interests of specific sections of the business community.

Some of these networks have developed into formal organizations such as trade associations and other examples are to be found in the financial services sector in such organizations as the Association of British Insurers. Further examples include The Association of British Travel Agents and the Institute of Bankers.

Like the Chambers of Commerce, these business networks and associations perform a number of important functions including:

- promoting the interests of the specific sector of the economy to the government and other agencies;
- providing services and business advice to member organizations;
- providing training programmes to members;
- establishing examination programmes which meet the requirements of the industry.

Activity

Undertake research activities in order to identify a range of business associations and networks which represent different sectors of the business community.

Describe the aims and objectives of one of the organizations and the services it offers.

There now follow some quick questions and revision exercises. They relate specifically to the chapter you have just studied. You are advised to attempt the questions without reference to the text, and then compare your answers and solutions with those on pages 74–5.

QUESTIONS

1. What is a **proposal form**?
2. What is the **insurance premium**?
3. List the type of information contained in the **insurance policy**.
4. Why should the proposer declare all **material facts** when completing the proposal form?
5. What is **fidelity guarantee insurance**?
6. What risks are covered by **liability insurances**?
7. What is the difference between a **bank loan** and a **bank overdraft**?
8. List **6** services provided by the **commercial banks**.
9. List **3** services provided by **merchant banks** to the business community.
10. List **3** services provided by **Chambers of Commerce** to the business community.

EXERCISES

1. 'Insurance is a means by which business risks can be transferred.' Discuss this statement with reference to the business organization.
2. Describe how the activities of commercial banks and insurance companies can influence the level of business activity.
3. How can the banks and insurance companies assist small businesses?

Influences on business activity

ANSWERS TO QUESTIONS

1. An application form which details the information required by the insurance company, which it uses to assess the level of risk and associated premium rates which would be payable by the person seeking insurance.
2. The cost of insurance protection.
3.
   - Name of insured and relevant personal details.
   - Risks covered by the insurance policy.
   - Risks not covered.
   - Any policy excesses or endorsements.
   - A declaration signed by the insured to the effect that the information entered on the proposal form is truthful and correct.
4. Material facts are those facts which influence the decision of the insurance company as to whether or not they will accept the transfer of risks to them and, if so, the level of premium which would be payable.
5. An insurance policy which protects the business against the activities of dishonest staff who steal company funds.
6. Those risks which might arise as a result of a legal claim concerning a business organization's negligence. The risks may apply to the business in its role as an employer or as a provider of goods and services to the general public.
7. A bank loan is for a specific sum of money over a set period of time at a fixed rate of interest. A bank overdraft is a facility provided to holders of current accounts who are given permission by the bank to overdraw on their account up to an agreed limit. Interest payable on the overdraft is variable and there is no set time within which the overdraft needs to be repaid.
8.
   - Credit cards
   - Bank accounts
   - Financial advice
   - Bank loans and overdrafts
   - Specialized services for small businesses
   - Payroll services for businesses.
9.
   - Specialized financial advice relating to share issues
   - Accepting bills of exchange
   - Advice on mergers and takeovers.
10.
    - Information on overseas markets
    - Training services
    - Arranging exhibitions and organizing trade missions.

SOLUTIONS TO EXERCISES

1. Business activity involves risks, and the decisions made by the business itself will all contribute to the success or otherwise of the business organization. Additionally, the business environment itself contains a number of risks which may impact upon the business – fire, storm damage and theft, etc.

   One decision which needs to be taken by the business organization concerns the identification of those risks against which it wishes to insure – for example, it may wish to insure its stock against loss by fire damage or theft. Once this exercise has been completed, the business can take out an insurance policy which effectively transfers these risks to the insurance company upon payment of the insurance premium. As a result of this process, the business can engage in its operations safe in the knowledge that any losses which arise in connection with the insured risks will be borne by the insurance company.

2. Business activity concerns the process whereby productive factors are combined together in order to produce goods and services. The prime purpose of business organizations is to produce goods and services which satisfy consumer wants. In other words, there is a direct relationship between business activity and the role and purpose of business organizations. Both the commercial banks and the insurance companies offer a range of services which both directly and indirectly influence the level of business activity. Bank loans to private individuals can result in increased sales, and such loans to the business community can lead to growth, expansion and the development of new products. A range of payment services including credit cards and cheque books can stimulate consumer demand, and with it the production of goods and services, ie *business activity*. International business activity is encouraged through a number of services offered by the banks to those business organizations involved in international trade. On a smaller scale, the banks are particularly keen to promote the development of new business organizations in order to generate a bigger customer base. In the same way, insurance companies also influence business activity, since the existence of a range of specialized business insurance policies means that risks can be transferred from the business to the insurance companies. This encourages the growth of new business organizations as well as stimulating investment opportunities within existing businesses.

3. Banks and insurance companies assist small firms in a number of ways.

Influences on business activity

POINTS TO REMEMBER

- Business activity, particularly in the private sector, involves risks.
- Profit is the reward received for taking risks.
- The greater the risk involved in a business venture, the greater will be the expected profits.
- Insurance is a financial service which allows some of the risks inherent in business activity to be transferred to an insurance company.
- The insurance contract is based on 4 main principles – utmost good faith, disclosure of material facts, insurable interest and indemnity.
- The principle of indemnity allows the policyholder to be compensated only for a financial loss.
- The existence of the insurance sector promotes the development of business organizations thereby stimulating business activity.
- Commercial banks, or joint-stock banks, are the familiar 'high street banks' and are located in the private sector of the economy.
- Commercial banks accept deposits, provide loans and provide a range of related financial services to their customers which include private individuals as well as business organizations.
- The activities of the commercial banks have both a direct and indirect influence on the level of business activity.
- Merchant banks are specialized financial institutions which provide financial services to business organizations including international trading services, advice to business and share issues.
- Chambers of Commerce are voluntary associations comprising representatives of prominent people engaged the business community.
- The London Chamber of Commerce and Industry is the most important Chamber of Commerce in the UK.
- Trade Associations represent the interests of specific sections of the business community.

5

The influence of the government on the business environment

> **After carefully studying this chapter, you should be able to:**
> 1 *describe how and why the government may seek to influence the activities of business organizations;*
> 2 *explain the main economic indicators;*
> 3 *explain what is meant by the global market.*

> **Extended Syllabus references**
> 1.10 Describe how and why the government may seek to influence the activities of business organizations:
>   1.10.1   government expenditure
>   1.10.2   taxation policies
>   1.10.3   changes in interest rate
>   1.10.4   measures to promote international trade
> 1.11 Explain what is meant by the term global market
> 1.12 Explain the main economic indicators and how they can have an affect on business activity:
>   1.12.1   standard of living
>   1.12.2   cost of living
>   1.12.3   national income
>   1.12.4   economic growth
>   1.12.5   inflation
>   1.12.6   exchange rates

This chapter will centre upon the role of the government and, in particular, how it seeks to influence the business environment in furtherance of its economic objectives. The reader will also be introduced to a range of specialist business terms which will provide the focus for measuring the performance and general well-being of a nation's economy.

Introduction

In Chapter 1 we identified the public sector as that in which the productive factors are owned and controlled by the government. We showed that public corporations, or nationalized industries, were the main types of organization found in the public sector.

In this chapter we will consider the role of the government and its influence on the level of business activity by concentrating upon the following key areas:

- What are the economic objectives of the government?
- How does the government seek to achieve these objectives?

What are the economic objectives of the government?

For the purposes of our study we will identify 4 main economic objectives of government which are common to most countries:

- economic growth
- price stability
- job opportunities
- promotion of international trade.

Economic growth

Economic growth is central to a government's economic objectives. Indeed, it could be argued that without economic growth, none of the other objectives could be achieved.

What is economic growth?

Economic growth is the *rate of increase* in the output of goods and services in an economy over a given period of time as measured by the nation's *national income*.

National income

National income measures the total amount of goods and services produced as a result of combining together the productive factors – people, raw materials, equipment, and capital. National income is usually measured over a period of time, and this measurement provides the opportunity for a country to measure its economic performance against another country's performance. Both the *rate* of economic growth and the *level* of national income are used by the government to measure the success or otherwise of its own economic policies.

What factors influence the level of economic growth?

Later in this chapter we will describe the range of policies which a government may seek to introduce in order to promote economic growth. At this stage, however, it is useful to consider, in general terms, a range of factors which may influence a country's economic growth rates.

- *People*
  - level of skills, qualifications and training
  - adaptability and ingenuity
  - working practices.
- *Raw materials*
  - access to a range of raw materials which can be 'processed' to produce goods and services
- *Capital*
  - rate of investment in new plant and equipment
  - level of investment in new technology
  - quality of capital stock
  - production techniques
  - availability of finance to promote and support new investment opportunities.
- *General state of the economy*
  - is there sufficient consumer and business demand in the economy to promote the output of goods and services?
  - do businesses feel confident enough to invest long-term in new plant and equipment?
  - do consumers feel confident enough to spend their money or are they too cautious, preferring instead to save?
  - are profit levels within the business environment at a level which will stimulate business activity?

Price stability

In our everyday lives we will have become aware that, over a period of time, there is a tendency for the price of goods to increase. Such increases in prices can result from a number of factors:

- changes in the level of demand;
- increased costs for producers which are passed on to the consumer in the form of higher prices;
- shortages of particular products in the competitive market;
- changes in government tax rates.

In some respects, it can be argued that the general increase in the price level is a natural outcome of a dynamic and growing economy. However, most governments will seek to control the level of *inflation* and try to ensure that the general increase in the price level is kept within a certain percentage range. In order to do this, governments must have some means by which they can measure the rate of inflation, and it is for this reason that the concept of the *cost of living* has been established.

Measuring the rate of inflation – the cost of living

The *rate* of inflation, ie the rate at which prices are increasing, is measured in most countries by the *cost of living*. In turn, the cost of living is identified by reference to some form of *retail price index (RPI)*. In technical terms, the RPI can be defined as a weighted average of prices of goods and services in the economy, measured over time. In simpler terms it can be described by identifying the major purchases which consumers make on a regular basis, the so-called 'basket of goods', and measuring the increase in the prices of these goods over a set period of time, say quarterly, half-yearly or annually. The resulting increases in the index will, in effect, be indicative of the rate of increase in the general price level within the economy as a whole and, hence, the rate of inflation.

Again, besides being an important indicator of government policy, the RPI is also used as an international 'performance indicator', since one country can compare its own inflation rate against other countries'.

Why should a government be concerned with the rate of inflation?

Governments need to ensure that prices within the economy are relatively stable and keep within an acceptable range. If the rate of inflation is too high, it can have a detrimental effect on the government's ability to achieve its other economic objectives, to the extent that the economy as a whole begins to under-perform.

The influence of the government

Table 5.1 shows the impact of inflation on a number of key groups within the business environment.

Table 5.1 The impact of inflation on key groups within the economy

Group	Impact of inflation	Result
Employees	• real value of wages and salaries decrease • demands made for higher wages and salaries	• disputes may arise between employee representatives and business organizations • labour costs will increase if wage demands are successful
Business organizations	• increase in costs (raw materials and labour) • less competitive compared with international competitors • fall in the demand for goods which are produced for overseas markets	• business failures • job losses
Savers	• value of savings reduced over time • people discouraged from saving	• less funds available for investment purposes • fall in business investment • economic growth may be reduced

Table 5.1 identifies a number of adverse results which follow from high rates of inflation. It should be noted that, from a government perspective, inflation is also politically unpopular – no-one likes the experience of having to pay more for goods and services – and, as such, a government ignores the rate of inflation at its peril.

The table also makes reference to the '*real value of wages*' and the '*real value of income*'. What does this mean in practice? Earlier in this chapter we described the national income in terms of the output of goods and services in the economy. This provides a clue as to what is meant by *real wages* and *real income*.

In effect, wages or income have little value unless they can be used to purchase goods and services. Real wages and real income measure the total amount of goods and services which can be purchased from money wages and income. As such, we are able to purchase *less* in the way of goods and services with our money if prices increase.

An understanding of this concept is important if we are to understand another important economic indicator – *the standard of living*. An individual is likely to consider his or her own standard of living in terms of the amount of goods and services he or she owns. In effect, if we compare 'rich' and 'poor' individuals we are likely to do so on the basis of:

Influences on business activity

- their monetary income
- their real wealth
- the level of their savings.

For a country seeking to identify the standard of living of its citizens, the point of reference is the level of national income, ie the total amount of goods and services produced in the economy. If we give a monetary value to these goods and services and divide this amount by the number of citizens in the population, we arrive at the *per capita* (or *per head*) national income, ie the amount of goods and services which, on average, are consumed by an individual citizen. This is illustrated in the tables below.

Table 5.2   Comparison of national income between 2 countries

	Country A	Country B
National income	$1,000 million (US)	$750 million (US)

If we referred solely to the level of national income we could assume that Country A was 'richer', in other words it had a higher national income. However, if we take into account the population of the 2 countries and calculate their respective *per capita income*, as in Table 5.3, we find a different picture emerges.

Table 5.3   Comparison of the per capita national income between 2 countries

	Country A	Country B
National income	$1,000 million (US)	$750 million (US)
Population	50 million	20 million
Per capita national income	$20 (US)	$37.5 (US)

Table 5.3 clearly shows that *per capita income* is likely to be a better indicator of a nation's standard of living than its overall, aggregate national income (Table 5.2). However, we must strike a note of caution at this stage, since, although per capita income is a more appropriate indicator of a country's standard of living, it may not provide us with the full picture for the following reasons:

- We would need to know the *distribution* of national income between different groups of citizens.
- We would need to know the distribution of national income between consumer goods and capital goods.
- We would need to know something about the country's 'quality of life' – has the high level of national income resulted in pollution, congestion and other undesirable environmental consequences?

- has the increase in per capita income been brought about by people having to work longer hours rather than by the introduction of more efficient and effective production methods?

> **Activity**
>
> Compare the national income and the per capita income of 4 countries with your own country. The countries should incorporate the following:
>
> - a European country
> - a country from the Middle East
> - a country from southeast Asia
> - a country from the Indian sub-continent.
>
> What conclusions can you draw from your research?

Job opportunities

As with the level of economic growth and the rate of inflation, the level of unemployment in an economy is another important indicator of the economy's overall economic performance – and with it the success or otherwise of the government's economic policies. Put simply, an economy which is enjoying high rates of economic growth is likely to be generating new employment opportunities as existing business organizations expand their production and new businesses are established to meet the increase in demand generated within the economy. Conversely, high levels of unemployment are more likely to be experienced when there are relatively low levels of economic growth.

In truth, this analysis is oversimplified, since we can identify different *types* of unemployment, some of which will exist *regardless of the level of economic growth within the economy*. The different types of unemployment are summarized in Table 5.4.

Why is the government concerned with unemployment rates?

Later in this chapter we shall see why it is vital for the government to be able to identify the type of unemployment it is dealing with since different types of unemployment may require different government policies. But why, in the first instance, should the government concern itself with the level of unemployment? Certain key reasons stand out:

Influences on business activity

- the level of unemployment is an economic indicator of an economy's performance;
- high levels of unemployment are politically unacceptable;
- high levels of unemployment result in productive factors – people – not contributing to the economy; this is particularly significant if the unemployed are highly skilled and qualified;
- skilled people may leave the country to work in other countries, thereby contributing to the economy of potential competitors;

Table 5.4 Characteristics of the different types of unemployment

Types of unemployment	Characteristics	Examples
Transitional	• unemployment which arises as people change their jobs • usually of a short-term nature	
Seasonal	• unemployment which arises out seasonal changes	• tourist industry • building industry
Regional	• unemployment which arises when a region specializes in the production of a particular product which is then subject to a fall in demand or increased competition from new suppliers in other regions or different countries.	• those regions in the UnitedKingdom which specialized in the production of coal, iron and steel, shipbuilding and textiles.
Structural	• unemployment brought about by fundamental changes in the structure of an industry which give rise to long-term unemployment	• introduction of new technology • replacement of coal by cheaper forms of energy
Cyclical	• unemployment which is brought about by a fall in the level of economic activity within the national or international market economy • this type of unemployment will tend to effect *all* firms and industries in the economy and is therefore viewed as the most serious type of unemployment • cyclical unemployment is associated with '*mass unemployment*' which affects all sections of the community	• economic depressions, eg 'the Great Depression' of the 1930s and the more recent depression in the UK economy which occurred during the period 1979–82

- the investment made by the government to train and educate these people would be wasted;
- unemployment is related to high levels of poverty;
- the cost of the government's social welfare benefits programme may increase;
- long-term unemployment can have disastrous effects on the social cohesion between different social groupings, which may result in civil disturbances;
- it may be difficult for those who have been unemployed for a long period of time to return to work should job opportunities become available in the future, because of a lack of up-to-date and relevant skills or a lack of motivation.

Promotion of international trade

The promotion of international trade highlights the critical importance of the *international marketplace*. Dramatic improvements in technology, communications, and transportation have all resulted in the development of a mature *global economy* in which countries specialize in the production of goods and services which they then seek to exchange in the international marketplace.

Another feature which has become more important over the last half century has been the growth of trading blocs, trading zones, free-trade areas and common markets. The common feature of all these developments is that they seek to join countries together as 'preferred trading partners'.

The most extreme example of this trend is to be found in Europe, where 15 countries operate collectively within a European Union and plan to introduce a single currency, the Euro, as the common monetary unit, replacing the existing national currencies which operate in the individual member states.

Why should governments be so concerned to promote international trade?

The answer to this question is to be found in our discussions so far, since international trade allows a country to benefit from the following advantages:

- access to bigger markets;
- opportunities for business expansion;
- stimulates the national economy and helps to create jobs;
- increases competition;
- bigger choice of goods and services for the consumer;
- generates increased output for individual firms, thereby increasing the opportunity to benefit from economies of scale;
- promotes links between countries which results in mutual respect for each others customs and culture.

Influences on business activity

The international trading activities of a country are recorded in a special set of national accounts known as *the balance of payments*. This is a financial statement of account which records a country's export sales and its spending on imports along with any international capital movements including investments and foreign currency.

It is beyond the scope of this book to look in detail at the various components of the balance of payments but the following specialized terms are a useful reference guide to students of business practice:

- exports   collective term for goods and services sold to other countries
- imports   collective term for goods and services purchased from other countries
- visible exports   *goods* sold abroad
- invisible exports *goods* purchased from abroad
- invisible exports *services* sold to overseas purchasers
- invisible imports *services* purchased from overseas suppliers.

International trade should therefore be viewed as the exchange of goods and services within the international marketplace. It therefore follows that it will involve the flow of financial resources between countries as they engage in international trading activities. It is this element, in particular, in which governments are interested.

Activity

Complete the following table with reference to the UK economy, indicating whether the transaction is a visible export, visible import, invisible import or invisible export.

Transaction	Classification
A motor car produced in Japan and sold in the UK	
A computer manufactured in the UK and sold in Germany	
Swiss cheese sold in the UK	
A UK tourist purchasing holiday souvenirs in Hong Kong	
An American firm insuring its factory premises in Texas with a UK insurance company	
A Malaysian tourist purchasing theatre tickets for a London musical	
A UK manufacturer selling office equipment to the Chinese government	
A loan provided by a UK bank to an Italian fashion house	

The influence of the government

Consider a situation in which an individual, or indeed a business, spends more money than is earned. How can this 'deficit' or outflow of funds be financed? The following is a list of possible solutions:

- take money out of savings (reserves);
- borrow funds (from a bank, for example).

But what are the implications if the individual or the business continues to overspend?

- Savings will be depleted.
- May be difficult to obtain additional funds.

In the end, of course, if spending continuously exceeds income, either the individual or the business will effectively be declared bankrupt.

Such a situation is best remedied by one of 2 strategies:

- reduce spending;
- earn more money.

This simple example provides an insight into the government's concern with international trade and the balance of payments in particular. Put simply, the government must ensure that the balance of payments is not subject to continuous deficits, since this would indicate that a country is continuously spending more on imports than it is earning from the sale of its exports. Over a long period of time the country's reserves (in the form of gold and foreign currency) would be depleted, and few countries would then be willing to lend money to finance further overspending on imports.

In such cases, drastic action would be called for. On more than one occasion over the last 20 years or so, the International Monetary Fund (IMF) has been called upon to represent the international community by coming to the rescue of countries which have found themselves on the edge of an economic crisis. In the late 1990s, South Korea needed the help of the IMF to help it cope with problems of this nature, as the economies of southeast Asia began to feel the impact of the global economy, which links separate nations and their economies.

Before we leave this aspect of our study of international trade, we need to be aware of one other aspect of its organization. Despite the best intentions of those countries which are members of the European Union to develop a single currency, for the foreseeable future international trade will be conducted on the basis of a range of different national currencies. Given the number of different currencies in existence throughout the world, coupled with the volume of international trade which takes place on a daily basis, what are the implications for the individual business organization engaged in international trade?

In effect, each country's currency is valued against other country's currency. For example, £1 = 220 Japanese Yen. What does this mean in practice for the business organization engaged in international trade? Consider the following examples:

Influences on business activity

> **Example 1**
>
> A UK business organization imports raw materials from Japan when the exchange rate stands at £1 = 220 Japanese Yen.
>
> Cost of raw materials = 50,000 Japanese Yen
>
> Cost of raw materials for the UK business = 50,000 ÷ 220 = £227.27
>
> **Example 2**
>
> A UK business organization sells office furniture to Japan valued at £10,000.
> Cost of office furniture to Japanese firm = 10,000 × 220 = 2,200,000 Japanese Yen

The exchange rate of a country is in effect the *price* of one currency in terms of another. As such, like all other prices, a country's exchange rate is dependent upon the forces of demand and supply. A deficit on the balance of payments will result in a fall in the value of a country's currency, since more of its currency will be *supplied* to the foreign exchange market. Conversely, a surplus on the balance of payments will result in an increase in *demand* for a country's currency, as other countries try to obtain (demand) the currency in order to purchase imports. We are therefore likely to see exchange rates fluctuating in response to the dynamics of a country's economic performance.

> **Activity**
>
> Using Examples 1 and 2 (above), calculate the cost of the raw materials and the office furniture if the exchange rate is £1 = 150 Japanese Yen.
>
> What conclusions can you draw from this activity regarding the influence of exchange rates on the price of imports and raw materials?

Those business organizations engaged in international trade will keep a keen eye on exchange rates. Having completed the previous activity you should now be in a position to understand why a fall in a country's exchange rate will lead to an increase in the price of imports and a fall in the price of exports, whereas an increase in a country's exchange rate will result in the opposite – a fall in the price of imports and an increase in the price of exports.

> **Activity**
>
> Chart the exchange rate of your own country's currency on a weekly basis over the period of your study of business practice. Account for any major fluctuations in your country's exchange rate.

HOW DOES THE GOVERNMENT SEEK TO ACHIEVE ITS ECONOMIC OBJECTIVES?

The aim of this section is to describe the range of policies which a government may seek to introduce in order to achieve its economic objectives. This is no easy task since we are likely to discover a number of *policy conflicts* – in other words, a policy which is introduced to further one objective may impact adversely on another of the government's economic objectives. Policy conflicts occur because the factors which we have considered in this chapter – economic growth, national income, inflation, the standard of living, exchange rates and the like – are all interrelated. Indeed the predominant feature of the business environment and the national economy is the range of relationships which exist between the individual components. Let us consider these interrelationships in more detail. Consider the following economic indicators:

- national income
- economic growth
- standard of living.

What is the relationship between them? At its simplest, we might say that economic growth leads to an increase in national income and thereby to an increase in the standard of living. Figure 5.1 illustrates this relationship.

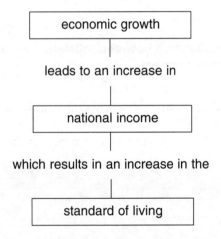

Figure 5.1 Relationship between economic growth, national income and the standard of living

Now let us take the relationship between the level of inflation, the balance of payments and the level of unemployment. Again we can show in diagram form the relationship between these 3 elements of the economy (see Figure 5.2, overleaf).

Influences on business activity

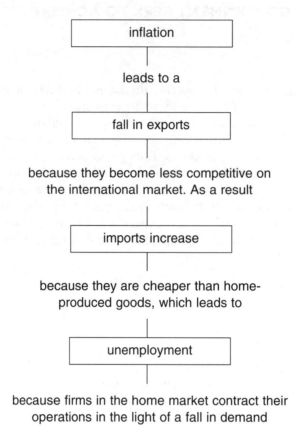

Figure. 5.2 Relationship between inflation, international trade and unemployment

It is because of these relationships that governments have developed a range of *policy tools* to further the achievement of their economic objectives. In broad terms, the most important of these policy tools can be classified in 2 main areas:

- fiscal policy
- monetary policy.

Fiscal policy

Fiscal policy is concerned with changes in government expenditure (spending) and taxation plans. Government expenditure can be used to manipulate the level of demand in the economy as a whole – for example, an increase in government spending on roads, houses, schools, and hospitals will result in an increase in demand for a whole range of specialized services. The resulting business opportunities will lead to job creation, economic growth, and increases in the national income and the related standard of living.

The influence of the government

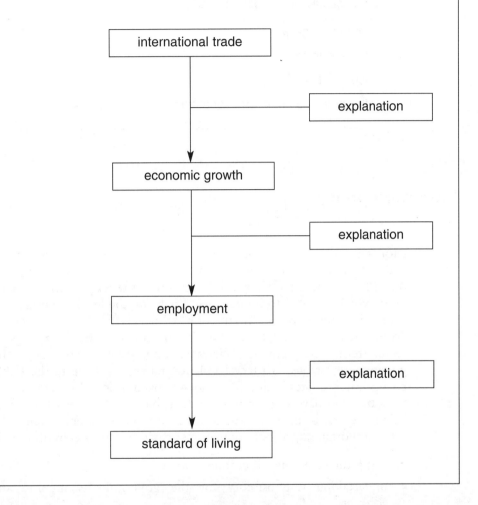

Conversely, an increase in *direct tax* (a tax on incomes) will reduce demand (consumers have less money to spend), and increases in *indirect tax* (a tax on spending) will also reduce demand (consumers will have to pay more for their goods.): both will exert a downward influence on price levels and the general level of inflation.

Fiscal policy is administered by a government finance minister and in the UK this is the role undertaken by the Chancellor of the Exchequer who is responsible for presenting the government's expenditure and taxation plans to parliament on an annual basis in the *budget*.

Influences on business activity

> **Activity**
>
> It is likely that, at some time during your Business Practice course, the government will announce its income and expenditure plans via a budget statement. Undertake the necessary research and identify how any measures announced in the budget can assist
>
> - economic growth
> - price stability
> - job creation
> - the promotion of international trade.

Monetary policy

Monetary policy can also be used to manipulate the level of demand in the economy and with it the level of business activity. However, monetary policy involves less direct intervention by the government, since it relies primarily on changes in interest rates, which are used to influence and regulate the level of business activity. In most economies there is a central bank which is under the direct control of the government; for example, in the UK, the Bank of England plays a central role in administering government policies relating to monetary policy. In the UK, the government establishes a target inflation rate and it is up to the Bank of England to change interest rates in line with movements in prices. In other countries, the central bank may not have such an independent role, and interest rates may tend to be fixed by the central bank on instruction from the government. Central banks undertake other important aspects of control over their country's economy, notably:

- being the sole issuer of currency notes;
- undertaking responsibility for the government's income and expenditure accounts;
- regulating the activities of the commercial banks;
- acting as guardian for the country's gold and currency reserves.

However, for the benefit of our analysis and the prime focus of the Business Practice programme of study, our main emphasis is on the role played by interest rates which are administered by the central bank, since changes in interest rates can influence the level of business activity undertaken by business organizations within the business environment.

Consider a situation in which a country is suffering from high levels of inflation, which results in fewer exports being sold abroad because they are more expensive than goods produced by other countries. If interest rates were increased, loans would become more expensive, which would lead to consumers borrowing less money. If consumers borrow less, they have less money available to buy goods and services and, as a result, there is a downward pressure on prices resulting in the country's exports becoming more competitive.

Policy conflicts

Unfortunately, government economic policy is not so easy to implement as the above analysis suggests. Owing to the interrelationship between the key economic variables, we are likely to see some unfortunate and unwanted 'side-effects' as a result of both fiscal and monetary policies.

Consider again the example just given (under 'monetary policy'). Although loans will become more expensive for consumers, as a result of the increase in the rate of interest, they will also become more expensive for the business organization, which may cut back on planned investment in new plant and equipment. Consequently, although exports will be cheaper, the country may not have the productive capacity to respond to the increase in demand.

Let us now take the problem of cyclical unemployment. We previously described cyclical unemployment as that which occurs when the level of demand in the economy is insufficient to generate the output of goods and services which will lead to 'full' employment. What does our analysis of fiscal and monetary policy indicate that the government should do when faced with cyclical unemployment? The following 'mix' of policy tools may be appropriate:

- increase government expenditure
- reduce interest rates
- reduce direct taxation.

A combination of these policy tools will result in an increase in demand which will stimulate production and jobs. But what if goods and services cannot be produced in large quantities in the short term, or what if too much demand is generated? Both of these circumstances could have adverse effects on the country's economy:

- inflation may increase due to excessive demand
- if consumers cannot purchase goods produced in the home market, they may demand more goods from overseas which could lead to a balance of payments deficit (overspend).

In truth, all aspects of government economic policy will tend to have 'side-effects' as the activity on the following page indicates.

It is largely because of these policy conflicts, and the associated problems and difficulties which can arise, that many governments have chosen to reduce the level of their *direct* involvement in the economy.

One aspect of this trend is to be found in the policy of *privatization* which was referred to in Chapter 1. We saw then that many previously nationalized public corporations have been privatized and returned to the private sector in the form of

Influences on business activity

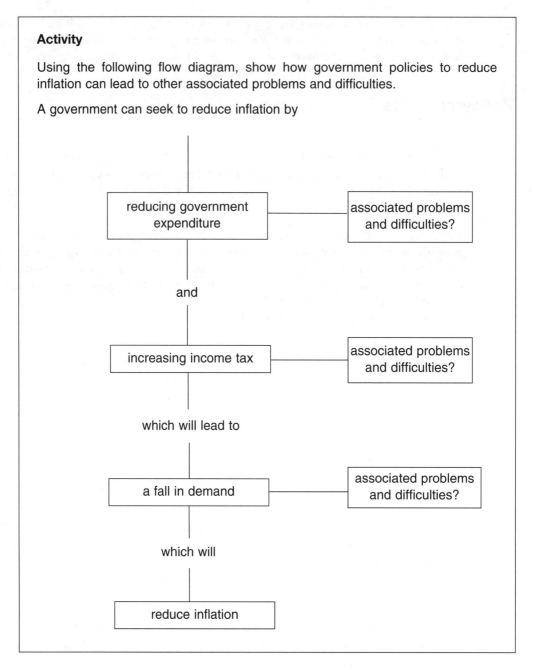

large, public limited companies owned by shareholders. Nowadays it seems that the role of the government in influencing economic activity is to be found in terms of providing the necessary conditions within which business organizations can prosper and develop, free from the direct interference of the government. This does not mean that the government does not still seek to influence and stimulate business activity; indeed there are many policies which may be used to unfluence the business environment including:

- grants for training;
- financial assistance to the unemployed;

The influence of the government

- grants to regions suffering from high levels of unemployment;
- trade missions to overseas countries to promote exports;
- promotion of health services to ensure a healthy and productive workforce;
- privatization of public sector organizations;
- tax advantages to promote the development of small firms;
- advice to firms on overseas trade and associated markets;
- direct financial assistance to individual firms;
- policies to protect the environment re-pollution and congestion;
- regulatory bodies to control those organizations which seek to use their power against the interests of the consumer.

However, despite the undoubted importance of such measures, we are increasingly led to conclude that increases in the growth of the private sector, in the competiveness of the marketplace, and in the power of the consumer – corporate and private – are now exerting more important influences on the business environment than ever before. Modern business practice recognizes this and throughout our study we shall constantly return to the policies and strategies which are employed by individual business organizations to influence their own environment.

Many commercial banks have specialist divisions which deal directly with the needs of the small firm. Specialist bank staff will have responsibility for assisting the business draw up its business plan prior to an application being made for start-up capital. Once the business commences trading it may be able to obtain on-going specialist advice along with preferential bank charges for a specified period of time. Should the business employ staff, the bank is also able to offer a payroll service which will administer all matters relating to salaries and wages.

A range of specialized insurance policies provided by the insurance companies significantly reduces the risks inherent in starting up a business. Liability insurances, financial insurances, property insurance and motor insurance will all result in a significant reduction in risks for the small firm, and life insurance, pension plans and associated savings schemes can all serve to provide long-term financial security for the owner and the owner's family.

> *There now follow some quick questions and revision exercises. They relate specifically to the chapter you have just studied. You are advised to attempt the questions without reference to the text, and then compare your answers and solutions with those on pages 97–9.*

Influences on business activity

QUESTIONS

1. List the **4** main objectives of government.
2. Define **national income**.
3. What is meant by the term **economic growth**?
4. What is the **cost of living** and how is it measured?
5. List **4** types of **unemployment**.
6. What is the difference between **structural unemployment** and **cyclical unemployment**?
7. What is meant by the **global economy**?
8. What is the difference between **invisible trade** and **visible trade**?
9. What is meant by the **exchange rate of a currency**?
10. What is the difference between **fiscal policy** and **monetary policy**?

EXERCISES

1. Describe the ways in which the government may seek to reduce inflation.
2. Show, with relevant examples, the difficulties a government may face in trying to reduce unemployment.
3. Explain the relationship between economic growth and the standard of living.

> *While attempting to answer the questions and exercises on this page, you are strongly advised not to read on and to cover the answers and solutions on the following page with a sheet of paper.*

The influence of the government

ANSWERS TO QUESTIONS

1.
   - Economic growth
   - Price stability
   - Job opportunities
   - Promotion of international trade.

2. National income is the total amount of goods and services produced in a country over a specific period of time, usually one year, and expressed in monetary terms.

3. Economic growth is the rate of increase in national income over a given period of time as measured by the nation's national income.

4. The rate at which prices are increasing. The cost of living is usually measured by some form of retail price index which seeks to measure the movement in prices over time. In simple terms, the price index usually relates to a cross-section of goods which are purchased by consumers on a regular basis. The prices of these goods are then monitored over specific time periods in order to measure the cost of living.

5.
   - Seasonal
   - Regional
   - Structural
   - Cyclical.

6. Structural employment is brought about by fundamental changes in the structure of an industry which gives rise to long-term unemployment. Cyclical unemployment is associated with the general level of economic activity which takes place within the economy, and is related to periods where there are low levels of aggregate demand.

7. The international marketplace which recognizes the importance of international specialization, international trade, international business organizations, and international communication systems.

8. Visible trade is trade in goods whilst invisible trade is trade in services.

9. The price of a country's currency in relation to another country's currency.

10. Fiscal policy is concerned with changes in government expenditure and taxation, whilst monetary policy is concerned with changes in interest rates and the money supply.

SOLUTIONS TO EXERCISES

1. The government can seek to use both fiscal and monetary policies to reduce inflation. The aim of both policies would be to regulate the level of demand in the economy whilst, at the same time, laying the foundations for an increase in economic growth.

Influences on business activity

Fiscal policy seeks to regulate the level of demand in the economy by changes in government expenditure and taxation. A reduction in government expenditure coupled with an increase in direct taxation leads to a fall in demand within the economy. Since inflation is generally associated with high levels of demand, such a policy will serve to reduce the overall level of demand in the economy, thereby exerting a downward pressure on prices.

Monetary policy, on the other hand, seeks to achieve the same goal by changing the level of interest rates. In the UK the general level of interest rates is determined by a special committee attached to the Bank of England. Changing the rate of interest will influence the level of demand in an indirect way. For example, an increase in the rate of interest will mean that loans become more expensive so people are deterred from borrowing money. Over a period of time this will result in a downward pressure on demand and prices and, with it, inflation.

2 A government seeking to reduce unemployment must, in the first instance, determine the type of unemployment it is dealing with, since different types of unemployment will demand different policy responses. Structural unemployment, which is closely related to regional unemployment, is brought about by fundamental changes in the structure of an industry. The replacement of coal by cheaper sources of energy and the impact of new technology are 2 examples of how structural unemployment can be caused. Government policies to reduce structural unemployment can involve the re-training of workers, and issuing government grants in the regions affected to encourage the development of new business organizations, along with grants and subsidies to attract new firms into the area concerned. Developments in the infrastructure can also be used to facilitate new business development.

Cyclical unemployment requires a different response, since it is caused by an insufficient level of demand across the economy as a whole and, as such, to some extent, affects all industries and all regions within the country. Both fiscal and monetary policy can be used to reduce cyclical unemployment by a combination of increasing government expenditure, reducing direct taxation and reducing interest rates, all of which will serve to increase the overall level of demand in the economy. In turn this will stimulate the production of goods and services which will generate employment opportunities.

The major problem which governments experience in trying to reduce unemployment is, firstly, to be confident that they can determine the type of unemployment they are dealing with and, secondly, to ensure that they use the appropriate policy tools. However, perhaps the most serious problem encountered by government is when they seek to 'fine-tune' the economy on the basis of regulating the level of demand. Far too often, it would appear, governments have generated too much demand, resulting in inflation which, in turn, leads to a fall in exports accompanied by an increase in unemployment – the very problem the government was seeking to address in the first instance.

3 Economic growth measures the rate at which the national income is increasing over time. This is an important economic indicator since economic growth and the national income will both influence a country's standard of living. The

standard of living is an indicator of the overall wealth of a country's citizens and, in general terms, when we speak of a 'rich country' we are in fact referring to the overall standard of living of its citizens.

An indication of a country's standard of living is to be found by measuring the per capita national income. This is calculated by dividing the country's national income by its total population. An increase in the national income will result in an increase in economic growth and, with it, an increase in the standard of living. Such figures must be used with care since both the composition of the national income and its distribution amongst the population can both serve to influence the standard of living of a significant number of people within the population.

Influences on business activity

POINTS TO REMEMBER

- The 4 main economic objectives of government which are common to most countries are to encourage economic growth, to maintain price stability, to generate the conditions which result in the creation of job opportunities and to promote international trade.
- Economic growth is related to increases in national income.
- National income is the total amount of goods and services produced by a country over a given period of time.
- Changes in national income have an influence on a country's standard of living.
- Inflation is an indicator of the rate at which prices are rising.
- Inflation can be measured by a retail price index which, in turn, is an indicator of a country's cost of living.
- The standard of living and the cost of living are both important economic indicators which identify the general well-being of a country's economy.
- It is important for the government to be able to identify the types of unemployment which may exist in the economy in order that it can adapt its economic policies accordingly.
- International trade leads to international specialization within the global economy.
- The balance of payments is a financial statement of account which records a country's export sales and its spending on imports, along with any international capital movements including investments and foriegn currency.
- The balance of payments incorporates details of visible and invisible exports and imports.
- The exchange rate of a country's currency will have a direct impact on the price of its exports and imports.
- A government can use both fiscal and monetary policies to achieve its economic objectives.
- Fiscal policy is concerned with changes in taxation rates and government expenditure patterns.
- Monetary policy relies primarily on changes in interest rates which influence the level of money supply.
- Monetary policy is implemented by the Central Bank on behalf of the government.
- Both fiscal and monetary policies are likely to result in unwanted 'side effects' which lead to policy conflicts whereby government measures to promote a specific policy objective can have an adverse effect on another of its objectives.

Part 2
The functions and organization of business

6

The internal organization of the business

After carefully studying this chapter, you should be able to:

1 *describe the main functional areas within organizations;*

2 *identify the objectives associated with the main functional areas and the duties of principal staff;*

3 *explain how organization charts can aid understanding of specialization and separation of responsibilities of staff;*

4 *describe the advantages of specialization to the business organization;*

5 *compare and contrast the organization of business functions in small and large organizations;*

6 *explain why an international organization may need to organize itself in different ways.*

Extended Syllabus references

2.1　Describe the main functional areas within organizations:
　　　2.1.1　personnel/human resources
　　　2.1.2　production/operations
　　　2.1.3　purchasing
　　　2.1.4　finance/accounts
　　　2.1.5　sales and marketing
　　　2.1.6　administration
　　　2.1.7　research and development

2.2　Identify the objectives associated with the main functional areas and the duties of principal staff

(continued)

The functions and organization of business

> **Extended Syllabus references (continued)**
>
> 2.3 Explain how organization charts can aid understanding of specialization and separation of responsibilities of staff
>
> 2.4 Describe the advantages of specialization to the business organizations
>
> 2.5 Compare and contrast the organization of business functions in small and large organizations
>
> 2.6 Explain why an international organization may need to organize itself in different ways as a result of:
>
>   2.6.1 legal systems
>   2.6.2 Government policy
>   2.6.3 international communications needs

The focus of this chapter is on the internal organization of the business. Specifically, we will consider the various *functions* which need to be undertaken in order for the business to deliver and support the production of goods and services. The central theme which will run through the chapter concerns the part played by *specialization* and how the internal organization of the business seeks to exploit the advantages of specialization within each of the identified functional areas.

Business functions

In Section 1 we became familiar with some of the key concepts and ideas which provide the framework for our study of Business Practice. Two of these concepts are important in the context of this chapter – the *production process* and the *trading cycle*. Figure 6.1 shows a simplified version of the production process and identifies 3 basic stages – inputs, process and output.

Since it is a *simplified* version of the production process, Figure 6.1 does not provide

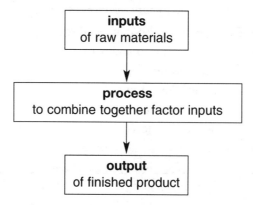

Figure 6.1 Simplified version of the production process

The internal organization of the business

us with a comprehensive understanding of the business functions which must be undertaken to ensure that the process is delivered and supported. Figure 6.2 on the other hand combines the basic idea of the production process with the elements of the trading cycle described in Chapter 1. It thus allows us to identify some of the functions which are required to be performed by the business if it is to successfully engage in productive business activity.

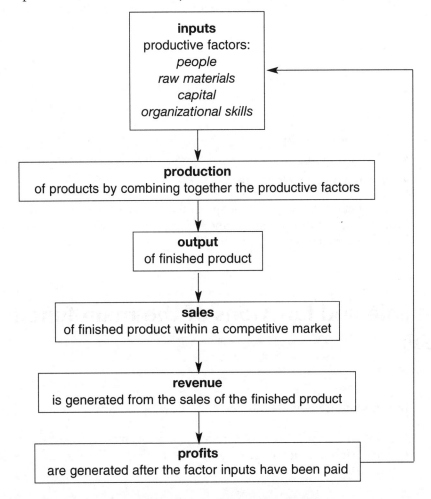

Figure 6.2 **The production process and the trading cycle**

Let us look at the process outlined in Figure 6.2 in order to determine some of the essential business functions which support the production process and the related trading cycle:

- the business will need to *purchase* raw materials and equipment;
- the business will need to employ *personnel*;
- the business will need to *produce* goods and services;
- the business will need to successfully *market* the goods if it is to achieve *sales*;
- the business will need to keep *financial* records concerning, amongst other things, its costs, revenue and profits;

The functions and organization of business

- the business will need to have *administrative* systems and procedures which support and coordinate the whole process;
- the business will need to engage in *research and development* activities in order to develop new products.

In other words, we can identify a number of key *business functions* related to business activity. For the purpose of our study of Business Practice, we will identify 7 of these functions:

- personnel/human resources
- production/operations
- purchasing
- finance/accounts
- sales and marketing
- administration
- research and development.

Depending on the range and scope of the business activity in which they are engaged, business organizations will exhibit organizational characteristics which cover some or all of these functions and, for this reason, they are referred to as *functional areas*.

The role and functions of the main functional areas

In this section we will consider the following aspects of each functional area:

- the role of each functional area
- what each functional area contributes to the achievement of the objectives of the business.

The personnel/human resources function

The role of the personnel function is to ensure that the business has sufficient numbers of staff who possess the necessary skills to enable them to contribute to the success of the business. In other words:

> *Making sure the business has the right people to do the right jobs.*

The internal organization of the business

In order to ensure that this role is undertaken efficiently and effectively, the personnel function is engaged in a number of key activities primarily concerned with the following 2 areas:

- manpower planning
- personnel management.

Manpower planning involves assessing the staffing needs of the organization with reference to its proposed development plan and identifying ways in which these staffing needs can be met.

Personnel management, on the other hand, is more concerned with the day-to-day management and administration of personnel or staffing issues. These may include such elements as:

- recruitment practices;
- training and development;
- redundancy issues;
- health and safety matters;
- maintaining confidential information on staff relating to employment history with the company;
- advising staff on employment issues and procedures relating to staff.

The personnel function has a critical role to play in ensuring that the company's policies relating to its staff make a positive contribution towards the overall success of the organization. Forward-thinking business organizations appreciate the contribution which their employees make to achieving *business goals and objectives*, and the concept of *human resource management* signifies the importance of company staff as a *resource* which makes a positive contribution to the business. As such, it is now appreciated that investment in staff means more than simply employing labour. Investment in staff incorporates every aspect of company activity including initial recruitment, ongoing training and development, fringe benefits, consultation, and communication.

Bearing these points in mind we can now identify a number of key activities which come under the broad area referred to as the personnel function:

- Manpower planning will involve *labour market analysis* within the region in order to identify existing skills and potential skill shortages over time.

- At the recruitment phase, the personnel function involves undertaking *job analysis* which enables the company to identify the skills and qualities required by a member of staff to undertake a specific job within the company.

- The personnel function will also engage in a *training needs analysis* in order to provide information for the business organization's *staff development and training programme*.

- The personnel function will establish and monitor the organization's *staff appraisal scheme* in order to ensure that personal targets are established for individual members of staff, supported by relevant staff training activities.

The functions and organization of business

- The personnel function will play a leading role in dealing with trade unions, professional associations and staff associations. These *industrial relations* will form the basis of *collective bargaining* which centre upon negotiations relating to pay, *fringe benefits* and the *terms and conditions of employment*.

- The role of the personnel function also involves monitoring the *legal responsibilities* which are involved in the employment of staff. This will involve ensuring that the business is meeting its legal responsibilities towards its employees as laid down by the various employment laws.

- Some companies are particularly keen to promote *equal opportunities* within their employment and recruitment practices and, in this respect, the personnel function may be called upon to supply the necessary statistics relating to the current workforce in terms of age, gender, and ethnic mix.

- The personnel function acts as a referral point for those staff who wish to obtain information on company employment practices. Additionally, some business organizations may seek to use the personnel function to promote the *welfare* of staff via sports and social clubs, company pension schemes and general support for those staff whose work may be adversely affected by their own personal circumstances.

The production/operations function

The role of the production function is to ensure that the business produces its output as efficiently as possible within given timescales and resources in order to ensure that the output of goods is in sufficient quantities and of the right quality to meet sales orders. In other words:

> *Making sure that productive factors are combined in such a way as to produce an output which meets the required specifications within the available budget.*

The production function is mainly associated with those business organizations which are engaged in the manufacturing sector of the business. In a developed economy we are likely to see more use made of capital equipment in the form of large-scale machinery and equipment. In its most developed form, this process of *automation* has resulted in the introduction of new robotic technology leading to a production line on which the numbers of staff are reduced as their repetitive work roles are taken over by programmed machines. However, this does not detract from the number of critical decisions which need to be considered by business managers:

- *production planning* involves the way in which the production process has to be organized in order to ensure that orders are met;
- *production control* ensures that the production plan is put into operation and that production runs smoothly;
- *maintenance* ensures that equipment and machinery are fully operational and that regular servicing is carried out on a scheduled basis;

- *stock control and purchasing* ensures that sufficient supplies of raw materials are available to meet the needs of the production process;
- *quality control* involves establishing a system whereby quality checks and sampling are undertaken on a systematic basis on order to ensure that the finished product meets the required quality levels as laid down in the product specification.

The purchasing function

The role of the purchasing function is to ensure that all elements of activity in which the business is engaged are supplied with the necessary equipment and materials to enable the activity to be performed efficiently and effectively within available budgets. In other words:

> *Making sure the business has access to the necessary resources to undertake planned and productive activity.*

Although we have identified the purchasing function as separate from the other business functions, in practice it is likely that purchasing activities will be conducted by either the production function or the administration function. Certainly, the business must decide whether it wants the purchasing function to be *centralized* – in order to benefit from economies of scale arising from bulk purchasing and the associated discounts which might arise – or whether it will want purchasing decisions to be made by individual departments on a *decentralized basis,* so that the amount of paperwork is reduced and the exact requirements of the department are met. Whatever the company decides, for our purposes the purchasing function has been identified separately in order to highlight its critical importance to the business organization.

In essence, if the various elements of the business do not have access to a supply of raw materials and equipment, then productive business activity will be adversely affected. However, raw materials and equipment in the form of 'stock' are a cost to the business. Since it has used part of its resources to purchase stock, there is obviously an *opportunity cost* – for example, the business will have smaller reserves of cash on which it could earn interest.

Successful business organizations are those which appreciate the importance of the purchasing function to the extent that they instigate systems and procedures which are formulated within an overall *purchasing policy*. The elements of such a purchasing policy are likely to involve such aspects as:

- How to obtain *value for money* in purchasing decisions. This will involve decisions relating to such issues as *price, quality, number and range of suppliers, delivery times.*

- How to ensure that all business activities are adequately resourced to meet their requirements. This will involve such elements as *stock control systems, purchasing plans, inventories, delivery schedules, replacement schedules for out-of-date or obsolete equipment.*

The functions and organization of business

- How to ensure that systems and procedures are in place to manage the purchasing function effectively. This will involve decisions regarding *centralized or decentralized purchasing*.

The finance/accounts function

The role of the finance/accounts function comprises 2 related elements. Firstly, the function ensures that the business is able to record the financial costs and revenues related to its business activities. In this respect, financial record-keeping is of prime importance since it enables the business to monitor the success of its operations. Secondly, the function provides information to managers which enable them to have a clearer understanding of the financial implications of any management decisions which may be taken. In other words:

> *Making sure that the business maintains financial records of all its operations and providing financial information to managers which assists decision-making.*

In later chapters we will consider the finance/accounts function in more detail when we look at the range of financial records and other types of financial information which form the basis of this particular functional area.

For our current purposes it is sufficient to describe the 2 main types of activities undertaken by the finance/accounts function.

- *Financial accounting* is the traditional role undertaken by the finance/accounts function and centres upon the systematic and efficient recording of financial transactions. In its simplest form this involves bookkeeping and posting entries into designated ledgers. We must not underestimate the importance of the bookkeeping function, since it ensures that an effective cash flow is monitored within the business. Financial accounting also involves the preparation of the *profit and loss account* and the company's *balance sheet*. The working practices involved in accounting are monitored by an independent auditing system which ensures that the accounting procedures, systems and processes are efficient, effective and accurate.

- *Management accounting* centres upon the provision of financial information to managers to assist the decision-making process. As such, management accounting plays a key role in the budget-setting process within the organization and provides information to managers which assists them in monitoring their individual departmental budgets and enables them to take corrective action when necessary. Additionally, management information provides the business with information which can assist the planning activities relating to future business developments. This may involve providing information about likely profit levels, the costs of any proposed investments, and the implications of any changes in the business environment – for example changes in the rate of interest – which may have financial and resource implications.

The sales and marketing function

The successful business must ensure that it produces goods and services which are required by the consumer. It must therefore engage in activities which enable it to determine what the market requires and ensure that there are sufficient opportunities available for the consumers in the market to purchase those goods and services produced by the business. These are the key roles undertaken by the sales and marketing function. In other words:

> *Making sure that the business is able to be both informed of and influenced by market demand in order to generate sales which will result in profits for the business.*

Although it would be true to say that all the business functions we will consider are vital to the success of the organization, in the final analysis, if the business does not meet the requirements of its consumers and achieve successful sales, the business will ultimately fail. Chapter 8 will look in more detail at how the sales and marketing function informs management decision-making, but in this chapter we need to identify the activities listed below, associated with this particular business function.

- *Marketing research* involves trying to ascertain information on both current and future trends which will inform management decisions. It focuses on those elements which are likely to affect the demand for a product or service including
  - price
  - level of competition
  - promotion and advertising
  - consumer preferences.
- *New product development* involves participating in research activities which informs management of:
  - potential new areas of product development
  - testing consumer reactions to new products and analysing the results of the tests.
- *Promotional activities* are aimed at informing the consumer of the existence of products and attempts to persuade them to purchase the product or service. Promotional activities will therefore incorporate *advertising campaigns* which are both informative and persuasive. Additionally, such activities may involve decisions involving the type of media to be used, the relative costs and benefits along with a range of promotional events, special offers and free samples. The larger business organizations are also keen to engage in *sponsorship activities* which incorporate high-profile events including popular spectator sports which generate a lot of media interest. Finally, business organizations are increasingly involved in *corporate hospitality*, which extends from the presentation of small gifts to customers and clients to inviting important clients to special events. Again these events are usually those which generate a lot of media interest.

The functions and organization of business

The administration function

None of the functions of business should be viewed in isolation from each other. Successful business organizations are those which are able to coordinate the activities of each functional area in such a way as to develop a smooth, well-oiled organization. The task of coordinating the diverse range of business functions is undertaken by the administration function. In other words:

> *Making sure the business establishes systems and procedures which allow its activities to operate as smoothly as possible.*

The administration function is largely a support role provided for the other functional areas but, in recent years, its importance has grown to the extent that senior management posts have been given responsibility for the function and professional bodies and examination boards, including The London Chamber of Commerce and Industry, all recognize the professional duties and responsibilities inherent in the administration function. The scope and range of this function will largely depend upon the size and nature of the business organization, but the following features and activities provide a general overview of the administration function:

- Ensuring that effective *communications systems* are in place at all levels within the organization. This will include such elements as common house-styles for formal written communications, minutes, reports and letters.
- Drawing up a *planning schedule* for administrative support based on the future support needs identified and supplied by the functional areas.
- Ensuring that systems and procedures are *controlled and monitored* in order to meet the changing support needs of the organization. Such systems will cover a diverse range of services, including post, telecommunications, IT, security, and transport.

Administrative systems are increasingly reliant upon the use of information technology in terms of providing managers with up-to-date information and promoting an efficient and effective communications system. The administration function will be responsible for drawing up and implementing the plans relating to the company's *information technology strategy*.

The research and development function

In a competitive market economy successful business organizations will be characterized by:
- the emphasis they place upon designing and developing new production techniques which lower costs of production;
- their desire to invest in new product development.

The internal organization of the business

These two responsibilities are encompassed within the research and development (R&D) function. In other words:

> *Making sure that the business develops cost-effective improvements to the production process and engages in research which promotes the development of new products.*

Developing more cost-effective ways of producing goods will result in a reduction in costs of production which can be passed onto the consumer in the form of lower prices, which will give the firm a *competitive advantage* over its competitors. Developing new products can have a similar impact, in that the firm will be able to introduce to the market new and innovative products which will replace traditional products, which will be subject to a fall in demand.

Some business organizations, whilst appreciating the importance of research and development, do not have the necessary funds to undertake this particular function, whilst others take the view that they prefer to let other organizations take the risks associated with research and development.

Certainly R&D is costly and can involve taking risks. For these reasons, the function is usually associated with larger business organizations or with those companies which specialize in technical and scientific products. However, the rewards of successful R&D can bring significant advantages to the business, so long as the business follows an R&D programme which incorporates the following features:

- establish clear aims and objectives and associated performance targets;
- establish an R&D team which works within clear management guidelines;
- instigate strict budgetary controls;
- identify timescales for reporting on progress;
- be prepared to cease R&D activities in those areas which do not meet performance targets.

The internal organization of the business

How does the business organize the functional areas in such a way as to produce an effective organizational structure which meets its needs? We will next look at 2 ways in which the business seeks to ensure that the various functions work together to coordinate their activities, so that the contributions made by each of the functional areas are maximized. The 2 aspects we will consider are:

- the role of departments
- the importance of specialization.

It is difficult to separate these 2 aspects, since a departmental structure is, in effect, an example of specialization. In other words, many businesses seek to locate the responsibilities of the various functional areas into specific departments, each one of which *specializes* in a particular business function.

The functions and organization of business

> **Activity**
>
> Identify *3* ways in which each of the various business functions can contribute to the successful introduction of a new product. One of the business functions has been completed in order to help you.
>
> | Sales and marketing | <ul><li>engage in market research activities to determine the level of market demand</li><li>test consumer reactions to the new product through field studies and pilot testing</li><li>organize a publicity campaign incorporating appropriate strategies for media advertising, sponsorship and corporate hospitality</li></ul> |
> |---|---|

The internal organization of a business is best described by using an *organization chart*. This chart is a diagrammatic representation of the internal structure of the company. In its simplest form, it will just identify each department, but more complex organization charts may show:

- the specific job roles within each department;
- the names of people attached to key job roles and functions within the organization;
- the channels of communication within an organization.

Figure 6.3 (opposite) is an example of a simple organization chart. It is not difficult to identify the limitations of this simple chart. It does not tell us the scope of the activities undertaken by each of the departments, and it does not provide us with any detail of the specialist job roles and personnel located in each of department. In fact, all it tells us is that Teletech Ltd has 5 departments – personnel, production, finance, sales, and support services.

Figure 6.4 (opposite) provides much more detail of the internal structure of Teletech Ltd and would be useful for managers, employees, customers, clients and suppliers who could save a lot of time by referring to the organization chart when trying to find specific information relating to the organization's activities.

Finally, Figure 6.5 (see page 116) goes into further detail by identifying the specific job roles within one of the departments. Obviously, if this exercise were undertaken for each department, we would obtain a highly complex organization chart. Indeed it could be argued that some organization charts are so complex as to be of little use to the organization or their external customers and clients.

This being said, organization charts have a number of advantages:

- they are easily understood;
- they can draw attention to organizational defects;
- they form the basis from which any proposed changes to the organizational structure are made.

The internal organization of the business

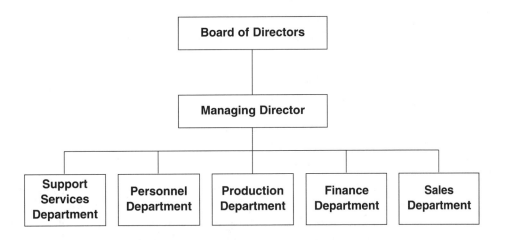

Figure 6.3 Simple organization chart of Teletech Ltd

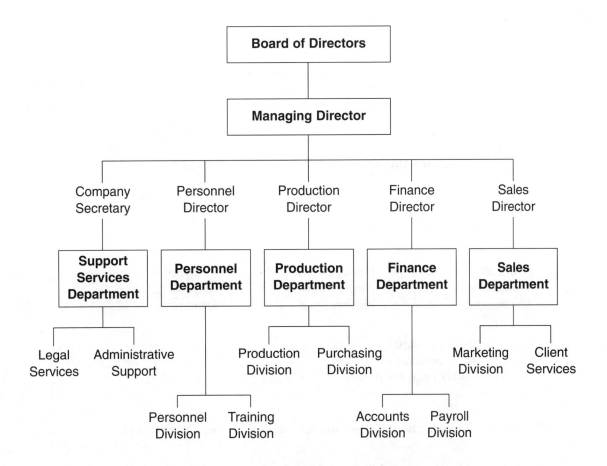

Figure 6.4 Detailed organization chart of Teletech Ltd

The functions and organization of business

> **Activity**
>
> Undertake research in order to construct an organization chart of a business engaged in either:
>
> - the manufacturing sector
> - the service sector.
>
> Identify the key job roles in *one* department or section of your chosen organization.

For the purposes of our study, the most important aspect of organization charts is that they identify the level of *specialization* which exists within the organization. In simple terms, the larger the organization, the greater will be the degree of specialization. This is directly related to other aspects of our study, notably:

- internal economies of scale
- the advantages of specialization.

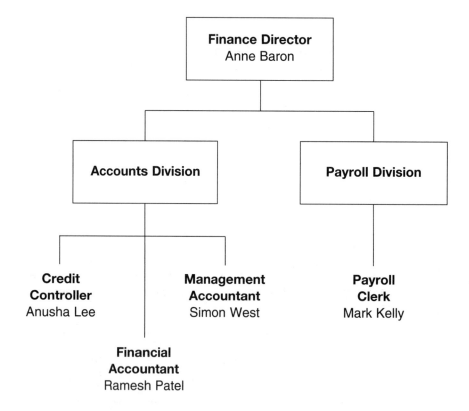

Figure 6.5 Organization of the Finance Department of Teletech Ltd

It should now be becoming clearer that there is a direct relationship between *business functions*, *specialization* and *internal economies of scale*. This relationship is outlined in Figure 6.6 (opposite).

The internal organization of the business

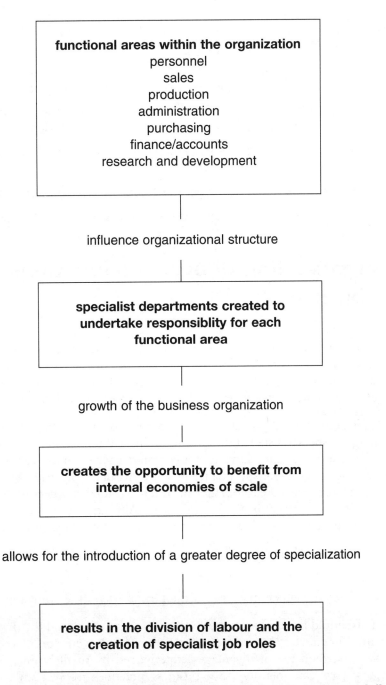

Figure 6.6 The relationship between the main functional areas, specialization and internal economies of scale

In Chapter 1 we described the advantages of specialization, and we should now view the division of labour as another example of specialization within the business environment. This being said, not all business organizations are large enough to benefit from the division of labour and the specialization inherent within a departmental structure. We must therefore consider how the smaller business organization seeks to undertake the business functions we have identified in this chapter.

Activity

Construct an organization chart for the Production Department using the following information and with reference to Figure 6.4 (page 115):

- John Howe is the Production Manager, who manages David Brown, the Maintenance Supervisor within the Production Division;
- The Purchasing Manager is Susan Higgins, who manages 2 invoice clerks, Kay Griffiths and Alan White;
- The Stock Control Manager within the Purchasing Division is Sonia Wong.

The organization of business functions in the small business

The fact that a firm is small does not mean that it can choose to ignore the main functional areas described in the previous section. Indeed, it could be argued that, for the small firm, it is vital that they understand the components which make up each of the specific activities undertaken by each of the functional areas.

This being said, the small firm is likely not to have sufficient resources to employ a range of specialist staff and may choose instead to *contract out* some of the functions to specialist consultancy services, for example, payroll services and accountancy services. On the other hand, the smaller business organization may choose to combine some of the functional areas together in order that they can become the responsibility of a specific person within the organization. Although there may be certain cost savings from this approach, there are a number of disadvantages including:

- work overload
- inefficiencies
- problems which may arise if the person leaves the company.

This should be familiar to the reader who has understood the first section of this book since, in effect, it covers the same aspects which were considered in Chapter 3 when we described the disadvantages experienced by small business organizations. Once again we can identify how business practice involves an understanding of the interrelationships which exist within the business environment. Chapter 7 will show another aspect of such interrelationships when we consider the main groups which influence, and are influenced by, the business environment and the activities which take place within it.

International business organizations

We have already identified from earlier chapters that the *global market* has led to the establishment of a number of *multinational corporations*, those business organizations which are represented in countries throughout the world. In the context of our present discussion, what factors will influence the way in which such corporations are managed and organized? In our study of Business Practice we will identify *3* factors which will influence these types of business organizations:

- legal systems
- government policy
- international communications.

Legal systems

Business organizations, like all other sections of the community, are subject to the various laws, statutes and regulations which govern social and economic relationships. For those business organizations represented in countries throughout the world, it is vitally important that they operate according to the rules and regulations of each of the separate countries.

Such regulations are likely to cover a host of specialized areas including:

- employment law
- health and safety regulations
- taxation policies
- consumer protection.

It is important that the business operates to the standards required in each country and, for this reason, we are likely to see *different organizational structures* in each of the countries in which the corporation may operate, in order that it can more easily meet the requirements of the host country's legal system.

Government policies

Most governments are concerned to promote competition, in order that no one business organization can become so dominant within the market that it can effectively establish itself as a *monopoly*. For this reason, most governments have established a regulatory framework within which they can monitor the size and importance of individual business organizations. Such a framework may involve specialized government agencies which advise the government as to the advantages and disadvantages of any proposed mergers and takeovers. Indeed, most countries have passed antimonopoly legislation or antitrust laws which prevent individual business organizations dominating the market.

The functions and organization of business

Given the size and scope of their operations, multinational corporations have to pay special attention to this aspect of government policy in order to ensure that they do not contravene the range of laws and regulations which are collectively referred to as *'competition policy'*.

International communication

In a later chapter we will consider in some detail the role and importance of new technology in promoting effective communications systems both *within* the organization and *between* business organizations. Our study of Business Practice will also identify the importance of business communications as a means of supporting business activities and operations.

Suffice to say that an international business organization will need to organize its global activities in such a way as to ensure that its senior management teams represented in countries throughout the world can readily communicate with each other in order to be kept informed of:

- important changes in company policy;
- receive instructions from the head office;
- receive management information;
- obtain advice and guidance on matters relating to specific areas of business;
- receive relevant updates and associated management reports;
- inform the head office of performance in key areas of the business, including costs, sales and profits.

The development of international systems of communication has enabled multinational corporations to extend their operations even further afield. The development of a global computer-based communications system – *the Internet* – enables managers to communicate with each other through an international e-mail system and exchange important documents at the touch of a computer key.

From this brief overview we can draw some important conclusions regarding the organization of international business organizations:

- multinational organizations will be organized on the basis of a *parent company* and a series of *subsidiary companies* located in different countries;
- the head office of the parent company is likely to be located in its country of origin, for example the head office of the Nissan Motor Company, the world's sixth largest motor company, is in Japan, whilst one of its major subsidiaries is Nissan Motor (GB) Ltd;
- the management and staff of the subsidiary companies are likely to be drawn from the host country;
- the organization of the subsidiary company and the specialized staff which it employs is likely to reflect the prevailing influences in the host country;

The internal organization of the business

- subsidiary companies are likely to be 'independent' organizations in terms of share ownership, with shares being traded openly on the host country's stock exchange;
- communications systems in international companies are of critical importance in ensuring the transfer of efficient and effective management information, and this is likely to be reflected in the way in which computer networks play a key role in their organizational structure.

Activity

Find the e-mail addresses of 3 of the following multinational corporations:

- Ford
- Nissan
- Toyota
- IBM
- Shell.

There now follow some quick questions and revision exercises. They relate specifically to the chapter you have just studied. You are advised to attempt the questions without reference to the text, and then compare your answers and solutions with those on pages 123–4.

The functions and organization of business

QUESTIONS

1. What is meant by the term **specialization**?
2. List the **7** key functional areas.
3. What is meant by the term **manpower planning**?
4. What is meant by the term **production planning and control**?
5. List **5** main features of a purchasing policy.
6. What is **marketing research**?
7. What are the main advantages of an **organization chart**?
8. What are **multinational corporations**?
9. What is meant by the term **competition policy**?
10. Identify **5** ways in which a global communications network can assist the operations of a multinational corporation.

EXERCISES

1. Describe the relationship between the production process and the trading cycle.
2. Outline the differences between financial accounting and management accounting.
3. Describe the relationship between the main functional areas, specialization and internal economies of scale.

While attempting to answer the questions and exercises on this page, you are strongly advised not to read on and to cover the answers on the following page with a sheet of paper.

The internal organization of the business

ANSWERS TO QUESTIONS

1. Specialization is the process in which the productive factors (*factors of production*) are organized so as to concentrate on specific aspects of the production process.

2. - Personnel/Human resources
   - Production/Operations
   - Purchasing
   - Finance/Accounts
   - Sales and Marketing
   - Administration
   - Research and Development.

3. Manpower planning involves assessing the staffing needs of the organization with reference to its proposed development plan and identifying ways in which these staffing needs can be met.

4. Production planning involves the way in which the production process has to be organized in order to ensure that orders are met. Production control ensures that the production plan is put into operation and that production runs smoothly.

5. - Value for money
   - Number and range of suppliers
   - Price and quality
   - Delivery schedules
   - Replacement schedules.

6. Marketing research seeks to identify current and future trends in a range of specific factors which will inform management decisions. Such factors will include price, the level of competition and consumer preferences, all of which will influence the size of the market.

7. - Easily understood
   - Can draw attention to organizational defects
   - Form the basis upon which any changes in the organization are proposed.

8. Multinational corporations are business organizations which have been established in countries throughout the world under the direction of a central head office.

9. Competition policy is a government policy which seeks to promote competition between business organizations in order to ensure that individual firms cannot dominate the market in such a way as to undermine the interests of the consumer.

10. A global communications network can assist a multinational corporation by ensuring that its senior management teams represented in countries throughout the world:
    - are kept informed of important changes in company policy;

The functions and organization of business

- receive instructions from head office;
- receive management information;
- receive management reports;
- inform head office of business trends.

SOLUTIONS TO EXERCISES

1 The production process in its simplest form is the combining of productive factors to produce goods and services. The trading cycle is a larger process in which the output of the production process is then sold in order to provide the financial resources for the business organization to be able to purchase more productive factors, in order for it again to engage in the production process.

2 Financial accounting centres upon the systematic recording of financial transactions and the production of financial records, including the profit and loss account and the balance sheet. Management accounting, on the other hand, is more concerned with providing management information which can assist the decision-making process. Such activities may include preparing draft budgets, monitoring budgets and identifying the likely costs of future business developments.

3 As a business grows and expands, it is able to organize its internal operations in a way that allows the essential business functions which support the production process to become identified as specialized units within the business. For example, the marketing function will become the responsibility of a specialized marketing department. The advantage for the large firm is that these specialized units can employ specialized staff with specific skills, knowledge and experience who can have a direct influence on business development and success. Therefore the growth of the firm leads to internal economies of scale, an example of which is the development of specialized functional areas within the business.

POINTS TO REMEMBER

- The production process in its simplest form involves the input of raw materials and other productive factors which are combined together to produce an output.

- A more sophisticated view of the production process is to identify certain specific functions which are required to be undertaken if outputs are to be generated.

- In the business organization, these functions are the responsibility of specialized functional areas.

- These functional areas will cover all aspects of business activities and operations including personnel, finance, administration, R&D, sales and marketing, purchasing, and production/operations.

- Organization charts are visual descriptions of the internal organization of the business.

- Large business organizations are able to organize the functional areas into specialist departments or sections, thereby benefiting from the advantages of specialization and internal economies of scale.

- Small firms may have to 'contract out' some of the functional responsibilities to specialized organizations, since they do not have the necessary resources to undertake such responsbilities on their own behalf.

- The global market has led to the development of global business organizations known as multinational corporations (MNCs) which are represented in countries throughout the world.

- The internal organization of MNCs will be influenced by the host country's legal systems and associated government policies along with international communication systems and networks.

7

The main groups involved in business activities

> After carefully studying this chapter, you should be able to identify the roles played by the major groups involved with the business organization.

> **Extended Syllabus references**
>
> 2.7 Identify the roles played by the major groups involved with the business organization:
>
>   2.7.1   shareholders
>   2.7.2   board of directors
>   2.7.3   managers
>   2.7.4   employees
>   2.7.5   customers and clients

This chapter aims to bring together the important themes which have been developed in the first 2 sections of the book. It will seek to identify the roles of the main groups involved with business activities in order to provide an overview of how they can influence the business organization.

Stakeholders

The previous chapter identified a range of functional areas which support the activities of the business organization whilst other chapters have been devoted to a range of factors which influence both the business environment and the individual business organization.

Groups involved in business activities

We briefly noted the importance of stakeholders in Chapter 1, and it is to this concept that we must now return if we are to obtain a full understanding of the wider context in which the business operates. For the purposes of our discussion we will highlight the role and influence of 5 key stakeholders – those groups which can both influence, and be influenced by, the activities of the business organization:

- shareholders
- the board of directors
- managers
- employees
- customers and clients.

Shareholders

It is appropriate to begin our discussion of the main stakeholders involved in the business by considering the role and influence of shareholders, since they are the owners of the largest and most important type of business organization – the public limited company.

Why should a person wish to be a shareholder? Three possible motives may be identified:

- to receive a share of the profits;
- in the hope that the value of their shares will increase over time;
- to influence company policy.

Let us take each of these motives in turn in order to ascertain the factors which influence both the shareholder and the business organization.

Share-out of profits

So far we have made the assumption that any profits made by a company will be distributed to all those holding shares in the business. In reality this is not always the case for a number of reasons:

- *types of share held* Public limited companies issue a number of different types of shares, each of which has a different level of risk attached to it:
  - *Ordinary shares* are the riskiest type of shares, since they are paid last in the share out of profits. Dividends on such shares are directly related to the profits made by the company. Because they are the riskiest shares, ordinary shareholders have the right to vote on company policy and to elect the board of

The functions and organization of business

directors at the company's annual general meeting (AGM). Although these shares carry the highest levels of risk, they also have the potential for the biggest gains in the form of both dividend payouts and the increase in the value of the shares on the stock market.

- *Preference shares*, on the other hand, have a fixed dividend, get paid first in the share out of profits but do not bring voting rights. Should no profits be made by the company, holders of preference shares will not receive any dividends. Additionally, if the company is wound up, preference shareholders will normally have preference over the ordinary shareholders should any capital be repaid.

- *Cumulative preference shares* carry the least risk, since not only do they carry a fixed dividend but, should they not receive a dividend in one year, they will be 'credited' with any arrears of dividend in future profitable years. Since they carry the least risk, they do not have voting rights at the company's AGM.

- *size of profits*

We can now understand why, in certain instances, shareholders may not receive a dividend. For example, the level of profits may be sufficient only to pay dividends to the preference shareholders. Additionally, the ordinary shareholders cannot rely on a fixed dividend since, even if the company does make a profit, dividends for the ordinary shareholders are likely to change each year.

- *retained and distributed profits*

Successful companies must ensure that they respond to changes in market conditions. For this reason, resources are required to develop new areas of business. One important form of finance which can be used for development and expansion are the profits generated from business activity. The business must therefore decide how much profit it should hold back to finance future expansion (retained profits) and how much it should distribute to shareholders (distributed profits). Once again we are drawn to the conclusion that an increase in profits does not, in itself, mean an increase in dividends for the shareholders, since the business may decide to retain a higher proportion of the profits in order to finance its expansion plans.

Shareholders are therefore keenly aware that profits and decisions relating to their distribution will have a direct impact on dividend payments. Equally, the level of dividend payments will have an impact on the *value of shares* and it is to this aspect which we now turn.

Share values

The previous section highlighted one influence which will affect the value of shares on the open market – the level of profits and the associated dividend payout to shareholders. Put simply, those firms which generate high profit levels and reward their shareholders accordingly are likely to see the price of their shares rise on the open market. In effect, the price of shares will be subject to the forces of demand and supply, the 'market place' for the shares being the various international stock exchanges.

In Chapter 1 you undertook an activity in which you were asked to chart the movement in share prices of a company of your choice and to account for any changes in the price of the share.

Besides the level of profits made by the company, your research may have identified some or all of the following reasons for changes in the price of shares:

• *takeover bids*	If the company is subject to a takeover bid, the value of its shares may rise as the demand for the shares increases.
• *rumours*	This is related to the previous point, since even rumours of a takeover can lead to an increase in share prices. Conversely, rumours which indicate that the firm's profits are not likely to reach previous forecasts – a so-called 'profits warning' – will cause their share prices to fall as holders of the shares attempt to sell them.
• *confidence levels*	Given the inherent risk in owning shares, shareholders' confidence in the share market and the economy as a whole, will be a direct influence on whether or not they wish to buy or sell their shares. Some financial markets have been subject to dramatic falls in share prices as a result of a lack of confidence – the collapse of the financial markets in southeast Asia in the late 1990s is a good example of this phenomenon.
• *government policies*	Government policies can have a direct impact on specific industries and individual companies. For example, the government may impose additional taxes on specific goods – cigarettes and tobacco and the like – which can affect share prices. In other instances, the government's overall

management of the economy may lead to unfortunate consequences – unemployment, inflation, poor trade figures – which may not only affect the overall movement of share prices but may also influence overall confidence levels in the economy, thereby exerting a downward pressure on share prices.

- *speculation*

    There are instances in which the activities of individual shareholders themselves may lead to share price changes which are not directly related to profit levels. Such instances arise when holders of large blocks of an individual company's shares sell them on the open market. As a result of the increase in the supply of the shares, their price begins to fall and this allows the original seller to purchase a greater volume of the same shares at the artificially reduced price. When the company makes its dividend payout, these shareholders will receive a larger proportion of the profits since they now hold a greater number of shares.

Our discussion so far has concentrated mainly upon how shareholders can be influenced by the business organization and the environment within which it operates. Are there instances in which the actions of shareholders themselves can influence the business?

Shareholders' influence on company policy

We have already identified one way in which the actions of shareholders can indirectly influence the company – they can sell their shares, which may result in a fall in the price of the shares on the open market. Are there any other, more direct ways, by which the shareholders can influence the business? In some respects this depends on the number of shares held by the shareholder. We have already noted that ordinary shareholders have voting rights. These voting rights, and the number of votes credited to each shareholder, depends upon the number of ordinary shares held – more shares means more votes at the company's annual general meeting.

In the largest public limited companies, it is unlikely that private individual shareholders on their own will hold sufficient numbers of shares to influence company policy directly. However, in recent years there has been an increasing number of cases where 'shareholder interest groups' have been formed, in which individual shareholders cooperate together to try to use their influence to change company policy, particularly on matters relating to the pay and remuneration of senior directors, environmental policies and the trading activities of the company.

On the whole, however, the largest shareholders are the financial institutions such as insurance companies and pension funds, which purchase shares in order to generate surplus funds which can be used to benefit their policyholders. In effect, this means that many people who, although not directly owners of companies (in that they do not personally own shares), can nevertheless be classified as 'stakeholders', since the money they pay towards their insurance policies and pension funds is channelled into business organizations.

Board of directors

One of the main features of public limited companies is that the ownership of the company is separate from its management and control. In essence, although the shareholders collectively own the company, they do not collectively manage and direct its operations. Instead, they elect a board of directors to perform this function for them. In effect the board of directors are the custodians of the company, directing and controlling its operations on behalf of the shareholders and, by implication, the other stakeholders involved in business activity.

The board of directors have a number of important functions:

- they determine the overall long-term direction of the company;
- they make policy decisions relating to how the business should be organized in order to achieve its long-term objectives;
- they appoint senior staff to manage the key functional areas;
- they decide how profits will be distributed;
- they make sure that the company is working within the law.

A closer examination of the board of directors will again reveal the importance of specialization. For our purposes we will show this with reference to 6 key positions:

- chair of the board and chief executive
- managing director
- company secretary
- executive directors
- non-executive directors
- worker directors.

Chair of the board – This person is responsible for the conduct of board meetings and acts in a representative capacity in dealing with the company's external relations – in large public limited companies this may involve dealings with the government and the press. Indeed a recent phenomenon is for the chief executive of some corporations to be directly involved in advertising campaigns in which, in effect, they stake their own personal and professional reputation on the quality of the service provided by the company. The chair of the board may also, in some companies, be the chief executive.

Managing director – This person has a pivotal role in the company and acts as the link between the day-to-day operations of the company and the board of directors. The managing director of the company will be a full-time appointment who will take an active role in management and provide regular up-date reports to the board of directors which identify the progress made with regards to the implementation of the

The functions and organization of business

company's policies and development plans. The Managing Director will be the chief executive in companies in which the chair of the board does not hold this position.

Company secretary – We have already noted in previous chapters that the public limited company is bound by a number of legal obligations with regard to its operations and disclosure of information. These include the various Companies Acts, employment legislation and various Health and Safety at Work Acts. As the person in the company responsible for legal matters, the company secretary ensures that the company is working within the law and within the framework of company practice as laid down in the Memorandum and Articles of Association.

Executive directors – These directors are usually full-time appointments and have direct responsibilities for the various functional areas within the business organization. It is their responsibility to ensure that company policy is implemented within their own areas of responsibility – e.g. personnel, sales and marketing, finance and the other functional areas within the organization. Like the managing director, executive directors will be expected to report regularly to the board of directors.

Non-executive directors – Whereas executive directors have a direct responsibility for the business activities and functions which take place within the organization, non-executive directors usually do not take an active part in management functions. Non-executive directors are usually appointed by the board of directors to provide an impartial view of company policy and, as such, they are usually well-respected figures in the business world who bring with them a range of skills and experience.

These non-executive directors are able to take on the role as 'ambassadors' for the company and to provide to the shareholders, along with the other stakeholders, the confidence that the business is in good hands. Sometimes, Members of Parliament are invited to take on the role of non-executive directors, since they have a wide experience and influence within the business world.

Worker directors – Some companies have experimented with introducing worker representation on the board of directors whilst others have chosen to establish works councils or joint consultation committees. Indeed, the European Union, via its Social Chapter legislation, has made it compulsory for firms over a certain size to implement procedures which allow for worker participation. Although worker-directorships are not common, we are likely to see an increase in the importance of worker representation as the concept of the 'stakeholding society' takes root.

Activity

Obtain the annual report of a large public limited company and identify the following:

- the name of the chair of the board of directors;
- the names of the executive directors and non-executive directors;
- the range of shareholdings in the company and the number of shares held;
- the total profits distributed to shareholders;
- the percentage dividend paid to shareholders.

Managers

Later chapters in this book will look in more detail at the role of managers, but by way of introduction we need to consider the functions they perform in relation to the following activities:

- planning
- controlling
- monitoring
- directing
- organizing
- forecasting
- motivating.

It is beyond the scope of this book to look at the theory of management, so instead we will consider these activities in the context of the areas of Business Practice which we have already covered. Indeed, by completing the activity overleaf you will be able to ascertain how far you have understood the main themes we have developed in the course of your studies.

Employees

We already noted, when we considered the role of the personnel function, that far-sighted business organizations regard their employees as a resource rather than as a business expense. Certainly, the way in which the business manages its staff will have a direct influence on how their employees view the company, their job role and whether they consider themselves as stakeholders within the business. Section 4 of this book will be devoted to the individual's contribution to the business and will provide us with the opportunity to look in more detail at these elements.

At this stage in our study, however, we need to set the scene by identifying the aspects (listed below) of the role of employees within the business.

- It is likely that employees will specialize in certain job functions.
- Teamwork can be used to identify shared goals and objectives.
- Motivation and job satisfaction can be influenced by both financial and non-financial strategies. *Financial strategies* may involve performance-related pay systems in which targets are set for individuals and linked to financial reward. *Non-financial strategies* for improving motivation may involve improving communication systems so that employees are better informed and implementing such systems so as to include the opportunity for feedback, consultation and participation.
- Training and staff development are of critical importance, and the resources committed to these elements should be viewed as an investment rather than a cost.

The functions and organization of business

- In many countries, employees have acquired 'employment rights' relating to such areas as contracts of employment, health and safety legislation, and minimum wages.
- Companies need to ensure that they monitor changes in the composition of their workforce and identify future labour requirements in order to meet the changing demands of industry, the business environment, and the overall development plans of the individual business.
- The way in which the business manages major changes in its organizational structure and any proposed future developments will have a major impact on employees.
- Many managers are, in effect, employees of the company and, although they have specialist job functions which may involve managing the work of other

Activity

State 3 activities undertaken by managers in each area identified in the table, and outline the benefits for the business organization of each activity you have stated. The first management function has been done for you to help you complete the rest of the table.

Management function	Activity	Benefits to the business
Planning	• work rotas • budgets • setting production targets	• ensure sufficient labour supply • identify resource requirements • ensures production meets sales orders
Controlling	• • •	• • •
Monitoring	• • •	• • •
Directing	• • •	• • •
Organizing	• • •	• • •
Forecasting	• • •	• • •
Motivating	• • •	• • •

employees, they can still be subject to the same internal and external influences as other employees, which will determine their view of the business organization.

In essence, employees will be influenced by a range of factors which will be present within the business organization:

- personnel practices and procedures
- communication systems
- internal organizational structures
- job design and work role
- management styles
- pay structures.

Customers and clients

We considered in Chapter 2 how customers have a direct influence on the business organization through their spending patterns in a competitive market. Now, however, we need to consider the role and influence of customers and clients from a different perspective.

Increasingly, business organizations are coming to realize that the pattern of consumer spending is not the only influence which their customers exert on the organization. Businesses now recognize that customers and clients are to be found both *inside the organization* as well as in the *competitive market* and, in this respect the notion of *external and internal customers and clients* has been developed.

External customers and clients

External customers and clients are those individuals and groups who purchase goods and services from the business organization. However, successful business organizations understand and appreciate that all external contacts and business relationships have the potential to develop into future sales. In this respect, *customer service* is seen to be of prime importance in meeting the needs of the existing customer base and influencing the future purchasing decisions of potential customers.

In much the same way, those other companies and organizations which provide services or supply goods to the business organization will also develop an opinion, based upon the organization's ability to pay, its efficiency in meeting payment schedules, and its conduct when negotiating contracts such as tenders or quotations for large-scale expenditure plans.

The functions and organization of business

Internal customers and clients

One of the biggest changes in recent times is the notion that customers and clients are represented within the internal structure of the business organization. The basic principle which underlies this notion is that the functional areas and the individual sections or departments responsible for undertaking functional activities are interrelated by the service they provide for each other. The personnel department provides a service to the production department by ensuring that appropriate staff are recruited and trained; the finance department provides a service to the other departments by maintaining up-to-date financial records and monitoring budget forecasts; and the marketing section provides a service to the administrative section by identifying the need for systems and procedures to monitor sales records in the different sales regions.

Since an individual department is providing a service to another department it follows that a 'client relationship' is established between the 2 departments. As with external relations, the client relationships which exist within the organization can be subject to the same level of customer service requirements, with each department or section establishing 'service standards' which can be used to monitor the level of service provided to their internal customers and clients.

> *There now follow some quick questions and revision exercises. They relate specifically to the chapter you have just studied. You are advised to attempt the questions without reference to the text, and then compare your answers and solutions with those on pages 138–40.*

QUESTIONS

1. Define the term **stakeholder** as it is used in the context of a business organization.
2. List **5** key stakeholders in business.
3. What are the main differences between **ordinary shares** and **preference shares**?
4. Define the terms **retained profits** and **distributed profits**.
5. List **4** reasons why share prices fluctuate.
6. List **3** functions of a board of directors.
7. List **7** functions of management.
8. What is the difference between an **executive director** and a **non-executive director**?
9. Define the term **external customer**.
10. Define the term **internal client**.

EXERCISES

1. 'It is important for the organization to recognize its employees as important stakeholders in the business.' Discuss this statement.
2. How can shareholders influence the business organization?
3. Describe the composition of a typical board of directors.

The functions and organization of business

ANSWERS TO QUESTIONS

1. A stakeholder is any person or group of people who may be affected either directly or indirectly by the operations and activities of a business organization.

2. - Shareholders
   - Board of directors
   - Managers
   - Employees
   - Customers and clients.

3. Ordinary shares are the riskiest shares since they are paid last in the share out of profits. Dividends on these shares are therefore likely to vary from year to year in the light of company performance. Ordinary shareholders have the right to vote at the company's AGM which will include the right to elect the Board of Directors. Preference shareholders, on the other hand, receive a fixed dividend before the ordinary shareholders are paid, and do not have voting rights.

4. Retained profits are the profits used by the company to finance future expansion or to add to their cash reserves, whereas distributed profits is the amount of total profits which are distributed to company shareholders.

5. - Speculation
   - Rumours
   - Takeover bids
   - Government policies.

6. - Determine the overall long-term direction of the company.
   - Appoint senior staff to manage the key functional areas.
   - Decide how profits will be distributed.

7. - Planning
   - Controlling
   - Monitoring
   - Directing
   - Organizing
   - Forecasting
   - Motivating.

8. Executive directors have a direct responsibility for business activities and functions and are usually full-time appointments, whereas non-executive directors are usually part-time directors who do not take an active part in management functions, acting instead in the capacity of advisors to the company and as its 'ambassadors' in the wider business world.

9 External customers are those individuals and groups who purchase goods and services from the business organization.

10 Internal clients are those individuals and groups within the business organization who make use of the services provided by the various functional areas within the organization.

SOLUTIONS TO EXERCISES

1 Far-sighted organizations regard their employees as a resource rather than as a business expense and recognize that the way in which the business manages its employees will have a direct impact on motivation, attitude and commitment. The business should regard its employees as stakeholders since the success or otherwise of the business will have a direct impact on them. If the business recognizes that its employees are stakeholders it will seek to:

- introduce a range of policies and procedures which can directly engage the workforce in elements of the decision-making process;
- ensure that communication systems and networks are efficient and effective so that its employees are kept informed of important company developments;
- promote opportunities for the staff to engage in staff-development and training activities;
- promote a management style which recognizes the importance of employees as stakeholders within the business.

2 Shareholders can influence the business organization in 2 main ways:

- the buying and selling of shares;
- voting patterns and shareholder interest groups.

Should a major shareholder sell shares in a company, it could result in a competitor gaining a controlling interest in the business. At the same time, selling large volumes of shares on the open market may lead to a fall in their price and, with it, a fall in the overall value of the company.

Holders of ordinary shares have the right to vote at the company's annual general meeting. In some instances this can result in a change in the composition of the board of directors resulting in a change in company policy. This can sometimes occur if shareholders organize themselves into informal 'interest groups'.

3 A typical board of directors is composed of:

Chair of the board who is responsible for the conduct of board meetings.

The managing director who will take an active role in ensuring that company policies are implemented within the organization.

The company secretary who is responsible for ensuring the company works within the law.

The functions and organization of business

Executive directors with responsibility for specific functional areas within the organization.

Non-executive directors who do not take an active part in the management of the company but who are able to provide an impartial view of company policies.

POINTS TO REMEMBER

- A stakeholder is a person or a group of people who are either directly or indirectly influenced or affected by the consequences of business decisions and activities.

- Shareholders are the owners of limited companies who receive a share of the profits, may be able to influence company policies and can benefit if the value of their shares increase over time.

- Different types of shares are issued by a public limited company, each with a different level of risk attached to them.

- Ordinary shares carry the most risk since dividends are directly related to profit levels.

- The price of shares on the open market can be influenced by both internal and external factors.

- Profit levels, order books and sales can all impact on share prices (internal factors), along with takeovers, rumours, speculation and government policies (external factors).

- The actions of shareholders may influence company policies since they could sell their shares or use their voting rights at the company's AGM.

- Shareholders elect a board of directors to manage the company on their behalf.

- Members of the board of directors take on specialized functions including chief executive, managing director, company secretary along with executive and non-executive directors.

- The board determines the overall long-term strategic direction of the company and agrees the overall structure of company policies which will serve to meet the corporate objectives.

- Managers are responsible for implementing the policies agreed at board level.

- Management functions will include planning, directing, organizing, forecasting, and controlling business operations.

- Employees within an organization will be influenced by a range of factors which will be present within the business organization including management styles, pay structures, communication systems and overall personnel practices and procedures.

- Customer service is a key business feature which recognizes the needs of both internal and external customers and clients.

- Internal customer service recognizes that the specialized functional areas within a business exist to provide an efficient and effective service to other parts of the organization.

The functions and organization of business

- **Customer service aimed at external customers and clients recognizes the fact that the price may not be the only factor which determines whether or not the consumer will purchase a particular product or service.**

Part 3
Business management

8
Business planning

> **After carefully studying this chapter, you should be able to:**
>
> 1 *describe the purpose of business planning;*
>
> 2 *describe the planning framework;*
>
> 3 *describe the main components of a business plan;*
>
> 4 *describe the differences between a strategic plan and an operational plan;*
>
> 5 *identify the differences between strategic and operational management;*
>
> 6 *identify the contributions made by the functional areas to the strategic planning process.*

> **Extended Syllabus references**
>
> 3.1 Describe the purpose of business planning
> 3.2 Describe the planning framework:
>   3.2.1 role of mission statements
>   3.2.2 SWOT and PEST analysis
>   3.2.3 target setting
>   3.2.4 timescales
>   3.2.5 quality guidelines
>   3.2.6 resource implications
>   3.2.7 finance
>   3.2.8 reviewing and monitoring activity
> 3.3 Describe the main components of a business plan
> 3.4 Describe the differences between a strategic plan and an operational plan
> 3.5 Identify the differences between strategic and operational management
> 3.6 Identify the contributions made by the functional areas to the strategic planning process

Business management

The purpose of this chapter is to provide a broad overview of the planning process undertaken by the business organization. We will consider why it is important for the business to plan and monitor its activities, and the contributions made by the functional areas to this process.

The purpose of business planning

Most of us at some stage in our lives have had cause to plan a journey or plan a holiday. How do we approach this task? Firstly we are likely to ask ourselves a number of questions:

- Where do we want to go?
- How do we want to get there?
- Are there alternative transport arrangements?
- How much will it cost?
- How much money have we got?
- How can we get more funds?
- When shall we go?
- What will we do when we get there?
- Are there any guidebooks to help us?

Upon our return, our friends and relatives are likely to ask if we enjoyed the holiday, and we will probably base our views on a range of factors which we experienced on the holiday, including:

- the weather
- holiday costs
- what we did and what we saw.

What does this tell us about *planning*? In simple terms, it tells us that planning is about:

- asking questions;
- making choices;
- obtaining information;
- managing resources;
- monitoring and evaluation.

How does this approach assist us in our understanding of the purpose of business planning? In effect, it shows us that the process of business planning incorporates all those activities we are familiar with in our everyday lives when we are seeking to ensure that we make logical and consistent choices from a range of alternatives.

In Chapter 1 we noted that the business organization is required to take a number of key decisions concerning a range of critical questions including:

Business planning

- What to produce?
- Where to produce?
- How to produce?
- For whom to produce?

We noted that, in considering these questions, the business is forced to make *choices*, each of which will involve an element of *opportunity cost*. We concluded that engaging in business activity could be viewed as a *risk*, since making the wrong choice could lead either to reduced profits or, in the most extreme case, to business failure.

One way in which the business can seek to reduce the level of risk is by engaging in a process of *business planning*. In essence, the purpose of business planning is for the business to undertake an in-depth, systematic analysis of its aims, goals, and objectives, and to identify the ways in which it will achieve them. In other words, we are likely to find that the approach to business planning will follow a similar approach to the one we described earlier on in the chapter:

- asking questions;
- making choices;
- obtaining information;
- managing resources;
- monitoring and evaluating.

Business planning is therefore a vital ingredient for business success and an analysis of the purpose of such planning will make this clearer.

Table 8.1 (overleaf) shows the range of factors which can be considered in each of the key planning areas. We can see that breaking down the planning process in this way will enable the business to have a much clearer view of its overall development plan. This will bring a number of benefits:

- the resources of the business can be channelled towards *profitable business activity*;
- *resources will not be wasted*, since the business will have a clear idea about its direction and development;
- staff employed within the business will be able to share in and contribute towards the development of the business, thereby increasing their *motivation*;
- *managers will have a clearer idea of how to direct business activities* in order that they can more effectively contribute to business goals and objectives.

All business organizations of whatever size engage in planning activities, but we are likely to notice major differences between individual organizations according to their size and complexity.

A standard tool in a large corporation is a formal strategic plan, which details its long-term goals and objectives, whereas a smaller organization is likely to have a less-detailed *business plan*, which could be presented to a bank manager as part of the process of obtaining business finance. Finally, even the smallest of business organizations, the sole trader, is likely to have an informal business plan, which may not even be written down but will still incorporate a basic idea and a 'wish list' of how to generate profits from business activity.

The next section looks in more detail at the main components of the planning process and identifies the framework upon which business planning is based.

Table 8.1   Key planning areas

Key planning areas	Scope and purpose
Asking questions	• what will be the main activities undertaken by the business? • how much will the productive factors cost? • what resources are available?
Making choices	• identifying potential markets • identifying potential customers • identifying suppliers • deciding how to plan the production process
Obtaining information	• engage in market research activities • is there a market for the product? • what is the level of competition? • how many consumers are there in the market? • how can we get the goods to the consumer? • how much profit will we make if our plans are successful?
Managing resources	• what resources will be required by the various functional areas? • how many staff do we require? • how shall we organize the business? • identify the role of financial and management accounting
Monitoring and evaluation	• monitor profit levels • monitor costs • monitor quality • monitor the level of customer satisfaction • monitor level of sales • monitor market share • evaluate business performance

The planning framework

We saw in Chapter 7 that business planning is integral to business success. However, business planning, if it is to be effective, should be based upon a framework which identifies the main factors to be considered within the planning process. We shall now consider these factors in more detail in order to build up a comprehensive picture of business planning.

> **Activity**
>
> You are considering purchasing a new computer. Complete the following table identifying the scope and purpose of the key planning areas which you will address, which will serve to inform your final decision of which computer you will purchase.
>
> **Purchase of a new computer**
>
> | Key planning areas | Scope and purpose |
> |---|---|
> | • asking questions | |
> | • making choices | |
> | • obtaining information | |
> | • managing resources | |
> | • monitoring and evaluation | |

The role of mission statements

Nowadays most organizations engaged in planning will identify their central, or core, objectives, values and principles in a *mission statement*. This is, in effect, a summary 'position statement' which informs all aspects of the company's operations and activities. As such, the mission statement concerns both the internal customers and clients and its external customers and clients. Once the mission statement is agreed, the rest of the planning process will try to determine how the mission can be accomplished.

SWOT and PEST analysis

Readers should now be familiar with the ideas of the external business environment and the internal structure and decision-making process which inform the nature of business activity undertaken by the business organization. Companies which are involved in planning are therefore strongly advised to consider the *context* within which these activities will be undertaken – both internally and with regard to the external business environment in which they operate. SWOT and PEST analysis are both simple techniques by which a company can address 3 basic questions:

(1) Where are we now?

(2) Where do we want to get to?

(3) What external factors do we need to take into account which will influence the operations and activities of the company?

Business management

Let us consider these questions in the context of SWOT and PEST analysis.

- *SWOT analysis* – SWOT is an acronym for the **S**trengths, **W**eaknesses, **O**pportunities and **T**hreats which can be identified within the internal operations, structure and activities of the individual organization. Senior managers who engage in SWOT analysis may think of a number of factors under each specific category when considering the place of their own organization in the business environment.

    Strengths: increased sales by 15% over the last year; introduced 3 new product lines.

    Weaknesses: high labour turnover; staff training programme not well-developed.

    Opportunities: expansion into overseas markets.

    Threats: increased level of competition.

- *PEST analysis* – PEST is an acronym for the **P**olitical, **E**conomic, **S**ocial and **T**echnological factors which may influence the activities of the individual company. For example, senior managers who engage in PEST analysis may consider the following factors which relate to the external environment within which their company operates:

    Political: what will be the impact of a change of government? what will be the impact of a change in government priorities and policies?

    Economic: will interest rates rise during the period of the plan? how will international factors impact upon the business, eg exchange rates, stability of international markets?

    Social: will changes in population have an impact on the demand for the company's products or services? will consumer preferences change over the period of the plan?

    Technological: what will be the impact of new technology, eg changes in telecommunications, importance of the Internet, development of 'home shopping'?

Once the business has identified the *context* of the plan, it can then set about identifying the practical implications involved when writing up the plan. This will involve the following aspects.

Target-setting

The business will need to establish measurable targets over the period of the plan which will enable it to ascertain whether or not it is achieving its objectives as laid down within the broad scope of its mission statement. These targets may include such broad areas as financial targets, sales targets and capital investments in new plant, and machinery.

Timescales

Targets must usually be achieved by a specific date. Obviously establishing a target to achieve a 10% increase in sales within one year is very different from aiming to achieve the same growth over a 5 year period.

Quality guidelines

The business must ensure that the achievement of these targets is completed without having to resort to a reduction in quality. Indeed, it is likely that *quality targets* will be incorporated into the planning process, and that the resulting targets, timescales and quality guidelines will form the basis of responsibilities allocated to the functional areas and to individuals with specific management responsibilities.

Resource implications

The business activities which will result from the implementation of the plans will involve the use of productive factors. The business must therefore take account of the resource implications of its proposals. It must therefore:

- identify the main resources required;
- identify the current resources which may not be required in the future
- identify the 'hidden costs' of resources, eg new computer hardware may mean that the company will have to purchase new software and implement a full-scale staff training programme.

Finance

The financial aspect of the planning framework is closely linked to the resource implications, and should identify the financial basis of any proposed developments incorporated into the plan. It will cover elements such as:

- identifying possible sources of finance to fund the plan;
- identifying the cost of any loans;
- drawing up draft budgets and accounts and, in effect, undertaking a 'financial health check' on the viability of the proposals within the plan.

Business management

Monitoring and evaluation

Regular checks will need to be made on the progress which the company has made towards meeting its targets. With this in mind, systems and procedures will need to be established which allow those responsible for meeting the targets to check on their progress. These systems may take the form of regular update reports or information updated on a regular basis by on-line access to computer networks.

Inevitably things can go wrong, or circumstances may arise outside the control of the business, which affect its ability to meet its targets and plans. For this reason, monitoring procedures are introduced which allow the business to identify any factors which may require it to implement alternative strategies, or change direction, or switch to other areas of business not previously considered within the planning process.

The foregoing analysis of the planning framework is likely to be undertaken by a large business organization which has the necessary resources and expertise to engage in an in-depth *strategic analysis*, the outcome of which will be a detailed *'strategic plan'*. The plan will build upon the company's current strengths and identify clear objectives which will determine its development plans for a number of years. Smaller organizations, and particularly new business organizations, will follow a similar planning framework but are likely to be less ambitious, producing instead a highly practical *business plan*. This plan can be particularly useful if additional resources need to be borrowed from one of the main financial institutions, the commercial banks. The next section describes in more detail the structure and format of these business plans.

Activity

With reference to the organization in which you are employed, or a well-known international company, complete the following tables by identifying 2 separate factors under each heading.

The internal influences

Strengths	Weaknesses	Opportunities	Threats
•	•	•	•
•	•	•	•

The external environment

Political	Economic	Social	Technological
•	•	•	•
•	•	•	•

The main components of a business plan

If we put ourselves in the position of a bank manager who has been presented with a business plan and a request to provide 'start-up' capital for a new business, what information would we require in the plan in order to satisfy ourselves that it provided the basis for a successful business venture? It is likely that we would require answers to the following questions:

- Who are you?
- What are you planning to do?
- Wy do you think your business will succeed?
- How will you organize your business?
- What will it cost and how will you generate profits?

In effect, these questions form the basis for the business plan, which can be identified as containing 5 key sections:

- *Background information* will cover such things as:
  - the name and address of the company
  - the product or service being offered
  - the legal status of the business
  - the owners of the business
  - the rationale for producing the product or offering the service: what makes it 'different' from other similar products which may be on the market, ie what is the product's 'competitive edge'?
- *Business objectives* will provide detailed information on:
  - targets
  - timescales
  - quality indicators
  - what is the 'mission' of the business?
- *The marketing plan and market research* will give details of the company's market research, presented and analysed with relevant conclusions. It will identify the level of demand for the product along with any relevant factors such as the degree of competition in the market. The plan will also include information on how the company proposes to sell and distribute the product or service to the customer including any elements of after-sales service.
- *Resource implications* will detail the range of productive factors required to implement the business plan. This will include such things as labour costs, including any specialist staff who may be needed, raw materials, capital equipment and machinery and premises costs. The plan will also detail how production will be planned (the production plan) and how the productive factors will be organized to produce the finished product or service (the production process).
- *Financial information* will detail a range of financial targets, including profit levels,

Business management

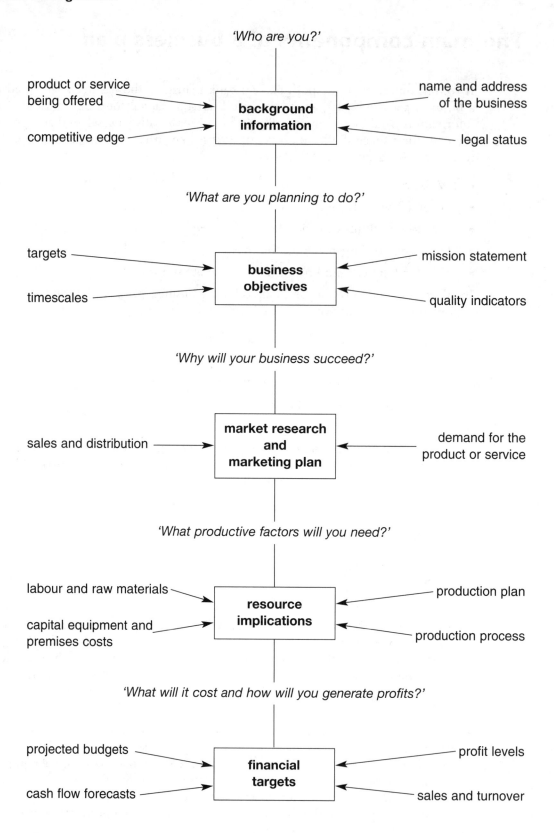

Figure 8.1   The main components of a business plan

projected sales volumes, and cash flow forecasts, which will form the basis of projected budgets and outline income and expenditure streams.

Figure 8.1 (see previous page) provides a summary of the main sections of the business plan. Additional information on business plans can be obtained from most commercial banks, which provide a range of useful leaflets and booklets to assist small businesses seeking financial assistance by submitting a business plan.

So far, we have distinguished 2 types of plan:

- the strategic plan
- the business plan.

We shall now consider 2 other types of plan which are incorporated into the planning framework:

- the operational plan
- the administrative plan.

In order to show how the different types of plan are linked, we must first identify 2 different management functions.

Strategic and operational management

In considering the differences between strategic and operational management we turn again to the principle of *specialization*. The board of directors is responsible for agreeing the company's mission statement and the overall direction of the company. Their work involves strategic planning, and requires senior board members to engage in strategic management decisions – in other words, the *broad* plans and areas of development which the company will seek to implement and achieve. However, these broad plans need to be broken down into *manageable targets* and *associated plans of action*. This task falls to the *operational managers* who are responsible for the day-to-day organization and implementation of business activities.

At the same time, these day-to-day operations need to be supported by systems and procedures which enable the business to function effectively – purchasing systems, communication networks, supplies, and a range of company policies which support business activity – all need to be put into place. In other words, there is a need for a plan which will provide the administrative support within the business. This administrative support will be based on an *administrative plan* drawn from the description of the needs of the company in its strategic plan. Table 8.2 (overleaf) shows the relationship between the strategic plan, the operational plan and the administrative plan.

How does the planning process relate to the other elements we have covered so far in our study of business practice?

We have already seen that planning will involve the following aspects, all of which have been covered in previous chapters:

- decision-making
- choices
- opportunity costs
- specialization
- organizational structure.

In the context of this chapter we can now show how the functional areas we described in Chapter 6 can also contribute to the planning process.

Table 8.2 The relationship between the strategic plan, the operational plan and the administrative plan

Strategic plan	Operational plan	Administrative plan
Broad plans and areas of development	Specific targets and action points to meet the strategic objective	Develop administrative systems to support the specific targets identified within the operational plan
3-year strategic objective: • to develop new overseas markets	Year 1: engage in market research to identify potential new overseas markets	• process data from market research
	Year 2: devise a marketing plan relating to the new overseas markets	• develop communication networks to incorporate staff engaged in overseas markets
	Year 3: implement the marketing plan and aim for the new overseas market to generate 5% of total sales volume	• establish distributive networks for the finished products

The contribution of the functional areas to the planning process

It should now be clear that, if the business is to engage in a planning process which will yield successful results, there needs to be a coordinated and collective effort from all those engaged in the management of the business, and the staff who undertake the productive tasks involved in business activity.

We are already aware that business activity is supported by the key functional areas and, in the context of the planning process, these areas perform 3 important roles:

- they provide the information upon which plans can be devised;
- they undertake activities which support the planning process;
- they are responsible for ensuring that the various operational and administrative plans are implemented and monitored.

In effect, the departmental structure which we considered in Chapter 6 describes these roles in more detail and provides another opportunity for us to see the interrelationship between the planning process, the functional areas of business and the role of individual departments.

There now follow some quick questions and revision exercises. They relate specifically to the chapter you have just studied. You are advised to attempt the questions without reference to the text, and then compare your answers and solutions with those on pages 159–60.

Business management

QUESTIONS

1. What is a **mission statement**?
2. What is **SWOT** analysis?
3. What is **PEST** analysis?
4. Define **strategic management**.
5. How does **strategic management** differ from **operational management**?
6. What is an **administrative plan**?
7. List **3** ways in which the functional areas can support the planning process.

EXERCISES

1. 'Business planning is a vital ingredient of business success.' Discuss.
2. Describe the main components of a business plan.

> *While attempting to answer the questions and exercises on this page, you are strongly advised not to read on and to cover the answers and solutions on the following page with a sheet of paper.*

Business planning

ANSWERS TO QUESTIONS

1. A mission statement is a summary statement which seeks to identify an organization's key objectives, values, and principles.

2. A 'planning tool' which seeks to identify an organization's *strengths* and *weaknesses* along with any *opportunities* it may seek to exploit and the accompanying *threats* to the achievement of its business plans and operations.

3. A 'planning tool' which seeks to identify a range of *external* factors which may influence the business organization's operations, plans and development. Such factors are classified as *political, economic, social* and *technological.*

4. Strategic management involves determining the broad plans and areas of development which the company will seek to develop, implement and achieve over the long term.

5. Whereas strategic management is more concerned with long-term, broad development plans, operational management concerns the implementation of these plans on a day-to-day basis by identifying targets and associated action plans.

6. An administrative plan identifies the administrative support needs required by the business in order to implement its operational plans.

7.
   - Provide information
   - Undertake activities which support the planning process
   - Take responsibility for implementing the various aspects of the operational and administrative plans.

SOLUTIONS TO EXERCISES

1. Business activity involves taking risks. One way the business can seek to reduce the level of risk involved in business activity is to involve itself in business planning. The purpose of business planning is to undertake an in-depth analysis of the organization's operations and to devise a plan based upon the results of this analysis. Business planning will therefore need to consider a number of factors which influence the activities of the business. Such factors can broadly be classified as those under the direct influence of the business (internal factors) and those which are beyond the control of the business (external factors). If the business does not involve itself in the planning process it will run the risk that, over the long term, it will not reach its full potential or be able to respond to changes in market conditions.

2. The main components of a business plan are:
   - background information on the company;
   - company objectives, targets and overall mission;
   - a detailed marketing plan based upon effective market research which identifies the opportunities available for the business;

- the resource implications, should the plan be implemented;
- the specific financial targets which will be used to monitor the success of the plan.

POINTS TO REMEMBER

- The purpose of business planning is to undertake an in-depth and systematic analysis of the organization's aims, goals and objectives and to identify the ways in which it will achieve them.

- Effective business planning will reduce the risks inherent in business operations.

- Business planning will result in managers having a much clearer picture of how to direct business activities.

- Planning should follow a logically consistent framework which commences with a clear view or mission of the company and its objectives.

- SWOT and PEST analysis provides the opportunity for the business to analyse both the internal and external influences on its operations.

- Target setting and monitoring mechanisms within the planning process will cover such aspects as quality indicators, measures of financial performance and associated timescales.

- A well-formulated business plan is particularly important for those business organizations seeking 'start-up' capital or for more established enterprises who are seeking additional funds for investment.

- Strategic planning involves the broad plans and areas of development which the company seeks to implement and achieve.

- Operational planning involves breaking down the strategic plan into manageable targets and associated action plans and timescales.

- Administrative plans concern the systems and procedures which need to be in place to support the implementation of the operational action plans.

- Each of the functional areas plays a role in the planning process by providing information, undertaking activities and implementing the action plans.

9

Business finance

> **After carefully studying this chapter, you should be able to:**
>
> 1 *explain why companies need financial information;*
>
> 2 *distinguish between financial and management accounting, and the contribution of each to the decision-making process;*
>
> 3 *understand the purpose of the trading and profit and loss account;*
>
> 4 *describe key financial terms.*

> **Extended Syllabus references**
>
> 3.7 Explain why companies need financial information
> 3.8 Distinguish between financial and management accounting and the contribution of each to the decision-making process
> 3.9 Understand the purpose of the trading and profit and loss account
> 3.10 Describe key financial terms:
>   3.10.1 gross profit
>   3.10.2 net profit
>   3.10.3 depreciation
>   3.10.4 assets
>   3.10.5 liabilities
>   3.10.6 turnover
>   3.10.7 cash flow

The purpose of this chapter is to provide a broad overview of the role of the finance function. The main focus of the chapter concerns the contribution made by the finance/accounts function to the business organization and how the various financial records produced by this specialist area of business can assist in the planning and monitoring of business activity. The chapter will also introduce a number of important terms used in the study of business finance which can be referred to when dealing with a range of other aspects of Business Practice.

The need for financial information

Chapter 8 highlighted the importance of business planning and the role of managers in the decision-making process. We have stressed throughout our study of Business Practice that decision-making involves making choices from a range of alternatives and that making the wrong choice can have serious consequences for the business. Having access to up-to-date, accurate and relevant information is crucial if the decisions made by the management team are to benefit the business organization. In this respect, the finance/accounts function can play a pivotal role.

The financial information required by the business organization covers every aspect of its operations. In general terms, the information can be classified in 5 broad areas:

- financial information relating to expenditure;
- financial information relating to income;
- financial information relating to proposed business developments;
- financial information relating to business targets;
- financial information which assists managers to monitor their budgets.

Later in this chapter we shall look at some of the financial records which are produced by the finance/accounts function, which incorporate specific types of financial information required by the business. Additionally, we shall identify the range of specialist financial documents from which the information is drawn. For the purpose of this introduction, however, we can conclude that financial information enables the business to:

- plan its activities;
- make decisions;
- control its business activities;
- monitor its progress;
- inform managers of potential problems.

Let us look at these aspects in more detail, paying particular attention to the decision-making process within the business organization.

Business management

The finance function and the decision-making process

When we looked at the role of the functional areas we identified 2 specialist areas within the finance function:

- financial accounting
- management accounting.

Financial accounting

We have already identified that financial accounting is concerned with keeping detailed financial records of all aspects of business activity which results in either income or expenditure. In order to assist the process of financial accounting, specialized financial documents are used, each of which contains specific information.

We can look in more detail at the range of these financial documents by referring to the simple business activity of purchasing goods – for example, the purchase of such items as raw materials, equipment or office consumables.

The purchasing process will involve some, or all, of the following documents:

- purchase order
- invoice
- statement of account
- credit note
- cheque
- bank statement.

Activity

Complete the following table and identify the financial information contained within each of the documents.

Document	Financial information
Purchase order	
Invoice	
Statement of account	
Credit note	
Cheque	
Bank statement	

Financial accounting deals with more than just the purchasing aspect of the business organization's operations. The business will also be involved in selling activities, and so the sale of goods will be accounted for by sales invoices and any outstanding credit notes. Additionally, documents used in this process will enable the business organization to identify outstanding debts and to follow-up any *bad debts* which have accumulated over time.

At every stage in the purchasing process and the sales process, financial transactions will be entered into special accounts books known as *ledgers* – the whole activity being referred to as *bookkeeping*.

Most purchases and sales will not be cash transactions, and there may well be a delay between when goods are ordered and when they are paid for. The business must ensure that it keeps a tight check on its *real* financial position, rather than relying purely on periodic statements produced by its bank.

Such bank statements only show those financial commitments which have actually been presented to the bank; they do not incorporate commitments which are in the process of being paid. This could mean that the business's bank account shows a healthy balance whereas, in reality, commitments made to purchase goods could result in a negative balance – in effect, a *bank overdraft*. An important function of financial accounting is therefore to ensure that the business has an up-to-date picture of its cash balances in the bank, and to do this it undertakes a process known as *bank reconciliation* – essentially, checking the bank statement to make sure that the entries are correct and to identify those payments and receipts which have yet to be entered into the business account.

Two other activities will also be undertaken by staff engaged in financial accounting – those concerned with small cash transactions being made on behalf of the company by its employees and those transactions which result in purchases of major pieces of equipment. There may be occasions when an individual employee may purchase items on behalf of the company – postage stamps and travel expenses in connection with business trips are two such examples. Most companies keep a reserve of cash to reimburse employees who have incurred such expenses from *petty cash*. Once again, special documents must be completed to ensure that the process is monitored. Employees will also be required to present sales receipts or other confirmation documentation such as rail tickets, restaurant bills and hotel bills in order to make a valid petty cash claim.

On the other hand, the business may undertake large-scale investment in new equipment and machinery. This will be recorded in a special *assets register*, which will provide details of:

- description of the equipment;
- when the equipment was purchased;
- cost of the equipment;
- serial number;
- location.

Asset registers are a useful source document in calculating the value of the company's assets, and are also referred to in the event of the loss or damage to the asset which may result in an insurance claim.

Financial accounting also plays a central role in providing information to the management team on the methods and costs of raising finance which can be used to finance business developments. All business organizations require capital to finance their operations. Such capital is required to purchase *fixed assets*, for example buildings and land, and in addition funds are required to finance *working capital*, including the purchase of raw materials. Finally, should the business wish to expand, additional capital may be required to finance the necessary *investment in new plant and machinery*.

Private sector business organizations can obtain finance from a variety of sources. Such finance can either be *short-term* (money raised for a period of less than 1 year – for example *bank overdrafts*), *medium-term* (for a period of 1 to 5 years – for example *bank loans*) or *long-term* (for a period in excess of 5 years – for example shares). There are a number of other methods of finance which can include short-, medium- and long-term sources of finance.

Short-term sources of finance

- *Factoring* allows the business to 'sell' its debts to a specialist firm known as a 'factor'. Such a service will produce, in effect, a cash sale and lead to an injection of cash into the business.
- *Trade credit* allows the business to obtain goods on the basis that it will pay its suppliers at some agreed future date, by which time it may have already received the money for selling them (or the product made from them).

Medium-term sources of finance

- *Hire Purchase (HP)* enables the firm to obtain assets and purchase them over a period of time, by making a 'downpayment' or *deposit* followed by *regular monthly repayments*. Such payments are the subject to interest charged by the HP company. In such cases, the asset is owned by the hire purchase company until the final payment is made.
- *Leasing* is a method of obtaining the use of equipment – office machinery, computers, company vehicles and the like – by agreeing to make *regular payments*. Unlike HP, the business *never legally owns the equipment*. As such, leasing is similar to a rental agreement and is particularly useful when equipment is liable to become rapidly obsolete or out-of-date, eg computer equipment.

Long-term sources of finance

- *Mortgages* are provided by large financial institutions to businesses which wish to purchase *land and buildings*. The property is used by the lender as *security* for the loan. Mortgages may be repaid over a long period of time, in many cases in excess of 20 years.

In all the above examples, the financial accountant will be required to provide the business with a range of advice and information about the costs and suitability of certain types of sources of finance which will enable the management team to decide on the most appropriate course of action.

From this brief overview of some of the activities undertaken within the financial accounting function we are able to draw the following conclusions:

- the business must keep a constant check on its expenditure;
- the business must ensure that it records all its financial commitments;
- the business must identify and follow up any outstanding debts which are owed to it;
- the business must ensure that all the payments which it makes have relevant documentary evidence in the form of invoices and receipts;
- the business must ensure that all its financial records are up to date;
- the business must have access to up-to-date, relevant, specialist advice regarding the most cost-effective way of financing its business activities.

Financial record-keeping is at the heart of the financial accounting process and it is from these records that the business can identify 2 crucial aspects of its operations:

- how much profit is being made?
- what is the current financial position of the business?

Two of the most important summary documents which can be produced from the wealth of financial information recorded within the financial accounting process are:

- the profit and loss account
- the balance sheet.

The profit and loss account – how much profit is being made?

Profit is one of the central indicators of business success. In simple terms it can be defined as the surplus of sales revenue over costs, but, for our purposes, we need to identify the way in which the business identifies the level of profit it has generated, and how this profit is used to meet the objectives of the business. Since the financial accountant's team is responsible for keeping records of all income and expenditure, it is their job to draw up the *profit and loss* account for the business.

Business management

Three separate stages are involved in producing the profit and loss account

- calculating the *gross profit*;
- calculating the *net profit*;
- identifying what will happen to any profits which are made.

Calculating the gross profit

In essence, gross profit is derived by calculating the value of sales revenue and subtracting the cost of those sales. For example:

Sales revenue	=	£380,000
less Cost of sales	=	£130,000
Gross profit		**£250,000**

This information is to be found in the company's *trading account*.

Although gross profit is a useful piece of information to enable the business to judge its performance, it is, in truth, only a partial indicator of how well the business is performing. In order to obtain a more realistic figure we need to understand that business activity does not only include purchasing goods and selling them on for a profit. We also need to be aware that a number of other expenses, which are also *costs*, are generated as a result of engaging in business activity. Such expenses include such elements as:

- wages and salaries
- heating
- lighting
- advertizing
- insurance
- premises.

In addition, the business may be liable to pay tax on its profits to the government. This 'corporation tax' is, in effect, a business expense, since it serves to reduce the overall level of profits available to the business. If we take into account the expenses of the business we are able to calculate the *net profit* as shown in Table 9.1.

Once the business has ascertained the level of its net profit (ie gross profit, less expenses), it then has to decide what it will do with these funds. It has, in effect, 2 choices:

- retain the profits to finance future plans;
- distribute the profits to its shareholders.

In practice, it is likely to do both, because the shareholders will realize that future

Table 9.1 Profit and loss account showing how expenses reduce the gross profit

Profit and Loss Account for Westway Toys Limited for the year ended 2 April

		£	£
	Gross profit		250,000
less	Expenses		
	Wages and salaries	100,000	
	Lighting	10,000	
	Advertizing	2,000	
	Insurance	5,000	
	Heating	15,000	
	Premises costs	30,000	
			162,000
	Profit before tax		88,000
less	Corporation tax		38,000
	Profit after tax		50,000

Table 9.2 Profit and loss account showing how profits are apportioned

Profit and Loss Account for Westway Toys Ltd for the period ending 2 April

		£
	Sales revenue	380,000
less	Cost of sales	130,000
	Gross profit	250,000
less	Expenses	162,000
	Profit before tax	88,000
less	Corporation tax	38,000
	Profit after tax	50,000
	Dividends paid to shareholders	20,000
	Retained profits	30,000

profit, and with it future dividend payments, is determined to a large extent by profits being re-invested, or 'ploughed back' into the business. We are now in a position to draw up the full profit and loss account for our company as shown in Table 9.2.

How can the information in the profit and loss account assist the business? Five broad areas can be identified:

- it can show trends in profit levels over time;
- it can highlight potential efficiency savings with regards to its expenses;
- it can highlight if some expenses are too high in relation to others;
- it can be used to compare performance with that of other firms;
- it can show profit as a proportion of sales revenue.

> **Activity**
>
> Draw up a profit and loss account for SAJ Electronics Ltd based on the following information. Show clearly the level of profits retained by the company.
>
> - Sales revenue   £800,000
> - Cost of sales   £200,000
> - Wages and salaries   £100,000
> - Premises costs   £50,000
> - Insurance   £15,000
> - Advertizing   £10,000
> - Telephone and postage   £5,000
> - Corporation tax is 20% of profits
> - Shareholders receive 25% of after-tax profits.

The balance sheet – what is the current financial position?

If the business wants an indication of its financial position at a given point in time, it can request that the financial accountant draws up a *balance sheet*. Once again, the information collected through bookkeeping is central to the process of drawing up the balance sheet.

In our study of business practice we will concentrate upon 2 main aspects of the balance sheet:

- the information contained in the balance sheet;
- how the balance sheet assists the decision-making process.

Information contained in the balance sheet

The balance sheet records what a business owns (its *assets*) and what it owes (its *liabilities*) at one point in time. It also contains information relating to the owner's capital (for sole traders) and shareholders' funds (for limited companies).

- *Assets* will include *fixed assets* such as premises, fixtures and fittings and any company vehicles. They also include *current assets* such as stock, cash reserves in the bank and money owed by debtors.
- *Liabilities* will include company debts and any taxation or dividends owed.
- *Shareholders' funds* will provide details of the money the company has raised from its shareholders.

How does the balance sheet assist the decision-making process?

The balance sheet assists the decision-making process in 3 main ways:

- it identifies if the business can afford to pay its debts when they become due;
- it identifies if there is potential for the business to issue more shares;
- it identifies what assets are available to cover the business's debts.

Both the profit and loss account and the company's balance sheet are of particular interest to those individuals and businesses who are involved with the company – both existing and potential shareholders will have a particular interest in the level of profits being made by the company, whilst those businesses who supply goods and services to the company will be keen to ascertain from the balance sheet if the company can cover its existing debts. Additionally, the annual reports required by law to be published by public limited companies must contain a statement of profit or loss and the company's balance sheet.

Management accounting

If the primary purpose of financial accounting is the efficient and effective recording and presentation of financial records, then *management accounting* can be considered as the *interpretation of financial information* in order to assist the decision-making process within the business organization. Management accounting also provides *ongoing monitoring procedures* regarding business activities. In this section we will consider 2 elements in which these aspects of management accounting are used:

- budgetary control
- pricing strategies.

Budgetary control

We are now familiar with the notions that the business uses productive resources when it engages in business activities, and that using these resources will generate costs of production. It is important for the individual business organization to keep a regular check on the resources it is using in order to ensure that its activities are within the financial resources available. Put simply, the business needs to make sure that it keeps within its financial means.

On a day-to-day basis, this is particularly important for those managers with budgetary responsibilities. Each year when the departmental or section budgets are agreed, the managers are given the responsibility of ensuring that their expenditure is kept within limits. They do this by submitting a 'budget profile' at the start of the financial year which identifies how they propose to spend their budget on a month-by-month basis. The management accountant will then issue regular reports during the year which identify how far 'actual' expenditure is in line with the 'budget profile'.

This process acts as a *monitoring mechanism* which enables the managers to identify if they are likely to overspend their budget and to take appropriate corrective action when necessary. The following activity provides the opportunity of looking at this process in action in order to determine if corrective action might need to be taken in order to prevent a budget overspend.

Activity

The following financial report has been produced by the management accountant.

Write a memo to the Head of Marketing outlining any concerns which you identify from the budget statement.

Marketing Department – Budget report up to July

Month	Budget profile (£)	Actual expenditure (£)	Variance (£)
January	400	300	−100
February	600	700	+100
March	200	400	+200
April	800	600	−200
May	1,000	1,500	+500
June	400	1,200	+800
July	800	2,000	+1,200
August	2,500		
September	500		
October	4,000		
November	1,000		
December	3,000		

Pricing strategies

The successful business operating in the private sector of the economy must make a profit from its business activities if it is to survive within the competitive market. We saw from the information contained within the profit and loss account that, as a result of selling goods and services, sales revenue can be used to pay business expenses and generate profit.

However, the profit and loss account is based upon actual sales and expenses and, as such, is a historical record of *past* business activity. Management accounting on the other hand can assist the business by considering the impact of different pricing policies on *future* profit levels. It does this by engaging in an activity referred to as

Business finance

break-even analysis. This section looks as this financial modelling tool in more detail in order to show how it informs the pricing strategies of the business.

Break-even analysis

The concept of break-even analysis is based on an understanding that business costs can be classified as *fixed costs* or *variable costs*.

- *Fixed costs* must be paid by the business even if the spending does not result in the production of goods. Examples of fixed costs include such items as rent, rates or interest on loans. Fixed costs are also referred to as *overheads* or *indirect costs*.
- *Variable costs* vary directly with output. In other words, if output increases then variable costs will also increase and, conversely, if output falls then variable costs will also fall. Examples of variable costs include such items as raw materials, labour and transport costs. Variable costs are also referred to as *direct costs*.

If we add together fixed costs (FC) and variable costs (VC) at any level of output, we will arrive at the total costs (TC) of producing that output. In other words:

total costs = fixed costs + variable costs

or

tc = fc + vc

As a result of selling the goods a *sales revenue* or *sales turnover* is generated, calculated by multiplying the number of sales by the price charged for the individual goods. In other words, the total revenue (TR) is found by multiplying sales by price:

total revenue = sales x price

or

turnover

or

sales revenue

Business management

> **Activity**
>
> (1) Calculate total costs, fixed costs or variable costs from the following data:
>
> | Fixed costs (£) | Variable costs (£) | Total costs (£) |
> |---|---|---|
> | 150 | 450 | |
> | 200 | | 3,450 |
> | | 2,000 | 8,550 |
> | 450 | | 1,050 |
> | 1,100 | 850 | |
>
> (2) Calculate price, output and total revenue from the following information:
>
> | Price (£) | Total sales | Total revenue (£) |
> |---|---|---|
> | 10 | 4,000 | |
> | 25 | | 25,000 |
> | | 5,000 | 150,000 |
> | 5 | 10,000 | |
> | | 1,500 | 30,000 |

Like the management accountant we are now in a position to construct a break-even chart which will identify the point at which the company's costs equate to the revenue received from sales. In order to do this we need to construct a series of graphs (Figures 9.1–9.4, pages 174–5) which can then be combined together to produce the break-even point (Figure 9.5, page 176).

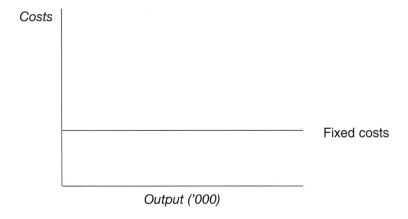

Figure 9.1 Fixed costs

Business finance

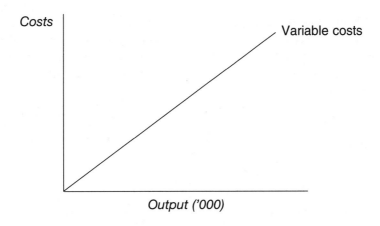

Figure 9.2 Variable costs

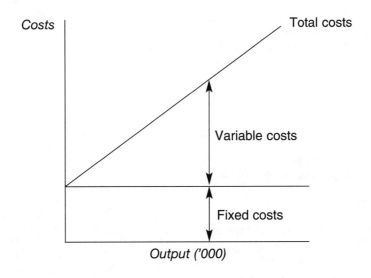

Figure 9.3 Total costs

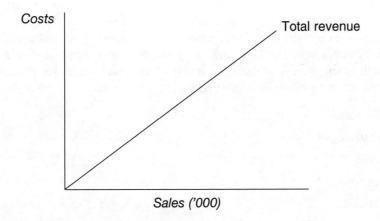

Figure 9.4 Total revenue

175

From these 4 graphs, we can now construct the break-even chart as identified in Figure 9.5. This shows that, at an output of OB, total costs and total revenue are equal (OA). Using this chart, the management accountant is able to provide important information which the firm can use when it is considering issues relating to *costs, price, output* and *sales*.

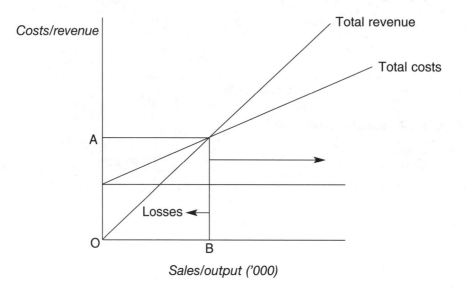

Figure 9.5   Break-even chart

Let us take 2 situations which may arise from the break-even chart in Figure 9.5:

- the firm sells an output *below* OB;
- the firm sells an output *greater* than OB.

If sales are *above* OB, then total revenue will be *greater* than total costs and the firm will be making profits. However, should the firm achieve a level of sales *below* OB then total revenue will be *below* total costs and the firm will be experiencing losses. Since we are aware that total revenue is dependent upon sales and price, the management accountant will be able to provide information to the management team regarding the effects of different levels of sales and prices on profit levels, thus enabling the team to make informed decisions relating to:

- business policies
- pricing strategies
- sales levels
- output levels
- cost structure.

Business finance

The language of business finance – key terms

Serious students of Business Practice must be able to use specialist financial terms with confidence in a variety of settings and contexts. The following list is a summary of financial terms we have used or referred to in this chapter:

- *Gross profit* – sales revenue minus the cost of those sales.
- *Net profit* – gross profit minus expenses.
- *Assets* – items or property owned by the business which have a money value.
- *Liabilities* – money owed by the business, ie business debts.
- *Turnover* – the value of sales revenue calculated by multiplying the total number of sales by the price of those sales.

Finally, in the context of our study of Business Practice we need to be familiar with 2 other specialized terms used by staff engaged in the management of the business.

- *Depreciation* – The concept of depreciation recognizes the fact that capital equipment – machinery and other fixed-assets – wear out as a result of being used in the production process. In order to arrive at the real costs of production, the business therefore includes an amount for depreciation in its accounts.
- *Cash flow* – The business must ensure that it has sufficient funds to pay its short-term liabilities. The purpose of monitoring cash flow is to identify any periods when sales income may not be sufficient to cover short-term outgoings. If this is planned in advance through a *cash flow forecast*, the business can ensure that sufficient funds are drawn from other sources to meet the shortfall.

Activity

Choose *1* of the following products and draw up a simple business plan:

- a new computer software package which can be used by small firms to monitor their finances;
- a new range of modular office furniture.

There now follow some quick questions and revision exercises. They relate specifically to the chapter you have just studied. You are advised to attempt the questions without reference to the text, and then compare your answers and solutions with those on pages 179–80.

QUESTIONS

1. List **5** reasons why the business requires financial information.
2. What is the purpose of an **invoice**?
3. What are **ledgers**?
4. What is meant by the term **bank reconciliation**?
5. What are the differences between **gross profit**, **net profit** and **distributed profit**?
6. List **5** ways in which the profit and loss account can assist a business.
7. What is the **balance sheet**?
8. What are **assets** and **liabilities**?
9. List **3** ways in which the balance sheet assists the decision-making process.

EXERCISES

1. Distinguish, with examples, between short-, medium- and long-term sources of finance available to the business organization.
2. How does break-even analysis assist the business organization?
3. In what ways can the finance/accounts function enable managers to perform their role more effectively?

> *While attempting to answer the questions and exercises on this page, you are strongly advised not to read on and to cover the answers and solutions on the following page with a sheet of paper.*

ANSWERS TO QUESTIONS

1.
   - To plan its activities.
   - To make decisions.
   - To control its business activities.
   - To monitor its progress.
   - To inform managers of potential problems.

2. To request a customer's payment for goods or services supplied by the business.

3. Specialized account books in which the business enters financial transactions relating to its purchasing and sales activities.

4. Checking bank statements to make sure that the entries are correct and to identify those payments and receipts which have yet to be entered into the business account in order to confirm the closing balance.

5. *Gross profit* is profit calculated by ascertaining the value of sales revenue and subtracting the cost of those sales. *Net profit* is calculated by subtracting expenses and taxation from the gross profit. *Distributed profit* is the amount of profits distributed to shareholders in the form of dividends.

6.
   - Can show trends in profits over time.
   - Can highlight potential efficiency savings with regard to its expenses.
   - Can highlight if some expenses are too high in relation to others.
   - Can be used as a source of comparison with other firms.
   - Can show profit as a percentage of sales revenue.

7. The balance sheet records what a business owns (its assets) and what it owes (its liabilities) at a given point in time. It also contains information relating to the owners' capital and shareholders funds (for limited companies).

8. Assets include fixed assets such as premises and current assets such as stock, cash reserves and money owed by customers and other debtors.

   Liabilities include the full range of company debts along with any taxation or dividends owed.

9.
   - Identifies if the business can afford to pay its debts when they become due.
   - Identifies if there is potential for the business to issue more shares.
   - Identifies what assets are available to cover its debts.

SOLUTIONS TO EXERCISES

1. Short-term sources of finance involve money raised for a period of less than 1 year, for example bank overdrafts, trade credit and factoring – a process by which company debts are sold to a third party thereby providing the business with cash. Medium-term sources of finance extend for a period of 1–5 years and include bank loans, hire purchase and leasing. Long-term sources of finance last for periods in excess of 5 years and include shares and mortgages.

2. Break-even analysis is a financial modelling tool used by the business organization to identify the level of sales and output at which costs of production will exactly equal sales revenue at different price levels. It works on the basis that costs are made up of both fixed and variable costs and that sales revenue is derived from selling products at a particular price. Since it is likely that different price levels will generate different levels of sales, it follows that the break-even point will alter with each different level of price thus allowing the business to determine the most appropriate price to charge for its product.

3. The finance/accounts function comprises 2 main elements, each of which can enable managers to perform their role more effectively. Financial accounting is concerned with financial record-keeping and the production of financial documents, such as profit and loss accounts and balance sheets. Management accounting, on the other hand, is more concerned with monitoring, predicting and forecasting. The manager's role consists of a number of interrelated functions including planning, controlling, monitoring, forecasting, directing and organizing, each of which is likely to concern making decisions which will have a direct impact on company performance. It is therefore of vital importance that the finance/accounts function plays a key part in business planning and, on a day-to-day basis, provides managers with relevant financial reports on management targets and associated department or section budgets.

POINTS TO REMEMBER

- Access to reliable financial information is a key requirement of the business organization engaged in planning, monitoring, measuring, and reviewing its performance.

- Financial accounting is concerned with keeping detailed financial records of all aspects of business activity.

- Activities associated with financial accounting include bookkeeping, bank reconciliation, maintaining an up-to-date assets register and providing information to the management team on the methods and costs of raising finance.

- Sources of finance can be classified as short-, medium- or long-term, each of which will be associated with different aspects of the business organization's operations.

- The profit and loss account contains information relating to a business organization's costs, sales, expenses, and apportionment of profits.

- From the profit and loss account we can determine the sales turnover, the gross profit, and the net profit.

- The balance sheet records what a company owns (its assets) and what it owes (its liabilities) at one point in time, taking into account a level of depreciation.

- Management accounting can be considered as the interpretation of financial information in order to assist the decision-making process.

- Management information can assist the business by monitoring budgets and by considering the impact of different pricing policies on future profit levels.

- Budgets can be monitored by comparing actual expenditure against the planned budget profile.

- Budgetary control allows the organization to monitor its cash flow in order to ensure that sufficient funds are available to cover short-term out-goings.

- Break-even analysis seeks to identify the level of output and sales at which fixed and variable costs will be covered. Sales above this level of output will generate profits.

Part 4
Personal contribution to business effectiveness

Part 4

10

Strategies for improving business performance

> After carefully studying this chapter, you should be able to explain the ways in which business performance can be improved by:
>
> - *target-setting;*
> - *customer service;*
> - *maximizing efficiency;*
> - *training and development;*
> - *multiskilling;*
> - *motivating staff.*

> **Extended Syllabus references**
>
> 4.1 Explain the ways in which business performance can be improved by:
>
>   4.1.1 target-setting
>   4.1.2 customer service
>   4.1.3 maximizing efficiency
>   4.1.4 multiskilling of staff
>   4.1.5 training and development of staff
>   4.1.6 motivation of staff

Personal contribution to business effectiveness

The purpose of this chapter is to consider some of the ways in which the business can improve the effectiveness of its activities, operations and performance. The chapter seeks to build upon the knowledge and understanding of our study of Business Practice and to introduce some of the key concepts and themes which will be developed in the final chapters of the book. One important theme which we will continue to explore is the contribution of the individual, either as an individual employee or as a team member, to the range of strategies which we will consider.

Business performance – an overview

It is perhaps worthwhile at this stage to restate a number of important conclusions which we have already drawn from our study of Business Practice. The following activity is designed to assist you in your understanding of Business Practice and will provide you with the opportunity to focus upon a number of key areas which we have looked at in previous chapters. When you are attempting this activity you should pay particular attention to the following aspects of Business Practice:

- the nature of business activity;
- the role of the productive factors;
- how the business is influenced by its environment;
- the role of stakeholders;
- the importance of business planning;
- the contribution of individuals and the importance of teams.

> **Activity**
>
> A group of new trainees has recently joined your organization and will be attending the local college to study Business Practice. Your employer asks you to speak to the trainees and outline to them the main topics they will study and how these topics relate to the day-to-day activities of the business organization. Compile a set of notes which you will refer to during your talk.

It is likely that the notes you have prepared in the activity will have made reference to the concept of *business performance*. What does this mean in practice? In essence, when organizations engage in business activity – in other words when they produce goods and services – the constituent parts which make up the whole process can be judged against certain criteria which, collectively, enable us to assess how well the business has performed. These criteria will include, amongst other things, such familiar factors as:

- the overall quality of the goods produced
- sales figures
- profit levels.

Improving business performance

Successful business organizations understand the concept of business performance and are able to introduce a range of strategies which enable them to influence the level of such performance. The same organizations are also critically aware of the competitive edge which high levels of business performance can generate. The rest of this chapter will concentrate upon some of the main strategies which can affect business performance and the way in which such strategies can influence, and be influenced by, the individual employee.

Target-setting

The starting point for any business organization which is seriously considering measuring its performance is to understand the concept of target-setting. A business seeking to introduce targets needs to answer 3 basic questions:

- *Why* do we want to set targets?
- In *what areas* will we set the targets?
- *Who will be responsible* for setting, monitoring and achieving the targets?

Why set targets?

Business organizations which set targets are likely to want to introduce a *'performance culture'*, in which all aspects of the business have targets. In an organization which uses target-setting as a management tool for improving business performance targets can be set for:

- individuals
- teams
- departments or sections.

The business will first need to identify its core aims and objectives which have been established as part of the *planning process*. We saw in Chapter 8 that this will involve looking at all aspects of the business's operations in order to determine the long-term plans and development of the organization.

If target-setting is not part of this process, the business will find it difficult to implement its long-term plans and will not be able to measure its performance over time.

If the business is successful in establishing targets as part of the planning process, then a number of other advantages will follow:

- targets enable the business to monitor business performance;
- targets can lead to a continuous improvement in business performance;
- targets can help to identify the contributions which individuals, teams and their respective departments and sections can make to improving business performance;
- targets can help to establish a 'performance culture' within the organization.

Personal contribution to business effectiveness

Given that individuals and teams will be directly affected by the target-setting process, it is important that the organization informs its staff of the reasons for introducing target-setting into the business's operations. If this is done in a constructive manner, which actively involves individuals and teams, the business is likely to find that staff will approach their targets in a positive way, confident in the knowledge that they can make a worthwhile contribution to business performance.

In what areas will the targets be set?

Once the business has established the principles of target-setting and the reasons why it wishes to introduce targets into its operations and activities, it will need to identify the specific areas in which the targets will be set. These areas might cover aspects such as:

- profit levels
- quality
- costs
- resources
- output
- staff training
- sales
- new product development.

Along with those targets directly related to the planning process there are a number of other ways in which the business may seek to use targets:

- to concentrate on particular aspects of quality which may be causing concern;
- to measure improvements in quality;
- to reward success, particularly for individuals and teams;
- to gain a competitive advantage.

Who will set the targets?

Setting and monitoring targets will be linked to the business's *'organizational culture'*. In some organizations, targets are set without reference to those who will be responsible for achieving them. In such instances, where there is no shared common purpose between managers and their staff, individual employees will not feel a sense of 'ownership' of the targets. If this is the case, the business is likely to find that, in the context of the targets, it will 'under-achieve'. Although in the final analysis the management team will be responsible for establishing the long-term development plans of the business, it is therefore advisable if the specific targets which are linked to these plans are discussed with individuals and teams. For the individual, staff appraisal can be used for this purpose whilst, for staff teams, discussions with team leaders, supervisors and team members can be used by managers to engage staff in the target-setting process. These discussions will result in specific targets being set which will enable the business to implement the following stages in order to ensure that the targets are met:

- draw up an action plan;
- allocate responsibilities;
- determine timescales;
- establish monitoring mechanisms.

The monitoring function is a particularly important management function, since it enables the manager to identify what action needs to be taken should it appear that targets are not being met.

> **Activity**
>
> Choose 4 of the following areas and give an example of a target in each of your chosen areas which would be appropriate for a firm wishing to expand its production over the next 5 years:
>
> - profits
> - quality
> - output
> - new products
> - costs
> - resources
> - sales
> - new markets.

Customer service

Customer service incorporates a range of services provided to the customer to promote customer loyalty and enhance the reputation of the organization. Business organizations in the service sector of the economy have always appreciated the importance of good customer service. However, in the modern business world, customer service is viewed as a vital component of all business success, to the extent that many organizations employ specialist staff to deal with customer enquiries and complaints. Indeed, it could be argued that customer service has become an additional *functional area* in much the same way as personnel, sales and marketing, finance and the other functional areas which we considered in Chapter 6.

Why has customer service grown in importance? Quite simply, the consumer is now looking at factors other than price to determine whether or not to purchase a particular product. For some products of a technical nature, advice and guidance given by well-qualified, trained and experienced staff can be of critical importance in achieving successful sales. This is particularly important in the field of business and office technology, where the pace of technological development and change generates a bewildering range of new products and product modifications. Those business organizations which produce or sell these products will gain a *competitive*

Personal contribution to business effectiveness

advantage if they are able to show to potential customers a high level of customer service in the form of knowledgeable sales staff.

Customer service will also incorporate good *after-sales service*. This will include such features as:

- availability of spare parts
- efficient and effective repair service
- advice and guidance on technical matters
- replacement of faulty goods
- money-back guarantees
- allowing the return of unwanted goods.

We can see from the above list that the customer service function can be classified as a *cost to the business organization,* since it will need to put into place an administrative system supported by a team of staff who will take responsibility for ensuring that relationships with existing and potential customers are maintained to the highest possible standards. The business is willing to *invest* in good customer service because of the advantages it generates for the organization. These advantages can be summarized as follows:

- improved sales figures
- repeat business
- enhanced reputation for the business
- improved services
- increased profitability
- increased market share
- customer loyalty.

In Chapter 13 we shall see how customer service, like all other aspects of the business's operations, can be subject to the target-setting process in order to achieve continuous improvements in quality and service. For now, we can conclude that the higher the level of customer service, the greater will be the rewards and benefits

---

Activity

(1) Find examples of 3 job advertisements which require an individual to work directly with the public. From the advertisements identify the following:

- type of organization
- job title
- key job functions and roles
- personal qualities required.

(2) What does this activity tell you about the importance of the individual in promoting customer service?

which will accrue to the business organization. In essence, the business can no longer simply pay lip service to the maxim that 'the customer is always right' but must be seen to be actively involved in service delivery.

Maximizing efficiency

Throughout our study of business practice we have constantly made reference to the fact that business activities should be performed *efficiently and effectively*. In this section we will concentrate on 2 main questions:

- What does 'efficiency and effectiveness' mean in the context of the activities of the business organization?
- Is there any way in which we can measure the efficiency and effectiveness of the business organization?

Efficiency and effectiveness

The prime function of business organizations is to combine productive factors in order to produce goods and services. In undertaking this function, the business organization must take account of a number of factors:

- the costs involved in producing goods and services;
- the revenue it receives from sales;
- how well it performs in relation to its targets.

These 3 elements provide us with an insight into what is meant by efficiency and effectiveness. In the context of our study of business practice, we will use the term 'efficiency' to describe the business organization's aim *to produce its goods and services at the lowest cost*, and the term 'effectiveness' to describe *how well the business performs against its targets*. In other words, whilst efficiency is a function of *cost*, effectiveness is a function of business *performance*.

Cost

It is vitally important that, in a competitive market, the business organization seeks to monitor and control its costs. Should costs begin to rise it is likely that profit levels will be reduced since, in a competitive market, the business cannot pass on increases in costs to the consumer in the form of higher prices – if they did, the consumer would be likely to switch to other, more competitively-priced products.

What strategies should the business consider if it is seeking to maximise efficiency?

Some organizations have taken efficiency savings to mean simply 'cutting costs' and, in this respect, have chosen to undertake a process known as *rationalization*. This involves looking at all aspects of the business and re-organizing the functions in such

Personal contribution to business effectiveness

a way as to lower costs of production. Rationalization may involve some or all of the following features:

- a management restructuring, which will involve taking management layers out of the organization in order to make a 'flatter' structure;
- closure of loss-making operations;
- reduction in staffing;
- 'contracting out' key services such as security, cleaning and payroll to specialist companies, rather than employing staff directly.

Since a firm seeking to implement efficiency savings may need to look at existing staffing levels and associated rates of pay, employees are likely to view the process with concern since they fear that it will result in job losses, lower pay and poorer conditions of employment.

There is no doubt that, during the 1980s, many organizations followed a process of *downsizing* – effectively reducing the size of their labour forces in their quest to lower costs and produce more efficiently.

However, in more recent times, far-sighted organizations have begun to realize that there are more subtle ways of promoting efficiency savings in the production process, some of which may actually involve an initial increase in investment. Such strategies may include some, or all, of the following:

- a staff-development and training programme which covers all levels of staff within the organization;
- a capital-investment programme which replaces obsolete equipment with new equipment based upon new technology applications;
- undertake an in-depth analysis of current suppliers and attempt to re-negotiate existing contracts;
- identify new suppliers;
- look at the existing product line and cease production of those products whose market performance is poor;
- transfer productive assets to the research and development function in order to develop new products;
- instigate a programme of growth and development in order to benefit from economies of scale which will generate efficiency savings in the form of lower unit costs of production.

Performance

Effectiveness in business, as we have already identified, is directly related to business performance. In effect, this involves analysing the organization's business plans and associated operational targets and identifying how far it has succeeded in achieving its corporate aims and objectives.

In this context, effectiveness is likely to be seen as involving quantitative, *measurable* performance indicators, and it is to this aspect of our study which we now turn.

Measuring efficiency and effectiveness

Maximizing efficiency and determining the effectiveness of business performance will involve the business organization identifying and measuring a range of important *performance indicators*.

Since efficiency is primarily concerned with costs, these performance indicators will centre upon such elements as:

- total costs
- output
- productivity
- unit costs
- financial performance indicators.

Let us consider these elements in more detail.

Total costs will involve both fixed and variable costs; how much labour costs are involved in the production process? How do these costs compare with other similar organizations?

Output will involve measurements of the total amount of goods produced in a given time period: how does this compare with previous time periods and with other similar organizations?

Productivity measures the *rate* at which goods are produced and is usually associated with the amount of labour employed by the business; 'high productivity rates' means, in effect, producing more goods from the same amount of productive factors in the same time period.

Unit costs measure the costs of producing one unit of output; this is a more reliable measure of efficiency than total costs since it enables the business to compare its efficiency rates over time and with other business organizations.

Financial performance indicators include such measures as unit costs but also incorporate other performance indicators such as *profit margins* – the percentage profit made on each sale – and the *return of net assets employed,* which shows how well the business has used the productive factors in order to generate profits.

Activity

From the financial and business press, identify 3 examples of how business organizations have attempted to improve the efficiency and effectiveness of their operations. Record the results of your research in a tabular format using the following headings:

- Name of the business organization
- Sector (retail, manufacturing, service, financial)
- Strategy for improving efficiency and effectiveness.

Personal contribution to business effectiveness

If the business has established targets in relation to these performance indicators, then it follows that measuring the effectiveness of business performance will involve determining how far the targets have been met.

Target-setting, customer service, and measures to improve the organization's efficiency and effectiveness all contribute to the overall performance of the business within the business environment. In the second part of this chapter we will consider 3 strategies which, if they are successfully incorporated into the business's operations, can all contribute to:

- the successful achievement of targets
- an improvement in customer service
- efficiency gains and improvements in the effectiveness of business performance.

The common feature of all these strategies is the emphasis they place on the contribution of the employee either as an individual member of staff or a team member. The 3 business strategies we will now consider are:

- training and development of staff
- multiskilling of staff
- improving the motivation of staff.

Training and development of staff

The responsibility for the training and development of staff usually rests with the personnel function and forms part of the business organization's *human resource management* (HRM) strategy. In Chapter 3 we looked in detail at the components of HRM and saw that it was important for a business organization to engage in manpower planning in order to ensure that it had sufficient skilled labour to meet its short-, medium- and long-term business needs. The training and development of staff should be seen as an integral element of this process which brings advantages to both the individual employee and the business as a whole.

For individual employees, staff training will:

- develop their skills and knowledge;
- increase job satisfaction;
- enable them to adapt to change.

For the business organization, investment in staff training may lead to:

- improvements in quality;
- an improvement in staff morale and motivation;
- reduced labour turnover;
- greater confidence in management;
- fewer accidents;
- improved job performance and effectiveness;

Improving business performance

- improved customer service;
- increased productivity as employees get better at their jobs;
- increased employee commitment to the business;
- matching the skills of staff to the requirements of the business.

Those business organizations which understand the importance of staff training are likely to implement a programme based upon the following criteria:

- staff training will relate to the targets established within the planning process;
- engage in a *training needs analysis* in order to ascertain the current skill levels of staff and identify any *skills gap* which may prevent the business from achieving its development plans;
- staff training will commence as soon as new employees join the company, when they participate in an induction programme;
- the staff training and development needs of individual staff will be subject to a formal review on a regular basis;
- the staff training programme will encompass all levels of staff within the organization including managers, supervisors, operatives and those involved in other specialist job roles;
- the staff training programme will be subject to regular reviews to ascertain its relevance and effectiveness in meeting company policies and to enable new priorities to be planned, developed and delivered.

The advantage of a 'company approach' to staff training is that it enables the business to harness the advantages of training for the benefit of all levels of staff within the organization which means that the collective efforts of both managers and staff can contribute towards the mission of the business.

Activity

Identify 3 advantages which may arise for the business organization as a result of the following training programmes:

- staff training in the use of *e-mail*;
- staff training in improving *telephone skills*;
- staff training in *understanding management accounts for new managers*.

Multiskilling of staff

One of the most important factors which can prevent a business organization from achieving its targets and business goals is the shortage of skilled labour. In Europe this has been recognized as a problem which impacts upon all those engaged in business activities. Current trends show that the population of Europe is ageing, whilst the development of new technologies require an increasing level of knowledge and understanding. Research undertaken by the European Union (source: EU Jobrotation Programme, 1998) indicates that in 2005:

- 80% of the European workforce will have an education or training qualification that is more than 10 years old;
- 80% of the technology will be less than 10 years old.

How can individual business organizations prepare themselves to meet the challenge of the 'skills gap'? One strategy which some organizations hope will alleviate the problem is to incorporate an element of 'multiskilling' into their staff training programmes. Multiskilling provides staff with the opportunity of gaining new skills which are not directly related to the specific job for which they were originally employed. The multiskilling approach to training recognises the fact that, in today's business world, the development of *transferable skills* will be beneficial to both the individual employee and the business organization. If multiskilling is incorporated into the training programme, the following advantages may arise for the business organization:

- employees become more flexible, which means that the business can save time in recruiting new members of staff to the organization;
- 'bottlenecks' in production will be reduced or prevented as employees are able to be switched more easily into new job roles;
- staff have more confidence in the business and the contribution which they can make to overall business performance;
- allows the business to feel more confident in introducing new technology into its operations and activities;
- staff teams will have access to a broader range of skills which can be used to meet team targets.

Activity

Identify the personal qualities and related skills which are required by staff engaged in 4 of the following functional areas:

- personnel/human resources
- sales and marketing
- production/operations
- administration
- research and development
- purchasing.

Motivation of staff

Our study of business practice has sought to identify the importance of the individual in contributing to business performance and the role of managers in planning, controlling and organizing business activities in order to ensure that the organization's plans are implemented. In order for managers to be able to perform their functions and get the best out of their staff, they need to ensure that individual employees and staff teams are *motivated*. In other words, managers need to implement strategies which result in their staff focusing their energies in the workplace for the benefit of the organization. A number of writers who have attempted to identify the factors which influence motivation. Chief amongst them are:

- Taylor
- McGregor
- Maslow
- Hertzberg.

We shall look in more detail at these writers in Chapter 12, but for the purposes of our current discussion we now need to identify their contribution to *motivational theory*. Taylor believed that people were only motivated by money, whilst McGregor considered that managers would treat their staff according to whether they believed them to be imaginative and creative or more concerned with avoiding work. Maslow and Hertzberg on the other hand, identified a number of elements which, collectively, can be referred to as *'motivational factors'*. At the heart of their analysis is the view that people have certain needs which need to be fulfilled whilst they are also motivated or de-motivated by a number of factors including:

- pay
- working conditions
- promotion prospects
- job satisfaction
- levels of responsibility.

Business organizations should be particularly concerned if they perceive that their staff in general are not well-motivated. Poor motivation is associated with a number of adverse results including:

- an organizational culture in which the achievement of business targets and objectives is not seen as a high priority;
- a lack of confidence in management;
- poor sales figures;
- low profit levels;
- low level of customer service;
- high levels of absenteeism;
- high labour turnover.

Those organizations which are seeking to address motivation amongst staff should therefore begin by identifying the *causes* of low levels of motivation.

A study undertaken in 1997 by the UK's Industrial Society, 'Maximising Attendance', identified low morale and boredom as 2 of the major factors affecting motivation, and with it an increase in absenteeism. Other causes identified in the study include:

- job insecurity
- long hours
- increased work loads.

The study also highlighted the strategies employed by firms to increase motivation and reduce absenteeism. These included such methods as:

- flexible working hours: all staff work core hours, say 10.00 am to 4.00 pm, but are otherwise free to make up the rest of their working week at times to suit themselves
- job-sharing
- term-time working for parents
- occasionally enabling staff to work from home.

These strategies highlight the range of factors which the organization and its managers need to take into account when managing individuals and teams. Indeed, we can devise a 'management checklist' which can inform organizational policies and management practices:

- communicating with staff is vitally important;
- many people like to be involved in decisions which affect their work;
- people are likely to respond positively to praise;
- people are motivated by a range of different factors not just financial rewards;
- working conditions and working practices will have a direct impact on motivation;
- staff will respond in different ways to different management styles;
- the needs of the individual and staff teams should be taken into account when planning work activities;
- job satisfaction is a prime factor in motivating staff.

A well-motivated workforce should be viewed as a valuable asset by the business organization since it will have a direct impact on business performance. In this chapter we have shown how target-setting, customer service and efficiency and effectiveness can all be influenced by employees who are skilled and motivated and who have the opportunity to engage in further staff training and development.

Activity

Place the following factors in their order of importance to you in your current, or future, job role:

- opportunity to develop new skills;
- flexible working hours;
- profit-sharing schemes;
- opportunity to be involved in decision-making;
- working in a team;
- performance-related bonus scheme;
- subsidized staff canteen;
- pay;
- social clubs and sports facilities;
- opportunities for career advancement.

Compare your responses with other students in your group. What conclusions can you draw from this activity which might need to be taken into account by managers in a business organization who are seeking to introduce strategies to improve motivation?

There now follow some quick questions and revision exercises. They relate specifically to the chapter you have just studied. You are advised to attempt the questions without reference to the text, and then compare your answers and solutions with those on pages 201–2.

Personal contribution to business effectiveness

QUESTIONS

1. What is meant by the term **'business performance'**?
2. List **6** areas of business in which **targets** can be set.
3. What is meant by **customer service**?
4. List **5** features of **after-sales service**.
5. What is meant by the term **rationalization**?
6. List **3** performance indicators which could be used to monitor the success of business.
7. List **3** advantages of staff training to the individual employee and the business organization.
8. Identify **5** motivational factors.
9. List **6** problems associated with poor staff motivation.

EXERCISES

1. 'Target-setting is the key to business success'. Discuss.
2. Describe the ways in which good customer service can benefit the business organization.
3. Outline the main features of an effective staff training programme.

> *While attempting to answer the questions and exercises on this page, you are strongly advised not to read on and to cover the answers on the following page with a sheet of paper.*

ANSWERS TO QUESTIONS

1. Business performance concerns the degree to which business is able to meet a range of targets and other performance indicators as identified in its business or strategic plan. The term is also used to describe how well a business performs in relation to other organizations, particularly its competitors.

2.
   - Profit levels
   - Quality
   - Output
   - Sales
   - New product development.

3. Customer service incorporates a range of services provided to the customer which promotes customer loyalty and enhances the reputation of the organization.

4.
   - Availability of spare parts.
   - Efficient and effective repair service.
   - Advice and guidance on technical matters.
   - Replacement of faulty goods.
   - Money-back guarantees.

5. Rationalization involves looking at all aspects of an organization's operations and activities and reorganizing business functions in such a way as to promote efficiency, eliminate waste and reduce costs.

6.
   - Unit costs
   - Output
   - Productivity.

7.
   - Increased job satisfaction.
   - Reduced labour turnover.
   - Increased productivity.

8.
   - Pay
   - Working conditions
   - Promotion prospects
   - Job satisfaction
   - Levels of responsibility.

9.
   - Poor sales figures
   - Low profit levels
   - Low levels of customer service
   - High levels of absenteeism
   - High labour turnover
   - Targets not met, resulting in poor business performance.

Personal contribution to business effectiveness

SOLUTIONS TO EXERCISES

1. A business organization seeking to engage in successful business activity, in which it produces its products at the lowest possible cost and maximizes sales in order to generate profits, will need to develop a business plan which identifies specific targets across the full range of its operations. This target-setting approach to business planning and development is based on the notion that all aspects of the business contribute to business performance, so that setting targets for them all allows the business to monitor the performance and contribution of the constituent parts of the business organization. This process will allow the business to identify those parts of the organization which are under-performing and to take remedial or corrective action to improve performance.

2. Modern business organizations appreciate that consumers are likely to consider a range of factors when determining whether to purchase a particular good or service. In other words, price is not the sole determinant of demand. For this reason, many business organizations are seeking to improve the quality of the service they provide to their customers, since such a strategy, they believe, will lead to increased sales and, in the long run, increased customer loyalty. Investment in customer service (for example by the development of company policies and the introduction of specially trained staff) can result in a number of benefits for the business including increased sales, repeat business, increased profitability and an increase in market share which, collectively, result in improved business performance.

3. An effective staff training programme is likely to include some or all of the following features:

    - the programme will be based on the planning process, which will have identified a range of targets related to the organization's human resource requirements;
    - staff training will commence as soon as new employees join the company, when they participate in the organization's induction programme;
    - the staff training programme will be subject to regular reviews, incorporating a training needs analysis, in order to ensure that it is meeting the needs of the company;
    - staff training will cover all levels of staff within the organization.

POINTS TO REMEMBER

- Business performance is assessed by monitoring the performance of the business against key performance indicators, including costs, profit levels, sales figures and measures of quality.
- Many business organizations will set targets against which they can measure their performance.
- Targets can be set for the business as a whole, or for its constituent parts including departments/sections, teams and individuals.
- Target-setting can lead to continuous improvements in business performance and to the establishment of a 'performance culture' within the business based upon shared goals and objectives.
- Customer service acknowledges that the consumer may consider factors other than price when making a decision about wether to purchase a particular product.
- Effective customer service can provide the business with a competitive edge, leading to measurable advantages in terms of repeat sales, improved sales figures, increased market share and bigger profits.
- Business efficiency describes how well the business performs against its targets and other performance indicators.
- The training and development of staff has a direct impact on business performance and should be seen as an integral part of the organization's human-resource management strategy.
- Shortages of skilled labour can prevent a business organization from achieving its targets and business goals.
- Multiskilling provides staff with the opportunity to gain new skills, which are transferable to a range of associated job roles and tasks, leading to a greater degree of labour flexibility.
- The organization must be aware of the factors which influence the motivation of staff.
- Poor motivation can result in high levels of absenteeism, high labour turnover, low profit levels and poor sales figures.
- Identifying the causes of poor motivation can lead to positive measures which improve working conditions, enhance the quality of communications within the organization and improve job satisfaction.

11

Individuals, teams and business performance

> **After carefully studying this chapter, you should be able to:**
>
> 1. *identify the ways in which the individual can contribute towards business performance;*
> 2. *understand the importance of individual targets and performance;*
> 3. *describe the contribution which teamwork makes towards improving communication and overall business performance.*

> **Extended Syllabus references**
>
> 4.2 Identify the ways in which an individual can contribute towards business performance:
>   - 4.2.1 effective communications
>   - 4.2.2 knowledge of company and company products/services
>   - 4.2.3 customer service
> 4.3 Understand the importance of individual targets and performance
> 4.4 Describe the contribution teamwork can make to improving communication and overall business performance:
>   - 4.4.1 commitment
>   - 4.4.2 innovation
>   - 4.4.3 quality
>   - 4.4.4 co-operation

The purpose of this chapter is to consider the role of the individual in the overall context of business operations. We shall look at how the individual can influence business performance both as an individual and as a member of a team.

The individual and business performance

So far, we have concentrated mainly on those factors which influence the establishment of a successful business organization. We have tended to view the business as an organization which spends money in order to produce goods and services which it then sells for a profit.

In our model, the successful business will be characterized by:

- efficient production methods
- effective organizational structure
- efficient financial recording methods
- high profit levels.

Additionally, we have identified the important role played by *specialization* in the business organization, particularly with regard to specialized business functions and associated job roles. We must now give closer attention to one of the most valuable resources utilized by the business – *the individual employee.*

In order to identify the contribution of the individual to overall business performance, we need to establish the relationship which exists between the employee and the business organization. This relationship should be viewed as consisting of :

- rights
- duties
- obligations.

Indeed, in most countries, the relationship between individual employees and the business in which they are employed is governed by a legally binding agreement in the form of a *contract of employment*, which lays down specifically the rights, duties and obligations of both parties involved in the employment contract. Table 10.1 (overleaf) outlines some of the main features of this relationship in the 3 areas noted above.

The contract of employment, however, does not tell us how the individual employee can make a positive contribution to business performance. Indeed, there may well be situations in which 2 different employees performing the same job role and with identical contracts of employment can make contrasting contributions to the business. In this introduction, we can highlight 3 main ways in which the individual employee can contribute to business performance over and above simply 'doing the job'. In today's competitive business world, business organizations must consider:

- the *quality* of the work produced by the individual employee;
- the level of *commitment* shown by the individual employee;
- the overall *effectiveness* of the individual employee.

Personal contribution to business effectiveness

Table 10.1 Rights, duties and responsibilities of the employee and the employer

	Employee	Employer
Rights	• receive wages and salary for work undertaken • safe working environment • holidays	• expect the employee to follow reasonable instructions • expect the employee to work the required number of hours
Duties	• perform duties in line with job role • work required number of hours • follow instructions • follow health and safety procedures	• provide a safe working environment • pay wages/salary at the agreed rate and at the specified time
Responsibilities	• participate in staff training activities • familiarize themselves with company policies and practices	• provide training opportunities • communicate company policies to staff

Target-setting and individual performance

We have just noted that an individual's contribution to the business is directly related to quality, commitment and effectiveness. We have also already noted that investment in staffing resources is a significant business cost. In the context of this chapter, we shall consider 2 aspects relating to individuals working within the business organization:

- how the contribution of individual members of staff can be measured and improved;
- how the organization of the workforce can directly contribute to improved business performance.

Measuring and improving individual performance

One method which can be adopted by the business to measure and improve individual performance is *staff appraisal*. A formal staff appraisal scheme is usually conducted on an annual basis and provides individual employees and their managers with the opportunity to consider in a formal, private setting a number of key areas of mutual interest. Staff appraisal schemes usually follow one of 2 basic approaches:

- staff appraisal based upon identifying individual staff training needs;

- staff appraisal based upon assessing individual performance.

In truth, the 2 approaches will have a significant overlap in terms of how they operate, and we are likely to find that a staff appraisal scheme based upon the assessment of an individual's performance is also likely to include the opportunity for the manager to identify a range of training needs relating to the individual employee. In practice, the difference in the 2 approaches to staff appraisal is therefore likely to be one of style and approach rather than specific detail. In general terms, both approaches to staff appraisal, whether based upon identifying staff training needs or assessing individual performance, provide the opportunity to gain a number of important advantages for the business, the manager and the individual employee. These advantages are identified in Table 10.2

Table 10.2 Advantages of staff appraisal

For employees	For managers	For the business organization
• provides the opportunity for individual employees to identify any concerns they may have about their jobs, working relationships with other colleagues, or changes in company policy • employees' achievements can be recognized • individuals' training needs can be identified	• enables the manager to get to know individual employees • employees' contributions to the business can be recognized • managers can use appraisal to praise and encourage individuals thereby increasing their commitment to the organization	• provides the opportunity to monitor the organization's recruitment practices and staff selection procedures • can identify those individuals who may be able to take on more challenging job roles through promotion, transfer or redeployment

A formal staff appraisal system should be viewed as much more than an informal chat between manager and employee. A formal staff appraisal scheme is likely to exhibit the following characteristics:

- standardized forms, documentation and recording procedures;
- an agreed timetable, eg staff appraisal undertaken on an annual basis with the opportunity for a six-month review;
- confidentiality;
- any 'action points' arising from the appraisal should be subject to agreement between the manager and the individual member of staff;
- staff appraisal is incorporated within the individual's contract of employment and, as such, the individual is required to participate in the process as part of their conditions of employment.

Staff appraisal provides the opportunity to establish action plans and targets relating to individual employees. Depending on the organization's approach to staff appraisal, such action plans and targets are likely to incorporate one, or both, of the following:

- a staff training plan based upon the training needs identified in the staff appraisal interview;
- individual targets based upon the employee's job role.

In the context of this section we will concentrate on the second of these areas – individual targets. If the appraisal scheme is to be effective, target-setting must be based upon the following SMART principles:

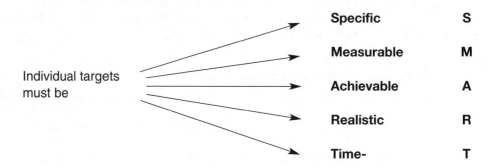

Above all, individual targets should be based upon the individual manager's skill in identifying how the individual employee can contribute to the overall objectives of the business as highlighted in its strategic plan. For example, a company may seek to increase its market share over the next 5 years. What will this mean in the context of the staff appraisal for the sales manager or for a member of the sales team?

Following our analysis, we must identify individual targets which follow our SMART rules. So, for example, a member of the sales team could be set the following appraisal targets:

1. to increase their total personal sales by 5% over the next year;
2. to generate 5 new customers each month over the next year.

Although it would be up to the individual manager and the member of staff concerned to agree that these targets are *achievable* or *realistic*, we can nevertheless still identify the *specific* and *measurable* factors which must be achieved in a given *timescale*.

Activity

In the context of your Business Practice course, agree 3 individual targets with your teacher which will contribute towards success in the final examination. These targets should relate to:

- homework
- reading
- revision.

Some business organizations use staff appraisal not only to identify staff training needs and establish individual targets, but also to assess the performance of individual employees. In these so-called *performance appraisal schemes*, not only are targets set and agreed, but managers are required to assess or grade the performance of the individual employee. Indeed, in some schemes, this assessment and grading can be linked directly to pay. This is one main reason why some staff may view the introduction of any staff appraisal scheme with anxiety. Although the focus of the scheme may, in the first instance, be on identifying staff training needs, there is always a concern that it might result in a pay structure which is directly related to performance. Therefore, despite the undoubted advantages of staff appraisal, those organizations which are seeking to introduce a formal staff appraisal scheme for the first time, are urged to proceed with caution. If a staff appraisal scheme is to be successful it must have the full support and confidence of all staff within the organization.

In order to achieve such support and confidence, the following factors need to be taken into account:

- management style
- organizational culture
- effective communications.

The study of Business Practice involves an understanding and an appreciation of all these elements. In the final analysis, however, a staff appraisal scheme must be judged on its ability to deliver the following:

- a high-quality performance from the individual;
- a high level of commitment from the individual;
- an increase in the effectiveness of the individual in job role performance;
- a recognition of the individual's contribution to the business;
- an identification of training needs.

Activity

Devise a simple form which could be used in a staff appraisal scheme which seeks to identify the training needs of individual members of staff.

The importance of teamwork in improving business performance

Although we have just commented on the importance of the individual's contribution to the business, many organizations have also sought to harness the collective efforts of individuals by promoting *teamwork* as a means of improving:

- commitment
- innovation

Personal contribution to business effectiveness

- quality
- cooperative working relations
- communications
- job satisfaction.

In this section we will consider how teamwork can, either directly or indirectly, contribute to all of these areas, by identifying some strategies which may be employed by the business to promote this way of working.

What is a team?

In the context of our study, a team is considered to be a small group of employees who work together to achieve a common goal. Many firms now realize that, although individuals may perform specialized functions and job roles within the organization, if these can be grouped together in such a way that common, agreed goals can be identified amongst a group of employees, then a number of advantages may follow for the organization.

How does a business promote and establish teams?

There are a number of ways in which the organization can encourage teamwork. In Chapter 12, we shall look at management styles, and at a type of business culture which seeks to encourage teamwork and participation and to promote the contributions of individuals and teams. Here we shall look at specific strategies which can be adopted by the business to promote teamwork and the advantages which may result. In particular, we will look at 3 main ways by which the business may seek to promote the development of teams in order to establish common goals which meet the needs of the organization:

- suggestion schemes
- quality circles
- empowerment.

Suggestion schemes

In some respects, suggestion schemes are the oldest and most traditional way of trying to establish a common purpose within the organization. Even today, many firms have a 'suggestion box' in which employees can deposit written suggestions for how business activities, operations or performance can be improved. We should not underestimate the importance of such schemes, since many organizations have been able to implement cost-saving measures based upon simple and straightforward suggestions made by members of staff who have a knowledge of the day-to-day operations of the business. Some organizations will positively promote such schemes by offering financial incentives for those suggestions which are successfully implemented. This being said, a number of progressive organizations have now realized that a more formal structure must be put in place which utilizes the ingenuity and experience of the workforce within the business.

Quality circles

Quality circles are one way in which a more formal structure for employee participation and consultation can be embedded into the conduct of the business. Quality circles, originally used to the advantage of Japanese companies, are small groups of workers, usually from the same section or department, who meet to:

- discuss practical work issues;
- solve practical problems;
- produce ideas for improving productivity or working conditions.

The groups meet in company time, and membership is voluntary. The main purposes of quality circles are:

- to improve quality;
- to suggest more efficient and effective ways of working;
- to generate new ideas;
- to develop a commitment amongst the workforce to the values, aims and goals of the organization;
- to promote an understanding of the benefits of cooperation between employees and their managers;
- to develop a team ethos within the organization;
- to promote effective communications between staff and their line managers.

Whilst a number of organizations have established quality circles, others still have taken the concept further and given groups and teams of staff much more responsibility for a wider range of business activities and functions.

Empowerment

'Empowerment' refers to a *process* rather than to a specific *policy*. In essence, the process has developed out of a trend which became prevalent in the late 20th century of 'de-layering', ie removing management levels from the organization in order to create a 'flatter' organizational structure. As management layers have been removed, so the workforce has been given more responsibility for a greater range of activities which have been traditionally associated with operational managers. These activities include such areas as:

- setting and monitoring targets
- customer service

Personal contribution to business effectiveness

- quality issues
- team meetings
- staff training
- work rotas and processes.

> **Activity**
>
> Compare and contrast the organization charts of 2 business organizations. Try to identify the different layers of management which exist within the respective organizations.

Benefits of teams to the business organization

It may be possible actually to *measure* the positive impact which teams can make upon business performance. Studies which have been undertaken on those organizations which promote teamwork would seem to indicate a number of advantages including:

- increases in output;
- falls in absenteeism;
- reduction in labour turnover;
- achievement of both team and individual targets;
- reduction in the number of accidents;
- fewer stoppages in productive activities.

Additionally, teamwork is often advocated on the basis of a range of factors which, although difficult to measure (in other words they are *qualitative*), are nevertheless central to the development of a successful organization. These factors include such benefits as:

- promotes consensus rather than conflict within the organization;
- encourages communication;
- develops cooperation;
- promotes consultation;
- enhances commitment;
- generates new ways of working.

All these factors affect the work environment in which individuals and teams are expected to perform. Since the business wishes to organize its activities in such a way as to enhance the quality and effectiveness of its operations, the strategies we have described in this chapter should be seen as essential ingredients which make for a successful business organization.

Individuals, teams and business performance

There now follow some quick questions and revision exercises. They relate specifically to the chapter you have just studied. You are advised to attempt the questions without reference to the text, and then compare your answers and solutions with those on pages 215–16.

Personal contribution to business effectiveness

QUESTIONS

1. What information is contained in a **contract of employment**?
2. What is **staff appraisal**?
3. What are **quality circles**?
4. List **6** main purposes of quality circles.
5. List **5** main features of a staff appraisal scheme.
6. What is meant by **empowerment**?

EXERCISES

1. Outline the advantages of staff appraisal for individual employees, their managers, and for the business organization.
2. 'Effective team work can lead to positive benefits for the business organization.' Justify this statement.

> *While attempting to answer the questions and exercises on this page, you are strongly advised not to read on and to cover the answers and solutions on the following page with a sheet of paper.*

Individuals, teams and business performance

ANSWERS TO QUESTIONS

1. A contract of employment identifies the rights, duties and responsibilities of the employer and the employee.

2. A formal staff-appraisal scheme provides the opportunity for a line manager to meet with each individual employee in a formal, private setting in order to consider the employee's performance, training needs and prospects.

3. Quality circles are small groups of workers, usually from the same section or department, who meet to discuss practical work issues, solve practical problems and produce ideas for improving productivity or working conditions.

4.
   - To improve quality.
   - To develop a team ethos.
   - To generate new ideas.
   - To promote effective communication.
   - To suggest more efficient and effective ways of working.
   - To promote understanding between employees and staff.

5.
   - Standardized forms, documentation and recording procedures.
   - Confidentiality.
   - Action plans and targets.
   - An agreed timetable within which appraisal is set.
   - Part of the employee's contract of employment.

6. Empowerment is the process by which the workforce is given greater responsibility for a range of activities which have been traditionally associated with management. Such activities will include setting and monitoring targets, quality issues and work rotas.

SOLUTIONS TO EXERCISES

1. Staff appraisal brings a number of advantages for individual employees, their managers and the business organization. For the individual employee, staff appraisal can be used to recognize achievements, identify training needs, and provide the opportunity to discuss work-related concerns with the immediate line manager. Staff appraisal also enables the line manager to recognize the achievements of individual members of staff and, in certain cases, agree individual work targets. For the business organization, staff appraisal can provide the opportunity to monitor recruitment policies and identify those individuals who may be able to take on more challenging roles.

2. A team is a small group of employees who work together to achieve a common goal. Organizing the workforce in teams within the business organization can bring both quantitative and qualitative benefits. Measurable improvements in business performance can be identified in terms of:

Personal contribution to business effectiveness

- increases in output;
- decreases in absenteeism;
- reduction in labour turnover;
- meeting business targets;
- fewer stoppages in productive activities.

Qualitative improvements in business performance centre upon improvements in staff morale, commitment, cooperation and communication.

POINTS TO REMEMBER

- A contract of employment identifies the rights, duties and obligations of the employer and the employee.
- Over and above the contract of employment, an individual employee's contribution to the business can be identified by the quality of their work, their commitment and their overall performance.
- Staff appraisal provides management with the opportunity to assess quality, commitment and effectiveness whilst, at the same time, identifying any specific training which may be required to enhance an individual's contribution and performance.
- Staff appraisal brings benefits to managers, their staff and to the business organization if it is structured, consistent and covers the whole organization.
- Staff appraisal can incorporate performance targets which can sometimes be used as part of an overall remuneration package.
- Staff appraisal schemes are influenced by management style, organizational culture and the quality of communications within the organization.
- A team can be considered as a small group of employees who work together to achieve a common goal.
- Quality circles are groups of workers who meet to discuss practical work issues, solve practical problems and provide ideas for improving productivity or working conditions.
- Empowerment is a process whereby teams are given more responsibility for a range of activities which have been traditionally associated with operational managers.
- Team working can have both quantitative and qualitative benefits for the organization with regards to increasing output, reducing labour turnover, achieving targets and promoting a positive business culture based upon consultation and cooperation.

Part 5
Business values and culture

12

Business culture

> **After carefully studying this chapter, you should be able to:**
> 1 *describe the influences on business culture;*
> 2 *describe different organizational cultures.*

> **Extended Syllabus references**
> 5.1 Describe how the following can influence an organization's business culture:
>   5.1.1 mission statements
>   5.1.2 corporate image
>   5.1.3 corporate identity
>   5.1.4 style of management
> 5.2 Describe different organizational cultures:
>   5.2.1 consultative
>   5.2.2 participative
>   5.2.3 performance or goal driven

The purpose of this chapter is to identify the factors which determine the image the business organization projects to its stakeholders – customers, employees, managers and shareholders – and to the wider community in which it operates. The chapter also considers how management styles can influence business policies and practices and, in turn, how such policies and practices influence relations between managers and their staff.

Business values and beliefs – the role of mission statements

Throughout this chapter we will refer to the *values* and *beliefs* of the business organization. This may sound strange, since values and beliefs are usually attributed to people rather than organizations. People, for example, may have religious or political beliefs which influence their values. As a result of these beliefs, people may value friendship, honesty and kindness which will, in turn, determine how they relate to others – family members, friends, relatives, and working colleagues.

There are a number of ways in which the business organization can communicate its values and beliefs to the outside world. We have already considered, in Chapter 8, the role of *mission statements* – published statements of intent which summarize the organization's core aims, objectives and purpose.

Some organizations have taken mission statements further by publishing specific statements relating to such issues as their commitment to the environment and equal opportunities and even the core values of their trading practices.

Other business organizations base their activities around core values concerned with their trading policies, particularly with developing countries.

The UK's leading Fair Trade company, cafédirect limited, a supplier of coffee-based products that incorporates Oxfam as one of its partner organizations, is keen to promote its goods as 'fair-trade products'. cafédirect is keen to inform its customers that: 'More of the money you pay for cafédirect coffee goes directly to the small farmers in Latin America and Africa. Fair trade means that the coffee-growing communities can afford to invest in healthcare, education and agriculture'.

There are many other examples of how business organizations seek to promote their values and beliefs. In some instances, this will involve published 'statements of intent' which have been translated into company policies. Examples of such policies may include:

- equal opportunities
- recruitment practices
- quality assurance
- customer service.

Another way in which the business organization can attempt to communicate its core values and beliefs to the wider public is by strategies which incorporate:

- company literature
- advertisements
- promotional activities
- sponsorship activities.

Even job advertisements can be used to communicate the company's beliefs and

Business culture

values – this is particularly important if the company is seeking to appoint staff who can both share and identify with the mission of the organization. Consider the following 3 extracts taken from recruitment advertisements.

Type of company	Sector	Extract from job advertisement
Furnishing company	Retail	'...a long reputation for providing discerning customers with contemporary furnishings of high quality and innovative style in a prestigious and imaginative shopping environment.' (Heal's, London)
Police service create	Public services	'... firmly committed to developing and improving its policing service to make (the area) a better place. A clear and strong emphasis is placed on working with the community, displaying integrity and openness to an effective partnership.' (Merseyside Police, England)
Software house	Computer services	'... we are a phenomenally successful systems and software house. We develop the highest quality software, providing systems expertise, operations support services and consultancy to clients worldwide. The exceptional growth of the group has generated outstanding career opportunities.' (VEGA Group PLC, UK)

Activity

Undertake research in relevant publications to identify business organizations which seek to promote their values and beliefs through their recruitment activities.

Corporate image and corporate identity

What does the previous section tell us about how business organizations operate? Why should the business be keen to promote its 'image'? Are there any other means by which the business can promote its image to the wider community? In order to answer these questions we need to return once more to the environment within which the business operates and to re-examine some of the influences which are exerted upon its activities.

All businesses are keenly aware that they operate in a *competitive environment*. In other words, they know that other organizations are producing a range of similar products which provide the consumer with a *choice*. The traditional way of analysing the competitive environment leads us to the conclusion that the consumer will seek to purchase those goods which have a competitive advantage in terms of *price*. Put simply, given the choice between a range of identical or similar goods or services, the consumer will purchase the one with the lowest price.

Although contemporary business practice recognizes the critical importance of price in determining consumer spending patterns, the traditional way of looking at the competitive market economy, based purely on price, has now given way to the view that there are other, more subtle, factors which can influence consumer behaviour. One of the main factors which can influence how the consumer views the business organization is the '*image*' projected by the company. Every organization will try to make that image favourable, manipulating it to project the values and messages they want. In other words, *corporate image* concerns how the business wishes to project itself to the outside world.

Corporate identity is a set of tools for doing this: it ranges from company and product names, to graphics, typefaces, uniforms, van liveries and colours, and can even extend to shop and office furnishings, music, humour and a whole range of public relations activities.

Herein lies the importance of corporate image and corporate identity as important 'influencers' on the behaviour of the consumer. The business will seek to project an image which mirrors the values and aspirations of consumers in its target market. If it can successfully achieve this objective then consumers will purchase its goods in preference to those of other producers, *regardless of any price differences*.

Activity

Choose 5 major items which you have purchased over the last year and identify 2 characteristics which you associate with the business organization responsible for producing or selling the product or service.

Do you consider that the *price* of the product or service mainly determined your purchasing decisions?

The influences on organizational culture

In practice, we can think of 2 ways in which an organizational culture is determined:

- by focusing on the organization's *internal relationships*;
- by considering the *external environment* in which the business operates.

The internal factors which can influence the organization's culture centre upon the relationship between managers and their staff. In this context, the focus would be on how the business shows that it is concerned about the welfare of its employees, their working conditions, the type of work they perform and their participation in the decision-making process. Specific policies within the organization can also enhance its image and status. A well-formulated staff training and development policy coupled with an equal opportunities policy can serve to enhance motivation and commitment amongst staff. Additionally, constructive relations with staff associations and trade unions can enhance the decision-making process and promote a common sense of purpose amongst management and staff.

Some organizations have developed a 'single status' culture in which there are few distinctions between management and staff. The provision of safe and pleasant working conditions, social clubs, staff restaurants and medical care facilities are also indicators of how an organization views the importance of its staff and the contribution they can make to business performance. The way in which an organization may choose to reward its staff can also influence its corporate image. High rates of pay, bonus schemes and profit-sharing agreements are all ways in which the business can show how it values its employees. Finally, many organizations are placing 'quality' high on the list of those factors which can influence corporate image.

Corporate culture can also be influenced by external factors and, in particular, will reflect the organization's relationships with people and other organizations in the wider environment and the community which it serves. As such, the organization's relationship with its customers, shareholders, suppliers, the local community, and the government will all influence its corporate culture. Shareholders, for example, will seek a fair return on their investment, whilst suppliers will require payment within agreed terms following open and fair contractual arrangements. The local community will be concerned that the business respects the environment and sets an example as a good employer, whilst the government will demand that the business observes its legal obligations.

Business values and culture

Table 12.1 provides an overview of some of the strategies and associated examples which can be implemented to promote a positive corporate image.

Table 12.1 Creating a corporate image/corporate identity

Strategy	Examples
High media profile	<ul><li>events and conferences</li><li>advertizing campaigns</li><li>sponsorship of national/international events</li></ul>
Company documentation	<ul><li>company stationery incorporates logo and</li><li>mission statement or slogan</li></ul>
Customer service	<ul><li>specialist Customer Service Manager</li><li>specialist section devoted to Customer Service</li><li>customer questionnaires</li><li>nationally recognised quality standards</li></ul>
Community links	<ul><li>work experience placements provided to local students</li><li>sponsorship of community events</li></ul>
Promotion of education	<ul><li>specialist Education Division provides materials to schools and colleges</li></ul>
Environment	<ul><li>environmental policy with associated targets</li><li>packaging</li><li>recycling initiatives</li><li>promotion of 'environmentally friendly' products</li></ul>
Promotion of good causes	<ul><li>sponsorship</li><li>charitable donations</li></ul>

Activity

Undertake research in both local and national newspapers and identify a range of appropriate articles which describe factors which you consider may affect the corporate image of an organization in either a *positive* or *negative* way.

Record your results in the following format:

Company	Brief description of article	Impact on corporate image (positive/negative)

Types of organizational culture

In an earlier chapter we noted that 2 individual employees with identical conditions of employment could make vastly different contributions to the business, largely based on their commitment, enthusiasm and their general approach to their job role. We saw how all these elements could contribute to the overall quality of the organization's output, operations and performance. Now we shall follow a similar model when comparing business organizations.

It would be true to say that most business organizations seek to promote a positive corporate image. Indeed, many of them will engage in the type of activities highlighted in Table 12.1. Additionally, the same organizations will be able to provide evidence of their positive commitment and support which they provide to their staff in terms of the range of policies which they have developed covering such areas as:

- training and development
- staff welfare
- recruitment practices
- staff appraisal.

However, most individuals who have experienced the world of work, are keenly aware that, despite the fact that, on the surface, two organizations may exhibit similar policies, the *organizational culture* in each may be vastly different largely due to the principles, ethos and general approach and *style of management* practised in each of the organizations. Organizational culture is therefore directly related to:

- the beliefs and principles upon which managers base their actions and operations;
- the way in which management duties, roles and functions are carried out;
- the policies and procedures of the organization.

Taken collectively, these 3 elements will form the basis of the organization's culture or, to put it more simply, *the way in which the organization expects its managers and staff to conduct themselves.*

The way in which the organization manages and organizes its workforce will therefore be a key factor in determining organizational culture.

Over time, a number of theories have been put forward by writers who have tried to compare and contrast different ways of organizing and managing the workforce, in order to suggest practical ways in which an organization can manage its operations more effectively. It is beyond the scope of this book to describe in detail the work of these writers but we need to acknowledge their contribution to the development of our study of Business Practice. Table 12.2 (overleaf) provides an overview of the pioneers of the main schools of thought which, collectively, are referred to as 'management theory'.

Business values and culture

Table 12.2 Management theories and their practical implications

Writer	Main conclusions	Practical implications
Frederick Taylor (1856–1915)	• advocated the division of labour and the specialization of tasks • workers are only interested in earning money and nothing else	• financial incentives • bonuses

Henri Fayol (1841–1925)	• advocated 'administrative management'
	• identified 5 main components of the manager's role
	  – planning
	  – organizing
	  – commanding
	  – coordinating
	  – controlling
		• clear instructions to workers
		• give managers authority and responsibility
		• treat people fairly
		• develop job satisfaction by promoting training opportunities
		• develop good team spirit

Mayo (1924)	• people work better when they are organized into small groups and are consulted about decisions	• measures to increase consultation with staff regarding company work practices and policies
McGregor (1960)	• managers adopted a management style depending upon their view of human nature	• people-centred management is likely to be more successful in motivating staff
Hertzberg (1966)	• identified factors which motivated workers and those which led to reduced job satisfaction	• staff can be motivated by a management style which recognizes the achievements of staff and promotes job satisfaction
Maslow (1968)	• individuals are motivated by a 'hierarchy of needs'	• pay an adequate wage in order for the worker to contribute more fully to the organization

Although there may well be some managers who will not be familiar with the writers identified in Table 12.2, their organizations will almost certainly have been *influenced* by them, including how they seek to organize, manage and motivate their staff – all of which are factors which influence differences in business culture. These differences in culture have been discussed by many writers, one of the most recent being Lesley Wright's *'Corporate Abuse' (1997)*. In it she details her own experience of working in 2 different advertizing agencies. As one reviewer of the book commented:

'The contrast between the two working environments could not have been starker. The Saatchi office had been run flexibly and creativity was encouraged. People were not afraid to make mistakes, and so the office flourished, ideas tumbled out, and business boomed. The other office was run along highly competitive, secretive lines. The result was that staff were afraid to speak up and simply became demoralized and apathetic. The business went downhill and one-third of the staff was eventually made redundant.'

(*Source:* The Guardian, *3 May 1997, review by Pauline Springett*)

Differences in organizational culture are therefore usually associated with the style of management practised within the business and the impact that this has on management – staff relations. In order to show how organizational culture is influenced by the style of management, we can identify a number of ways in which management responsibilities can be discharged. If we take the decision-making process, for example, we are likely to see a number of different approaches:

- the *autocratic manager* tells staff what to do and actively *discourages contributions and suggestions*;
- the *participative manager* will seek to ensure that staff have *responsibility for making decisions*, usually within the context of empowerment and teamwork;
- the *consultative manager* will actively *encourage contributions* from staff.

Most people like to be involved in those decisions which impact on their job roles and work activities and are therefore likely to support an organizational culture which is consultative or participative. Although this may lead to an increase in motivation and have a positive impact on business culture, we also need to be aware of the possible disadvantages of this approach to management:

- the decision-making process can become time-consuming if a number of individuals and staff teams have to be consulted;
- managers may become frustrated if they are unable to use their own initiative to take decisions;
- some individuals and teams may wish to take decisions which are motivated by self-interest rather than for the benefit of the whole organization;
- some members of staff may not consider it their responsibility to engage in the decision-making process;
- staff may not have access to the full range of information which enables them to make *informed decisions*.

Those business organizations which seek to develop an organizational culture which is based on either participative or consultative management principles, also have to take account of the *context* in which their managers are operating. Indeed there may be circumstances in which the management may have to exhibit *autocratic tendencies* particularly related to matters such as:

- health and safety
- statutory requirements
- staff disciplinary procedures.

Business values and culture

Business organizations are therefore best advised to set up *policies, procedures and systems* which determine the framework within which participation and consultation will take place, and which will provide for both managers and their staff a clear understanding of their respective roles and responsibilities in the decision-making process.

This is particularly important in organizations whose culture can be described as *performance – or goal – driven*. In these types of organizations, individuals, teams and managers will work to clearly defined goals or *targets*. The business will tend to frown upon those activities which do not directly contribute to the achievement of company goals and instead will seek to measure how each activity will contribute to the overall performance of the business.

Although this would seem to support some of the conclusions we have drawn from our study of Business Practice, an organizational culture based purely on the achievement of goals and targets can give rise to a number of issues including:

- anxiety and stress levels may increase amongst the workforce;
- management style may be less participative or consultative if managers are driven by the desire to achieve targets;
- managers may become more cautious and less willing to take risks if it means that goals may not be reached.

For the purposes of our study we are led to the conclusion that organizational culture will be influenced by the general nature of the management style exhibited by the senior management team and the organization's operational managers. In turn, management style will be influenced by the personal attributes and the professional skills, qualifications and experience of the management team.

Activity

A business organization wishes to introduce a staff appraisal scheme in which staff will have to agree individual targets with their line manager. How would you suggest the business attempts to secure the support of its staff in order to implement the scheme successfully?

There now follow some quick questions and revision exercises. They relate specifically to the chapter you have just studied. You are advised to attempt the questions without reference to the text, and then compare your answers and solutions with those on pages 232–3.

QUESTIONS

1. What is meant by the term **corporate image**?
2. What is a '**single status culture**'?
3. Identify **3** factors which may influence organizational culture.
4. Distinguish between an **autocratic** manager, a **participative** manager and a **consultative** manager.

EXERCISES

1. Outline the ways in which a company can influence its corporate image.
2. Describe briefly how the conclusions of some of the main management theorists have been translated into practice by business organizations.

Business values and culture

ANSWERS TO QUESTIONS

1. Corporate image is the way in which the outside world perceives a company. The company may take a number of steps to make that image favourable.

2. A business culture in which there are few status distinctions between management and staff.

3. - Management style
   - Level of customer service
   - Quality systems.

4. The *autocratic manager* tells staff what to do and actively discourages contributions and suggestions.

   The *participative manager* will seek to ensure that staff have responsibility for making decisions.

   The *consultative manager* will actively encourage contributions from staff.

SOLUTIONS TO EXERCISES

1. Corporate image can be influenced by a range of factors which, collectively, can be classified as either internal factors or external factors. Internal factors concern corporate culture, ie, those aspects of company operations which relate to its internal organization, policies and procedures and the general way it chooses to conduct relations with its staff. In this respect, management style can play a critical role in identifying the way in which the company is viewed by its staff. Specific influences on corporate culture may include staff facilities, rates of pay, working conditions and the way in which the company may seek to communicate with its staff. The role of employees in the decision-making process is also seen as a critical factor in shaping the culture of a company.

   Besides these internal factors, the company may also seek to project a positive corporate image in the wider community. A high media profile, community links, the promotion of education and high profile good causes along with an emphasis on good customer service can all contribute to a positive corporate image. A number of techniques and strategies are used to project and control the company's image in the outside world. They include business and product names, the style of the company's advertising, packaging and printed material, the decor and layout of any retail environments, the colours and logos on the company's delivery vans, etc.

2. The work and research undertaken by management theorists has had an important influence on the ways in which business organizations are organized and managed. Early writers, such as Taylor, advocated the division of labour and the specialization of tasks whilst Fayol identified the manager's role as being made up of 5 main components: planning, organizing, commanding, coordinating and controlling. Even in today's business environment we can identify the specialization of tasks and how the manager's role is still considered to be based, in part, on the 5 components identified by Fayol.

Other writers have sought to identify how individuals in the work place can be motivated in order to maximize their contribution to the organization. Mayo identified the importance of team work and consultation whilst Hertzberg stressed the need to recognize the achievements of staff in order to promote job satisfaction, a view shared by McGregor, who argued that people-centred management was more likely to be successful in motivating staff.

Business values and culture

POINTS TO REMEMBER

- A mission statement is a published statement of intent which summarizes the organization's core aims, objectives and purpose.
- Corporate image is the way in which a company seeks to present itself to the outside world.
- Corporate identity is a set of tools used by an organization for creating a corporate image. Such 'tools' may include company and product names, typefaces, uniforms and can even extend to shop and office furnishings. Public relations can play an important role in establishing a corporate image.
- Organizational culture concerns how the organization's values and beliefs are translated into practice by its owners, managers and staff and the way in which the business conducts itself in relation to the community which it serves.
- Differences in organizational culture, corporate image and corporate identity are closely associated with different management styles.
- Different management theorists have drawn a number of conclusions from their research which have led to the introduction of practical measures which have influenced business practice and, with it, organizational culture.

13

Quality systems

> **After carefully studying this chapter, you should be able to:**
> 1 *understand what is meant by internal and external clients;*
> 2 *identify the ways in which the organization seeks to improve the quality of its systems, products and services.*

> **Extended Syllabus references**
> 5.3 Understand what is meant by internal and external clients
> 5.4 Identify the ways in which the business organization can identify and seek to improve the quality of its systems, products and services:
>   5.4.1   survey standards and target setting
>   5.4.2   quality circles
>   5.4.3   staff appraisal
>   5.4.4   research and development
>   5.4.5   customer satisfaction surveys

The purpose of this chapter is to show how the business organization can measure, monitor and improve the quality of its operations. The chapter will also provide a broad overview of the main ways in which quality systems can be incorporated into business activities.

Internal and external clients

We noted in Chapter 7 that a number of organizations are now beginning to appreciate the notion of internal and external clients and customers. What does this mean in practice? The generally accepted view is that customers or clients are the *purchasers* of the goods or services produced by the business organization. Customers

Business values and culture

and clients therefore exert an important influence on business activities. Indeed, in our study of Business Practice we have identified them as key *stakeholders* in the business environment, whose actions influence, and are influenced by, the activities of the business organization. At this stage in our study, we can identify a number of ways in which these influences are exhibited:

- customers and clients will have a direct impact on turnover which, in turn, will influence profit levels;
- customers and clients will be influenced by the marketing activities of the business, including promotion and publicity;
- customers and clients will be influenced by business culture and the corporate image projected by the business organization;
- customers and clients are likely to view a corporate image based on quality and 'putting the customer first' as a positive feature which will influence their purchasing decisions;
- the business needs to be aware of changes in tastes, fashion or preferences which may influence the purchasing decisions of its customers and clients.

Customer loyalty

Customers and clients are therefore central to the activities of the business organization. They should be viewed as 'long-term assets', the central task of the business being to create outstanding value for money for customers so that they remain *loyal* to the business, thus generating long-term sales opportunities.

Generating sales enables the business to create the cash reserves to finance expansion which, in turn, will generate profits, which can then be used to reward shareholders and employees. This idea of rewarding shareholders and employees can be taken further, since if the business can generate a loyal customer base from which profits can be generated, then the customer can also be rewarded by being able to purchase better quality products from the business organization. Therefore, as we have already noted, the loyal customer or client, can be viewed as as much of a *stakeholder* in the business as can shareholders, managers and employees.

From this analysis we can draw the following conclusions:

- customers and clients have a direct influence on business activities;
- the business needs to generate a 'loyal' customer base;
- customers are important stakeholders in the business.

The same conclusions can be drawn if we consider the internal operations of the business organization.

If we consider the role of the functional areas and the associated operational units or departments, we see that, in effect, these departments are also offering a *service to their clients*. However, their clients are not external to the organization, but are the managers and employees who use the services of the various departments. The marketing manager, for example, will require financial information provided by the finance department, so that the marketing manager can be viewed as an *internal client* of the finance department. In exactly the same way as for the external client, the marketing manager's views of the organization will be based upon the quality and level of service provided by the various departments within the organization.

For this reason a number of organizations are now coming to realize that the quality of their activities and operations should be measured, monitored and improved in response to the views of both *external* and *internal* clients, and that procedures need to be in place which enable the business to identify *quality* as one of its *'core values'*.

Monitoring quality

The business organization has a number of different methods by which it can monitor the quality of its systems, products and services:

- quality control
- quality assurance
- total quality management.

Quality control is the traditional way in which a manufacturing company can choose to monitor quality. It involves the systematic inspection of a product or samples of products on a production line in order to ensure that standards are being maintained. Specialist staff are usually employed as *quality-control inspectors*, who inspect and test sample products using statistical sampling techniques.

Quality assurance involves a much broader range of business activities and functions incorporated into a quality assurance system or process devised by the organization. Responsibility for implementing the system rests with the workforce, which is usually organized into small groups or teams. It is important therefore that the business is able to persuade staff of the importance of quality as a core business value which has a direct impact upon products, services, sales, profitability, and, ultimately, business survival and continued success.

Total quality management (TQM) is a natural extension of quality assurance, but, as the term suggests, it covers *all* aspects of business operations. TQM is based upon 2 basic principles:

- the customer is at the centre of all business activities;
- creating a quality culture based upon continuous quality improvements.

If TQM is to be successfully implemented, it must result in a positive change to business culture, and one which recognizes both external and internal clients, each of whom can demand the highest possible level of quality from the business and its constituent parts – departments, teams, managers and individual members of staff. Japanese companies in particular have recognized the importance of TQM in establishing a competitive advantage for their products and, in Europe, German manufacturers have also been able to establish a reputation for high quality goods.

Business values and culture

TQM brings to the business organization a number of advantages which can also influence business culture and so enhance corporate identity. Such advantages include:

- teamwork;
- collective and shared responsibility for quality amongst staff – teams, individuals and the management team;
- improvements in quality can be measured;
- communications systems are improved;
- less waste;
- establishes a culture in which problems are solved by the team;
- the business is able to gain a deep insight into the needs of its customers in its target markets;
- staff can be encouraged to make constructive and positive suggestions to improve quality;
- fewer errors;
- reduced costs;
- improved business performance;
- better services and products;
- repeat sales.

Elements of all 3 methods of monitoring quality – quality control, quality assurance, and TQM – can be found in most successful business organizations.

What we will now consider is a range of specific measures which can be incorporated into business operations and how they can all contribute to improving quality. A number of these practical measures will now be familiar to the student, since we have covered some of them in earlier chapters:

- survey standards and target-setting
- quality circles
- staff appraisal
- research and development
- customer satisfaction surveys.

> **Activity**
>
> Choose a large business organization which is involved in the retail sector and identify the ways in which it seeks to highlight the quality of its products and services.

Survey standards and target-setting

Survey standards recognize the fact that a business seeking to create a quality culture within its operations has to take account of its internal clients as well as meeting the needs of external customers.

Many businesses are now incorporating survey standards into the operations of departments and their associated operational teams. Staff teams will be required to publish a series of *quality standards* relating to their particular areas of operational responsibility. The published quality standards will then be subject to a system of ongoing monitoring and evaluation, and members of staff will be surveyed in order to ascertain how far the department or operational team has met its published quality standards and associated targets.

Survey standards are an important way of identifying to the workforce the emphasis which the business places on quality, and such measures also serve to reinforce the idea that quality is a collective responsibility incorporating all levels of staff within the organization. At the same time, such standards provide the basis upon which continuous improvements in services can be maintained.

The following are examples of quality standards which may be incorporated into the activities of one of the main functional areas, finance/accounts:

- to process purchase orders in 3 working days;
- to distribute up-to-date management accounts to all budgetholders on the first Monday of each month;
- to settle expense claims within 15 working days.

Activity

Identify 3 quality standards which would be appropriate for either:

- a team of personal assistants
- a team of administrators.

How would you determine if the quality standards had been met?

Targets can be set for individuals, teams and their managers. Target-setting is best implemented by establishing a dialogue involving the manager and the individual members of staff, a process referred to as *management by objectives* (MBO). Such a system of establishing targets not only incorporates issues relating to quality but can also impact upon all other areas of business activity.

Business values and culture

Quality circles

Quality circles were considered in Chapter 11, in which we saw how they can make a positive contribution to business performance. In the current context, we can view such teams of staff as an integral feature of those organizations which wish to incorporate the principles of Total Quality Management into their business activities and operations.

Staff appraisal

It should now be becoming increasingly clear to the reader that the study of Business Practice concerns a series of interrelated activities and operations which all serve to enhance business performance, in order that the organization can meet its business objectives.

> **Activity**
>
> Complete the following flow chart to show the direct relationships which exist between a range of key components in Business Practice.
>
> A management style which seeks to involve staff in the decision-making process is referred to as P............................ Management
>
> ↓
>
> This style of management can involve the manager and the individual employee agreeing targets as part of an overall system of M...............B....O....................
>
> ↓
>
> These targets can be agreed in a formal interview between the manager and the individual employee as part of a system of S...............A....................
>
> ↓
>
> Some of the targets can be related to quality indicators as part of an overall policy of T.................Q................M.......................
>
> ↓
>
> This policy can incorporate staff teams organized into Q..................C....................
>
> ↓
>
> All of these measures, which place quality at the heart of business operations, will have a direct impact upon B.......... C.............. and, with it, the establishment of a C................. I...............

Research and development (R&D)

In Chapter 6, we described the main activities of the R&D function, stressing that its primary purposes were to:

- develop cost-effective improvements in the production process;
- engage in the research and development of new products.

Both of these primary functions are directly related to improving the quality of the organization's product base.

The R&D function can contribute to the overall improvement in quality standards in the following ways:

- incorporate high standards and specifications into new products;
- ensure that the production process is designed in such a way as to minimize the possibility of defective products reaching the market;
- utilize new technologies in the production process, in order to enhance the quality and effectiveness of new products;
- ensure that new product development is based upon clear criteria resulting from in-depth market research;
- identify ways in which the production process can be made more 'environmentally friendly', by creating less waste, using fewer factor inputs, and generating lower levels of pollution.

As a result of establishing an efficient R&D process, the business can design, develop and manufacture higher-quality products which can compete effectively in the competitive market economy, thereby meeting the needs of the most discerning consumer.

Customer satisfaction surveys

If quality systems place the consumer at the heart of the process of improving the quality of business systems, products and services, then it is not surprising to find that a number of organizations seek to establish ways in which the consumer can take an active part in monitoring quality. Put simply, this means asking the consumers for their views on company products and services. The most common method used to elicit the views of the consumer is the use of *surveys* and *questionnaires*. If a business is considering using questionnaires to measure consumer satisfaction it must ensure that they are designed to have the following features:

- explain why the questionnaire is required;
- try to allow for 'yes' or 'no' answers;
- keep it simple;
- do not use technical words;
- keep the questions as short and as few as possible;

Business values and culture

- do not ask leading questions;
- ask questions which provide a profile of the person who is completing the questionnaire;
- provide the opportunity for the consumer to 'grade' the quality of the service or product;
- ask the consumer if they would purchase the product or service again if they had the opportunity;
- undertake a pilot exercise in order to ascertain if the questionnaire meets the needs of the organization.

> **Activity**
>
> Obtain examples of 2 customer satisfaction questionnaires and comment on:
>
> - their common features
> - their suitability and effectiveness in assessing consumer views.

One leading UK business organization involved in the travel industry has established a policy of publishing the results of its customer surveys in its travel brochures. Potential holidaymakers have the opportunity to see how previous clients have rated their holiday experiences in terms of accommodation, location, food and the overall holiday package. The results are published in the form of a percentage rating scale and are based upon large samples of holidaymakers who have completed customer-satisfaction questionnaires.

This aspect of quality systems emphasizes the importance of communicating with customers and clients as part of an overall strategy of *business communications* – a topic which provides the focus for the final section of our study of Business Practice.

> **Activity**
>
> Devise a simple customer-satisfaction questionnaire which could be used by one of the following business organizations:
>
> - a restaurant
> - a manufacturer of electrical goods
> - a supermarket
> - a car manufacturer
> - a hotel
> - a sports centre.

Quality systems

There now follow some quick questions and revision exercises. They relate specifically to the chapter you have just studied. You are advised to attempt the questions without reference to the text, and then compare your answers and solutions with those on pages 245–6.

Business values and culture

QUESTIONS

1. List **4** ways in which customers and clients can influence the business organization.
2. Define **customer loyalty**.
3. Define **quality control**, **quality assurance** and **total quality management**.
4. List **6** advantages of total quality management.
5. List **5** ways in which quality can be monitored and improved.
6. What do the initials **MBO** stand for?
7. List **4** ways in which **R&D** can contribute towards quality improvements.
8. List **6** criteria which should be considered when devising a customer-satisfaction questionnaire or survey.

EXERCISES

1. Describe the relationship between customer service and customer loyalty.
2. Distinguish between internal clients and external clients. How can the business organization seek to measure the quality of its services to each of them?

> *While attempting to answer the questions and exercises on this page, you are strongly advised not to read on and to cover the answers on the following page with a sheet of paper.*

ANSWERS TO QUESTIONS

1. - Pattern of spending
   - Desire for quality products
   - Looking for good customer service
   - Changes in preferences and tastes.

2. The notion that customer spending decisions will be based on identifying a preferred supplier rather than on other factors such as price.

3. Quality control involves the systematic inspection of a product in order to ensure that standards are being maintained and that quality has been achieved. Quality assurance involves a much broader range of business activities and functions intended to achieve quality, which are the responsibility of small groups or teams within the organization. Total Quality Management covers all aspects of the business and is based on 2 basic principles: firstly, that the customer is at the centre of all business activities and, secondly, that creating a quality culture involves continuous quality improvement.

4. - Teamworking
   - Less waste
   - Improvements in quality can be measured
   - Reduced costs
   - Improved business performance
   - Better quality products and services.

5. - Survey standards
   - Quality circles
   - Staff appraisal
   - Customer satisfaction surveys
   - Research and development.

6. Management by objectives.

7. - Incorporate high standards into product specifications
   - Utilize new technology
   - Ensure that production planning and control are effective
   - Reduce waste and use high-quality inputs.

8. - Keep it simple
   - Do not use technical words
   - Do not ask leading questions
   - Provide the opportunity for customers to 'grade' the service
   - Keep the questions short and simple
   - Do not ask too many questions.

Business values and culture

SOLUTIONS TO EXERCISES

1 In today's highly competitive business world, business organizations have begun to realize that they will have a competitive advantage in the market if they can create a loyal customer base which promotes repeat business. Customer loyalty is based on the principle that the customer is both a stakeholder in, and an asset to, the company and therefore should be at the heart of all business activity. An important influence in developing customer loyalty is the promotion of policies and procedures which result in a high level and standard of customer service. If a business can gain a reputation for offering a high standard of customer service, it will not only win new customers, but is also likely to find that they remain loyal to the company in preference to other organizations and suppliers.

2 An internal client is an individual or group of individuals within an organization who are provided with a service by other individuals within the same organization. For example, the finance department may be viewed as providing a service to other departments in the organization. An external client, on the other hand, fits the traditional view of a business customer.

A business may seek to measure the quality of the service offered to both internal and external clients in a number of ways:

- survey standards
- questionnaires
- quality targets
- quality standards.

POINTS TO REMEMBER

- Customers should be viewed as potential long-term assets of the business, generating long-term sales opportunities.
- The business needs to generate a loyal customer base.
- Business needs to recognize the importance of both internal and external customers.
- Consumer loyalty can be enhanced if the business places an emphasis on the quality of its products or services.
- Quality can be monitored by quality control, quality assurance or a commitment to Total Quality Management (TQM).
- Quality control is the systematic inspection of a product or sample of products on the production line.
- Quality assurance involves establishing a quality assurance system or process which highlights the importance of staff teams in monitoring quality as a core business activity.
- Total Quality Management is based on the notion of creating a quality culture which places the customer at the centre of all business activities.
- Survey standards can be incorporated into the operations of team/sections/departments which they can use to monitor the quality of their performance against set standards and targets.
- Customer satisfaction surveys can be used to ascertain the views of consumers on company products and services. Such surveys can be used to monitor the quality of both the internal services provided by the functional areas as well as the quality of service provided to the customer.

Part 6
Communication in business

14

Business communication

> **After carefully studying this chapter, you should be able to:**
>
> 1 *understand the different forms and types of communication and their advantages and disadvantages;*
>
> 2 *identify the criteria applied to determine the appropriateness of different communication systems to meet specific needs.*

> **Extended Syllabus references**
>
> 6.1 Understand the different forms and types of communication and their advantages and disadvantages:
>
>   6.1.1   formal and informal
>
>   6.1.2   internal and external
>
>   6.1.3   verbal/written/other forms
>
> 6.2 Identify the criteria applied to determine the appropriateness of different communication systems to meet specific needs:
>
>   6.2.1   fitness for purpose
>
>   6.2.2   costs
>
>   6.2.3   perceptions
>
>   6.2.4   security

The purpose of this chapter is to identify the importance of communications to the business organization and within the wider business environment. We will consider the various types and methods of communication used in business and their suitability to specific situations.

Business communication and the study of Business Practice

Throughout our study of Business Practice we have described a number of key factors which we have identified as being of critical importance to the business organization. These have included such diverse elements as the role of specialization, the importance of maintaining financial records, and the increasing emphasis placed upon establishing a corporate identity based upon a positive business culture. Indeed, the set of factors which contribute to business success has been at the heart of our study of Business Practice.

However, if one feature is common to all these factors – a feature without which they would be unable to contribute to business success – we would have to highlight the pivotal role played by *business communication*.

For this reason, a study of business communication is central to an understanding of Business Practice. Our study of business communication will examine 3 aspects. In this chapter we will consider the types and methods of communication which are used in business. This will provide the background knowledge required to understand the second aspect, which will be the subject of Chapter 15: how efficient and effective communications can contribute to the achievement of business goals.

Finally, Chapter 16, *Information technology in the business environment*, will provide the opportunity to show how information technology applications can be used to enhance the effectiveness of business communication systems and to improve the overall quality of communication undertaken by the business.

The importance of business communication

Business communication is at the heart of all the activities in which the business organization is engaged. Communication will involve both *internal* and *external* activities and functions including:

- communication between the business and its customers and clients
- communication between the business and its suppliers
- communication between the functional areas
- communication between managers
- communication between teams and individuals
- communication between managers and individuals.

> **Activity**
>
> With reference to the range of stakeholders who are involved in business activity, and using the previous list as a guide, identify 5 other kinds of communication in which the business organization is engaged.

The starting point in our study of business communication is to consider the impact of poor communication systems on the range of internal and external relations which we have now identified. In other words, if communication is of poor quality and badly managed, what will be the impact on the overall efficiency and effectiveness of business performance? The next activity will provide the opportunity of establishing some of the problems which might arise for the business organization if it does not place 'effective communication' high on its list of priorities.

Activity

Consider the following situations and say what you consider the effect will be on the business organization:

- the business does not have a system for dealing with customer enquiries and complaints;
- business documentation does not conform to a common housestyle;
- the business does not have an up-to-date organization chart;
- individual managers implement staff appraisal using different systems, timescales and recording documentation;
- there is no common system for informing employees of changes to company policy on matters which may affect them;
- some letters sent out from the business are not of mailable quality;
- the business does not have a procedure for dealing with incoming telephone calls.

Having undertaken the previous activity, the reader should now be in a position to identify some of the *symptoms* of poor communication. These can be summarized as follows:

- confusion
- mistakes
- lack of coordination
- misunderstandings
- lack of motivation
- increase in customer complaints
- increase in staff grievances
- low morale
- apathy
- poor management control of operations.

For the student of Business Practice, such consequences should signal a major cause for concern since it is likely that poor communication will have a direct impact on business performance.

Communication in business

The result of poor communication on business performance can be summarized as follows:

- low productivity
- poor sales figures
- lack of financial control
- lower profit levels
- targets not met
- high labour turnover
- increase in accidents.

In the context of our study of Business Practice, we can now see the importance of effective systems of communication in business. Indeed, we can identify business communication as one of the main factors in establishing *corporate identity,* and, with it, a positive *corporate image* in which both the direct stakeholders in the business, together with the wider community in which the business is involved, have a clear understanding of its core beliefs and values.

> **Activity**
>
> Identify 6 ways in which the business may choose to communicate its beliefs and values to its main stakeholders and the wider community which it serves.

Communication systems

We have referred to the need for an *effective communication system*. What does this mean in practice? In order to answer this question we need to understand the *process* of communication. In essence, the simplest form of communication system involves a process whereby a *message* is *transmitted* or *sent* and *received*. We can therefore distinguish one person as the *sender* of the message and another person as the *receiver* of the message.

However, this simple communication system does not address a number of central questions which must be considered if we are to monitor the *effectiveness* and *quality* of communications. In order to enhance the effectiveness of the simple communication system we must pose a number of questions:

- Should the message be written or communicated orally?
- What is the best way of communicating the message – face-to-face or by indirect means?
- Do we require a response from the message?
- How do we know if the message has been received?
- How do we know if the message has been understood?

- Has the message been sent in the appropriate style, manner and language?
- What is the most cost-effective way of sending the message?
- How many people need to receive the message?

All of these various elements will form the basis of a communication strategy which can lead the business to develop a communications system which best serves its needs. The communication system which the business devises will be informed by an understanding that, within any organization, communication can be analysed by using the following specific categories:

- communication *channels*
- communication *routes*
- *methods and types* of communications.

We will now consider each of these categories in turn in order to identify how an understanding of them can serve to inform the development of a communications strategy.

Communication channels

In any organization we are likely to distinguish 2 channels of communication through which communications flow:

- formal communication
- informal communication.

Formal communication

Formal communication incorporates all types of communication which are sanctioned or authorized by the business organization. Examples of formal communications include:

- company policies
- company directives
- company literature
- company correspondence
- formal meetings
- company notices
- business plans
- reports produced by the functional areas
- organization charts.

Informal communications

Informal communication centres upon those 'messages' which are not officially sanctioned by the organization. These informal channels of communication are collectively referred to as 'the grapevine' – a term which symbolizes how such communications spread throughout all levels of the organization.

The term 'grapevine' is often used in a derogatory sense indicating that it carries rumour and gossip, which can often lead to an increase in anxiety amongst staff and a distrust of business practices and motives. However, although there may be occasions where the 'grapevine' may be disruptive to the business, such informal communication can, at times, be beneficial to both the company and its management team. Examples of how the business may use the 'grapevine' include:

- to counteract rumours;
- to ascertain if information has reached all 'interested parties';
- as a means of assessing staff morale;
- to determine if more information needs to be communicated;
- to monitor the quality and effectiveness of formal communication channels.

Communication routes

Communication routes are the way in which 'messages' – instructions, information, directives and the like – flow through the business organization. We can distinguish 2 communication routes:

- vertical communication
- horizontal communication.

Vertical communication involves 'messages' in the form of instructions, policies or directives being sent by those in a position of authority to those in the organization who are on a lower level in the command structure, along with any responses which may be generated.

Horizontal communication, on the other hand, involves communication between those on the *same level* within the organization.

Both vertical and horizontal communications are best understood with reference to an organization chart, a simple version of which is shown in Figure 14.1 (opposite).

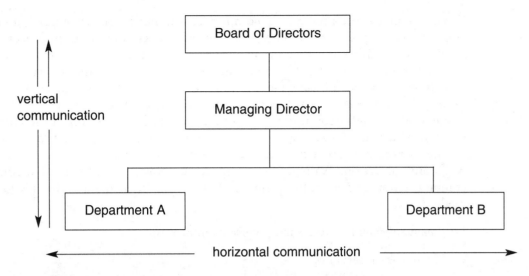

Figure 14.1 **Vertical and horizontal communication routes**

Activity

Classify the following communications in terms of formal/informal; vertical/horizontal:

- a set of management accounts distributed by the finance department to all heads of department;
- a company directive issued by the managing director banning smoking in the workplace;
- a conversation involving staff from the marketing department in which they discuss the likelihood of a company reorganization;
- a company newsletter produced by head office;
- a conversation in the staff restaurant involving a manager and a member of staff in which the manager reveals the possibility of the loss of a large order which may result in financial difficulties and job losses.

Methods and types of communication

A business organization seeking to establish an effective communication system also needs to be aware of the main methods and types of communication. For the purposes of our study of Business Practice we can distinguish 3 main methods of communication:

- oral
- written
- visual.

Communication in business

We shall consider each method of communication, but before we embark upon this task we must appreciate another element of the communication process. This involves ascertaining whether or not the message which is transmitted requires a response from the receiver. If it does, then we describe the communication as '*two-way*'; however, if the message does not require a response, for example an instruction or an order, we refer to it as '*one-way*' communication. There is nothing inherently wrong with one-way communication but, as we shall see later on in the chapter, a business which mostly uses one-way communication is likely to develop a business culture markedly different from one which strives to engage in a high level of two-way communication. With this in mind, let us now return to the 3 methods of communication and identify examples of the types of media associated with each method.

Oral communication involves such diverse examples as:

- face-to-face interviews
- meetings
- training sessions
- telephone calls
- committees
- staff appraisal.

> **Activity**
>
> Determine whether the following examples can be described as one-way or two-way communication:
>
> - a 'No Smoking' notice;
> - wage negotiations involving management and staff representatives;
> - quality circles;
> - a company circular providing details of staff holiday schedules;
> - a staff appraisal interview.

Oral communication brings to the business the following advantages:

- it is the most direct form of communication;
- it allows the sender and receiver to ask direct questions to clarify the meaning of the 'message';
- it allows the message to be enhanced by 'non-verbal behaviour' such as body language, facial expression as well as the 'tone' of the message;
- feedback on the message is direct and immediate.

This being said, oral communication needs to be used with caution since it can bring a number of disadvantages including:

- decision-making can sometimes be time-consuming if a number of people are involved in face-to-face communications;

Business communication

- sometimes there is no written record of what has been discussed and decided;
- disputes can arise if people interpret discussions in different ways;
- it is difficult to relay complex information using oral communication;
- sometimes managers have been known to make spontaneous remarks which they have regretted when they have had the time to reflect on their comments.

Written communication involves such examples as:

- letters
- reports
- memos
- agendas
- minutes
- newsletters
- notices.

Written communications generate a number of advantages for the business:

- they provide a permanent record of what decisions have been made; in some instances the reasons and rationale for the decisions can also be recorded;
- technical information can be communicated more easily because it allows the receiver time to consider and 'digest' the information;
- they are more easily enforceable by law, especially if they involve business contracts;
- they provide the opportunity for evaluation and analysis of complex ideas;
- there is less chance of the parties involved in the communication process misunderstanding the 'message' since points can be referred back to the sender for clarification and agreement.

As with other methods of communication, written communication can also result in a number of disadvantages including:

- costs;
- time-consuming;
- 'red-tape' and bureaucracy;
- instant feedback is often not possible;
- can be overly formal and lacking in character, warmth and familiarity;
- does not allow for an immediate response.

Finally, *visual communication* incorporates aspects which can enhance the quality and effectiveness of both oral and written communication. As such, visual communication includes examples such as:

- charts
- tables
- posters
- videos

- photographs
- graphs
- statistical data
- diagrams.

An effective diagram, graph or a chart can certainly relay complex, technical information in a form which is easily understood. However, these types of visual communication tend to be used in conjunction with oral or written communication. It should also be noted that some diagrams, charts and graphs require a certain level of analytical knowledge and understanding if they are to be of use to the intended audience.

Internal and external communications

The business organization engaged in establishing a *communication strategy* needs to take account of both its internal organizational needs, coupled with its relationships with its customers, clients, other business organizations and a range of external agencies.

It is important that the business identifies appropriate methods and types of communication when dealing with its internal and external customers and clients.

A policy adopted by a number of business organizations is to use a common 'house-style' in all aspects of business communication. Distinguishing features of a common house-style may incorporate some, or all, of the following features:

- common layout for reports, agendas and minutes;
- company logo on all external communications;
- common format for all printed advertisements;
- common typeface for all written communications;
- specially chosen 'company colours' and rules for how they can be used in external communication.

> **Activity**
>
> Compare and contrast the external communications used by 3 different organizations and list their common features.

Communication strategy

Earlier we noted that the company might wish to establish a communication strategy, and we are now in a position to highlight the essential features which inform the development of such a strategy.

These features can be summarized as follows:

- determine the company's mission statement;
- ensure that the mission statement incorporates the business's core values and beliefs which can be shared with the stakeholders;
- determine a common house style for all the main methods of communication;
- establish a formal committee structure with associated membership lists, terms of reference and reporting procedures;
- publish an up-to-date organization chart;
- determine the ways in which official communications channels can be established within the company, such as newsletters, bulletins and notices;
- ensure regular patterns of communication are established within the business;
- establish a system in which business communication is subject to regular review, evaluation and monitoring procedures.

Business communication as a cost of production

At the start of our study of Business Practice, we described business activity as the process whereby productive factors such as labour, raw materials and capital are combined by skilled organizers – the entrepreneurs – in order to produce goods and services which satisfy the needs of consumers and clients. We also identified that the productive factors are associated with costs – costs of production – which must be subject to a rigorous regime of cost control and monitoring in order to ensure that business performance is efficient and effective.

In the context of the current chapter it must be appreciated that business communication can also be viewed as a *cost of production*. Let us take as an example the costs of producing a report on a given subject – a piece of market research to ascertain the likely market demand for a new product which is currently being designed by the business. Table 14.1 (overleaf) identifies the stages involved in producing the report along with the associated costs.

As with all other costs of production, the business must ensure that it uses the most appropriate and cost-effective types of communication to meet its specific needs. If it is able to do this successfully it will find that it gains the maximum benefits from its communication system at the least cost – in other words it will have developed an efficient and effective communication system.

As we shall see in the final chapter, information technology now plays a significant role within the development of communication systems. Since business equipment based upon new technology applications is likely to involve significant costs for the business, it is important that purchasing decisions are made against agreed criteria. For most business organizations such criteria will centre upon the following elements:

- establishing the need for the equipment;
- identifying the contribution it can make to business performance;

- itemizing the direct and indirect costs of purchasing the equipment;
- identifying if the communications for which the equipment will be used are of a confidential nature, and, if so, how the equipment can be made secure.

The above criteria can be broadly summarized under the following 4 headings:

- fitness for purpose
- costs/value for money
- contribution to business performance
- security.

The best way to look at the application of these criteria is with reference to a specific purchasing decision in which many business organizations are now involved – the purchase of computers. Let us consider how the process of purchasing a new computer system meets the criteria we have established.

Table 14.1 Costs of producing a business report

Stages	Activities	Costs
Determine the scope of the report	• establish a team representing the various functional areas • determine the brief and scope of the proposed report	• time • staff costs
Undertake the research	• engage in primary research • gain access to secondary research	• engage research team and marketing consultants
Analyse results	• statistical analysis • establish trends • draw conclusions	• computer costs
Write up the report	• draft the report • present report to the planning team • incorporate changes and recommendations	• typing costs • photocopying costs
Publish the report	• decide on appropriate format for the report • agree distribution list	• administration costs • publishing costs • distribution costs

Table 14.2 (opposite) clearly shows that purchasing major pieces of equipment which will contribute to the development of communications systems within the business, involves 3 distinct elements:

- identify the possible benefits;
- itemize the full range of costs involved in the purchasing decision;

Business communication

- draw-up a series of recommendations and action points which can be presented to the relevant managers in the business who have budgetary responsibilities.

Table 14.2 Purchasing communication equipment

Stages	Computer network
Identify benefits	• client database • mailshots, publicity • financial record-keeping • positive impact on business image • payroll, personnel records • increase quantity and quality of management information
Itemize costs	• hardware • software • service/maintenance costs • staff training costs • security costs • insurance • consumables • updating costs • changes to accommodation • depreciation costs
Recommendations	• *fitness for purpose*: must result in positive measurable benefits to the business • *value for money*: ensure that the benefits outweigh the costs over a specified period of time • *costs*: determine the size of the budget
Action plan	• conduct a 'needs analysis' (identify the priorities for the business) • decide on the level of funds available • research the available systems • visit other companies to see the system in operation • consider the use of specialist outside consultants who will be able to offer advice and guidance • keep staff fully briefed on developments and actively encourage them to share their views and expertise on any proposals

---

Activity

Using appropriate business journals and catalogues, draw up a list of business equipment designed to improve internal and external communication in Satwick Enterprises, a medium-size business organization engaged in the production of children's clothes.

Communication in business

Business communication and management styles

In Chapter 12 we identified a range of management styles which are exhibited within the business environment – participative, consultative, autocratic, performance-driven, and the like. These types of management style provide an insight into the forms of communication which will exist within the organization.

In general terms, those organizations which seek to promote a participative or consultative style of management are more likely to engage in two-way communication with their staff. In this way they will take the opportunity to engage in a constructive dialogue with the workforce in order to elicit their views on company policy, with the aim of sponsoring a collective team spirit within the organization which encompasses a shared vision based upon common goals.

Activity

Complete the following table identifying the intended audience for the various examples of internal and external communication.

Internal communication	Intended audience
• agendas	
• minutes	
• notice boards	
• memos	
• reports	

External communication	Intended audience
• annual report	
• advertisements	
• press releases	
• catalogues	
• posters	
• sales brochures	
• job adverts	

Performance or goal-driven organizations, although they may exhibit some of the characteristics associated with two-way communication, are more likely to be focused on one-way communication, with targets or goals being determined at a senior management level and then communicated to the workforce who may have less opportunity to participate in the target-setting process.

It should be stressed that, in the context of a study of business communication, there is no 'preferred model'. As with all other aspects of business performance, we must assess an individual business organization's communication system and its management style on the basis of its efficiency and effectiveness in meeting its business goals, and it is this aspect of Business Practice which forms the basis of the next chapter.

There now follow some quick questions and revision exercises. They relate specifically to the chapter you have just studied. You are advised to attempt the questions without reference to the text, and then compare your answers and solutions with those on pages 267–9.

Communication in business

QUESTIONS

1. List **8** symptoms of poor communication.
2. List **6** disadvantages of poor communication.
3. Define **formal communication**.
4. Define **informal communication.**
5. List **6** examples of formal communication.
6. What is **the grapevine**?
7. List **4** examples of how the business can use the grapevine.
8. Define **vertical communication**.
9. Define **horizontal communication**.
10. Explain the difference between **two-way** and **one-way communication**.
11. List **4** advantages of oral communication.
12. Explain the term **visual communication**.
13. Explain what is meant by a **house-style**.

EXERCISES

1. Explain why business communication should be regarded as a cost of production.
2. Examine the relationship between business communication and management styles.
3. Describe the stages involved in purchasing communication equipment.

While attempting to answer the questions and exercises on this page, you are strongly advised not to read on and to cover the answers on the following page with a sheet of paper.

ANSWERS TO QUESTIONS

1.
   - Lack of motivation
   - Misunderstandings
   - Low morale
   - Increase in customer complaints
   - Poor management control of operations
   - Confusion
   - Increase in staff grievances
   - Lack of coordination.

2.
   - Low productivity
   - Poor sales figures
   - Lower profit levels
   - High labour turnover
   - Increase in accidents
   - Targets not met.

3. Formal communication incorporates all types of communication which are sanctioned or authorized by the business organization.

4. Informal communication covers those 'messages' which are not officially sanctioned by the organization and for which they cannot take direct responsibility.

5.
   - Company policies
   - Company directives
   - Formal meetings
   - Company notices
   - Business plans
   - Company literature.

6. An informal communication system that runs throughout the company and whose methods and 'messages' are not subject to company control.

7.
   - To counteract rumours.
   - As a means of assessing staff morale.
   - To determine if more information needs to be communicated.
   - To monitor the quality and effectiveness of formal communication channels.

8. Vertical communication involves 'messages' in the form of instructions, policies or directives being sent by those in a position of authority to those in the organization who are on a lower level in the command structure, and the responses returned to those at a higher level.

9. Horizontal communication takes place between those on the same level in the organization's command structure.

Communication in business

10. Two-way communication involves a response from the receiver whereas one-way communication does not require a response.

11. • Direct
    • The receiver can ask for clarification.
    • Feedback can be immediate.
    • The 'tone' of the message is more easily understood.

12. Visual communication incorporates all those aspects which can enhance the effectiveness of oral and written communication, including charts, graphs, pictures, posters and videos.

13. An official and uniform way of presenting all aspects of company documentation and literature.

SOLUTIONS TO EXERCISES

1. Business communication should be regarded as a cost of production since resources are utilized in the process of establishing an effective communication system. These costs can be classified as physical costs such as equipment, machinery and consumables; publishing and distribution costs, including photocopying costs; and the direct staff costs of those specifically engaged in the communication systems and procedures. However, perhaps 2 of the most important costs which are often overlooked when trying to ascertain the costs of communication are staff time and opportunity cost. The latter is particularly important since an ineffective communication system can have serious implications for the business organization.

2. There is likely to be a direct relationship between management styles and the forms of communication which are used within a business organization. Autocratic managers will tend to rely on one-way vertical communication in the form of notices, instructions and orders. Since such managers do not place an emphasis on employee participation or consultation, they will tend not to introduce forms of communication which promote feedback and discussion.

   Participative and consultative management styles will actively promote feedback within the organization and will place an emphasis on two-way communication and team work in such a way as to foster cooperative working arrangements and active participation in the decision-making process.

3. There are 4 main stages involved in the purchasing of communications equipment.

   Firstly, the organization must seek to identify the benefits of any proposed purchase and ascertain how it will contribute to the overall performance of the business. Secondly, there must be an in-depth analysis of costs. The business is best advised to itemize these costs and, in particular, to make sure that any associated costs are taken into account.

Once these first 2 stages have been completed, those wishing to make the purchase will be in a position to make recommendations to those responsible for purchasing decisions within the organization on the basis of the equipment's fitness for purpose, value for money and costs. Finally an action plan needs to be drawn up identifying the key responsibilities of those who will be responsible for monitoring the purchase and installation of the equipment.

POINTS TO REMEMBER

- Effective communication within a business organization will have a direct impact on the efficiency and effectiveness of its operations.
- Poor communication centres upon poor management control of operations and systems leading to a lack of coordination, low staff morale and an increase in customer complaints.
- The results of poor communication can seriously undermine productivity, sales, profits and financial control.
- Formal communications incorporate all types of communication which are authorized by the organization.
- Informal communications are those which are not officially sanctioned by the organization and are sometimes referred to as the 'grapevine'.
- Vertical communication involves communications between those in authority and those who are in a lower level in the organization.
- Horizontal communication involves communication between those on the same level within the organization.
- Many organizations seek to incorporate a common 'house style' into their written/visual communications so that they conform to an agreed format and layout.
- Many organizations seek to determine a communications strategy which identifies the way in which it proposes to implement and monitor an effective communications system.
- Business communications can be viewed as a cost of production which must be subject to a rigorous regime of cost control and monitoring in order to ensure that the effectiveness of such communications is maximized.
- Management styles will determine the nature and characteristics of communications within the business organization.

15
Communication systems and business performance

> **After carefully studying this chapter, you should be able to:**
>
> 1 *describe how effective communication can assist the achievement of business goals through information flows;*
>
> 2 *describe the importance of management information as a means of controlling and monitoring business activity;*
>
> 3 *analyse how communication can impact upon the understanding of company objectives and the effect it may have upon individual and team performance;*
>
> 4 *understand the need for administrative systems and procedures and how they affect business communications.*

> **Extended Syllabus references**
>
> 3.11 Describe the importance of management information as a means of controlling and monitoring business activity
>
> 6.4 Describe how effective communications can assist the achievement of business goals through information flows
>
> 6.5 Analyse how communications can impact upon the understanding of company objectives and the effect they may have upon individual and team performance
>
> 6.6 Understand the need for administrative systems and procedures and how they affect business communications

The purpose of this chapter is to show how communication systems can influence the achievement of business aims and objectives. Additionally the chapter will highlight the importance of the administrative function in developing systems and procedures which promote the efficient and effective communication of management information within the business organization.

Introduction

In previous chapters we have shown how the business organization will engage in a systematic planning process in which it will seek to establish a number of aims and objectives – its *business goals* – along with a range of specific targets, which, if they are met, will enable the business to implement and achieve its overall business plan.

We have also shown that the implementation and achievement of targets will involve a collective effort on the part of managers, teams and individuals organized into their respective functional areas. In the context of our study of business communication, 3 questions arise:

- How will the business determine the progress that it is making towards the achievement of its business goals and the associated targets?
- How will managers, teams and individuals monitor their own contributions to the overall success of the business?
- How can the specialist roles of the functional areas be combined in such a way as to maximize their contribution to the achievement of business goals?

These questions will form the basis of this second part of our study of business communication in which we will concentrate upon 2 aspects:

- business goals and the importance of management information;
- the role of the administrative function in developing communication systems.

The role of management information

It is now appropriate to return again to some of the central themes which were introduced in Chapter 1 in which we identified the importance of decision-making in the business organization. We also considered decision-making in Chapters 8 and 9, on business planning and business finance. In essence, the central theme which we have drawn from considering these different aspects of Business Practice is that making business decisions involves:

- risks
- costs.

It is important for the business to minimize both the level of risk and the costs involved in making business decisions. In order to do this it must have access to *information* which is:

- up to date;
- relevant;
- presented in an appropriate format;

- complete;
- concise;
- accessible to non-technical managers.

Such information is derived from *raw data* which has itself been derived from the various activities and operations in which the business is involved. However, in its raw state, data is of little use to the business organization, since, to be of any real use, data needs to be manipulated or *processed* in such a way as to produce meaningful *management information*. This leads us towards a broad definition of management information as *the information derived from processing raw data which can assist those managers who are engaged in the decision-making process*.

A management information system (MIS) is therefore a *management tool* which is used by the business organization to:

- *plan* its activities;
- *monitor* its targets;
- *evaluate* its performance;
- *inform* decisions regarding its future development;
- *coordinate* the main business functions.

Let us now look at these various aspects of management information in the context of the role of the main functional areas.

Management information and the functional areas of business

In Chapter 6 we identified 7 main functional areas:

- personnel/human resources
- production/operations
- purchasing
- finance/accounts
- sales and marketing
- administration
- research and development.

We saw that the activities of the functional areas are interrelated, so that their specialist roles need to be coordinated in such a way as to produce the maximum benefits for the business organization.

We shall now consider 2 main aspects of communication within the functional areas:

- the information requirements of each of the functional areas;
- how an effective communication system can serve to assist the functional areas by improving their access to management information;

Communication in business

Table 15.1 identifies the main information requirements of the functional areas and provides an insight into how the scope and range of this information can be used in the decision-making process.

From the table we can draw the following conclusions:

- the business organization generates vast amounts of raw data;
- from this raw data the business organization can access a significant volume of management information;
- managers with functional responsibilities are likely to produce management reports which include detailed recommendations, action plans and *decisions* based upon the information at their disposal;
- the more accurate and reliable the information, the better will be the quality of the decisions, activities and contributions of each of the functional areas;
- much of the information required by the business is in a numerical or quantitative format which needs to be analysed and presented in such a way as to be meaningful;
- the functional areas need to have access to historical data and information in order to determine *trends* which will, in turn, inform future forecasts.

In the next, and final, chapter of the book we will show examples of how information technology can be used by the functional areas to control and monitor business activity, but in this section we are more concerned to show how effective communication can be used to coordinate the *information flows* between the various functional areas.

Table 15.1 Range of information requirements of the main functional areas

Functional area	Data requirements	Decisions
Personnel	Personal details of staff • name, address, age • pension details • salary/wage rate • work number • section/department • employment history • staff development undertaken • qualifications • skill level	• payroll services • determine future labour requirements • identify skill shortages • devise appropriate staff development activities
Production/operations	• raw material costs • stock levels • availability of spare parts • order levels • new orders • quality indicators	• maintenance schedules • job rotas • production schedules

Functional area	Data requirements	Decisions
Purchasing	• prices • quality • supplier details • delivery times	• stock control systems • delivery schedules
Finance	• costs • sales income • factor inputs • capital expenditure • reserves • profits • interest payments on loans • depreciation	• financial records • financial forecasts • management accounts • investment appraisal • break-even analysis
Sales and marketing	• market demand • sales figures (by region/product type) • level of competition • number and type of consumer (age, gender, geographical region, social class, income level) • retail outlets (location, type, turnover, sales) • repeat sales	• sales campaigns • promotions • advertising • sponsorship activities
Administration	• stationery levels • inventories of equipment • records and files • maintenance requirements • technical data (computer networks and related business equipment)	• planning schedules • purchasing plans • communication networks and systems • replacement policies • reporting procedures
Research and development	• costs • budgets • technical and scientific data • statistical analysis	• new product development • new product design • product testing • product updating

The flow of information between the functional areas

Although Table 15.1 provides an overview of the data which is generated by each of the functional areas, and how this can be used to develop systems and procedures within each of the areas, it does not tell us anything about the *interrelationship* between the functional areas. For the purposes of our study of Business Practice, it is very important that we understand that data generated within one functional area is likely to be of use to a range of other functional areas. Indeed we should view data and the information which is generated from it rather like a stream which *flows through the organization*. In order to show how information flows through the organization, we can take as our example the raw data and corresponding information which is produced as a result of the business selling one of its products.

When a consumer purchases one of the business organization's products, a significant range of raw data is produced which may include some or all of the following:

- sales revenue
- sales receipts
- sales invoice
- method of payment – cash, cheque, credit
- credit terms
- type of retail outlet where the product was sold
- name and address of the consumer
- location of retail outlet
- stock figures
- delivery dates.

It is important that we distinguish 2 aspects of business operations which inform how this data can be used within the organization:

- the data is required *by a number of different functional areas;*
- the data needs to be processed in such a way that *it can provide information to a number of different functional areas.*

Once the data has been generated, the business must ensure that it has the systems in place which allow both the data, and the processed information which flows from it, to be accessible to all the constituent parts of the business organization. Not only will this allow the functional managers the opportunity to make *informed decisions*, but the flow of information will also act as *a means of monitoring and controlling business activity.*

Activity

Identify the raw data which is produced as a result of the business organization purchasing a consignment of raw materials.

Once this data has been processed show how it will assist the following functional areas:

- finance
- purchasing
- production/operations.

Controlling and monitoring business activity

In earlier chapters we described the importance of the finance function in the control and monitoring of business activity. We saw how both financial and management accounting have a critical part to play in this process since efficient and effective financial record-keeping will allow the business to monitor its financial targets, to inform managers of any anticipated budgetary difficulties, and to provide advice and guidance on any corrective action which may be necessary to ensure that profits are safeguarded.

The flow of management information between the functional areas also allows the business to control and monitor its business activities as part of its *planning activities*.

In order to show how this works in practice we will consider an aspect of business activity which is crucial to the long-term success of the business – the development and implementation of a *marketing strategy*.

A successful marketing strategy will be based on the raw data which will be generated from implementing the business's *marketing plan*. The marketing plan will generate a wealth of data relating to the marketing function, and will be based upon the following activities:

- market research – attempts to provide data on the behaviour patterns of the consumer and the important influences on consumer behaviour;
- sales analysis – attempts to provide data drawn from previous sales;
- market trends – attempts to provide data on the market from previously published data;
- customers – attempts to build up a 'customer profile';
- competitors – attempts to provide data on the competitive environment;
- pilot launch – attempts to provide data resulting from a selective small-scale launch of the product.

Activity

Complete the following table by identifying 3 pieces of data which may be generated from the marketing plan, and the associated information which the business would find useful when drawing up its marketing strategy.

Activity	Data	Information
Market research		
Sales analysis		
Market trends		
Customers		
Pilot testing		

Communication in business

The marketing plan will therefore generate the *data* which, when *processed*, will lead to *marketing information* which will, in turn, inform the business's *marketing strategy*.

In essence, the marketing strategy will identify the way in which the business will seek to achieve successful market penetration for its products and services.

As with all other areas of business activity, the development of the marketing strategy will involve the business organization in establishing ways in which it can:

- *control* and *monitor* its performance;
- access *information* which it can use to inform its *decisions*.

In this respect a successful marketing strategy will centre upon an understanding of 2 key concepts:

- the marketing mix
- the product life cycle.

The marketing mix

In the business world, business planning is the key to success, and nowhere is this more the case than in the marketing of goods and services. No business will succeed unless it can successfully sell its products to the consumer, and the 'marketing mix' enables the business to develop a strategy which incorporates the *control* of the 4 main essentials of successful marketing:

- product
- place
- price
- promotion.

The task of the business organization is to ensure that these 4 components, collectively referred to as the '4Ps', are combined in such a way as to produce the most efficient and effective means of ensuring that the product meets the needs of the consumer.

Product

The organization has to identify the products which the consumer wants. *Market research* is an important tool in ascertaining consumer preferences. A keen eye on the market can also lead to products being adapted or additional features being incorporated into the design. *Product guarantees, packaging* and *after-sales service* can also be used to stimulate demand for the product.

Place

This component of the marketing mix seeks to ensure that the product is in the right place at the right time and that efficient and effective *distribution channels* have been established in order for this to take place. It is vital that stock levels are maintained in order to ensure that sales are not lost to competitors.

Price

Obviously prices must be competitive in order to stimulate demand and sales. Attention must also be paid to the *size of the market* and *market segmentation,* along with the *disposable income* of specific consumer groups. There are a number of pricing strategies which can be used in this element of the marketing mix, ranging from a single percentage mark-up through to *discount pricing* – selling products slightly cheaper than other outlets – and *loss-leader pricing* – pricing some products below the normal price.

Promotion

This aspect of the marketing mix comprises all those elements relating to promotion, advertising, public relations, and personal selling. *Brand image* and *corporate image* are also useful promotional tools in establishing certain products as *market leaders*. Essentially, promotion is concerned with *marketing communication,* and involves the business in informing consumers about new products and reminding them of existing products in order that they might be persuaded to purchase them.

> **Activity**
>
> Choose an example from one of the following products and identify how the 4 components of the marketing mix have been incorporated into the business's marketing strategy.
>
> - a motor car
> - a piece of computer software
> - an electrical consumer good
> - the release of a successful Hollywood film on video.

It is important that all 4 components of the marketing mix are *monitored* and *controlled* in order to ensure that the business gains the maximum benefits from its marketing strategy.

Communication in business

At the same time, the business must also be aware that different products will require the 4 components of the marketing mix to be combined in different ways depending upon the position of the product in the *product life cycle*.

The product life cycle

The product life cycle identifies 4 stages in a product's useful 'market life':

- introduction
- growth
- maturity
- decline.

Introduction

At this stage, the product is being brought onto the market. There may be little competition within the market, but, at the same time, demand may be low. It is therefore important for marketing strategies to promote *product awareness*. One way of doing this is through aggressive pricing policies such as *penetration pricing*, which involves setting a low price in order to reach as large a market as possible. Advertising is also crucial at this stage on the product life cycle.

Growth

This stage in the cycle is characterized by an *increase in competitors* and *rising sales figures*. Given the increased competition it is important for the company to promote its own *brand image* and acquire *additional outlets* from which its product can be sold. The firm may also benefit from *internal economies of scale* as their output, and accompanying sales, increase.

Maturity

Although at the maturity stage it may be difficult for new competitors to enter the market, the level of existing competition serves to *reduce overall profit levels* for most producers. Sales increase at a reduced rate and *prices begin to fall* as businesses try to maintain their market share. Marketing strategies at this stage may incorporate *price discounting* and the business may also seek to *promote efficiency savings* which result in the benefits of lower costs being passed on to the consumer in the form of lower prices. It is also likely that, at the maturity phase, *new products will be introduced*, which will eventually replace existing products.

Decline

As the term suggests, this phase of the product life cycle signals *falling sales*, *reduced profit levels*, and, in some cases, *businesses leaving the marketplace*. Pricing strategies reflect the declining nature of the market and surplus stocks are sold at 'knock-down prices'. Figure 15.1 shows the product life cycle over time and its relationship to sales.

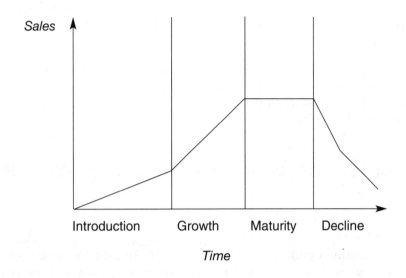

Figure 15.1 The product life cycle

> **Activity**
>
> Identify 4 products which are at different stages in the product life cycle. Provide examples to show how the marketing and promotion of these products takes account of their place on the product life cycle.

It should now be clear to the reader that the business which is seeking to establish a marketing strategy will need to take account of the following factors:

- establish the means by which data can be effectively 'captured';
- understand that data is generated from the activities undertaken by all the functional areas;
- process the data to generate management information;
- coordinate the flow of information throughout the organization in order to ensure that it is accessible to all managers in an appropriate format;
- base marketing decisions on management information which relates to the components of the marketing mix and the product life cycle;
- ensure that control and monitoring mechanisms are in place to ascertain progress towards meeting targets.

Closer examination of the above factors reveals that *effective communications* is of vital importance if the marketing strategy is to be implemented successfully:

- data needs to be processed and *communicated* to managers;
- managers need to have *access* to the information;
- up-to-date *management reports* need to be produced on a regular basis to monitor progress.

In the following chapter we will show the importance of information technology in generating management information and how new technology can be used to improve communication.

For the purposes of this chapter, however, we will focus on another aspect of communication which will directly influence business performance – how communication can affect the understanding of company objectives, and the effect it may have on individual and team performance.

Communicating business objectives to individuals and teams

In Chapter 11, we described the contributions which both individuals and teams can make to business performance. Here we shall describe how these contributions can be maximized if the business effectively communicates its business goals to its staff.

A forward-looking business organization will regard its staff as important *stakeholders* in its operations. At the same time, members of staff will be keenly aware that the success of the company in terms of its sales, profit levels and new product development will be directly related to their own job security, welfare, morale and general financial well-being. If a business can successfully persuade its staff that it regards them as one of the most important elements which contribute towards business success, then it will go a long way to ensuring that the contributions of the staff towards business activities and performance are maximized.

Our study of Business Practice has already identified a number of factors which influence the way in which employees will view the business:

- management style
- corporate image and identity
- motivational influences
- organizational structure.

To these factors we can now add *effective communication of business goals,* since, if the business can perform this task successfully, it will create a workforce which is better able to understand the motives and actions of the business and the management team.

A well-informed team of staff which has shared in the formation of business goals and objectives will bring a number of benefits to the business:

- staff will be better motivated;
- there will be a positive impact on staff morale;
- they will be able to understand the reasons which underlie management decisions;
- industrial relations will be improved;
- productivity will increase;
- their will be a positive impact on the achievement of targets;
- staff appraisal can be set in the context of overall business goals and objectives.

What strategies can the business employ to ensure that its goals and objectives are communicated and understood by its staff? There are a number of practical examples which can be drawn from a variety of different organizations which show the range of methods used by businesses to communicate their business goals. These include examples such as:

- company newsletters;
- a summary of the company's annual report distributed to all staff;
- the publication of an annual review of its activities;
- team meetings;
- mission statements;
- staff-development activities.

> **Activity**
>
> Obtain a copy of an annual report produced by a public limited company. From the report, identify what you consider to be the company's main business objectives.
>
> Describe one way in which these company objectives could be communicated to their employees.

The need for administrative systems

There is need to ensure that communication systems are developed, introduced and coordinated in such a way as to meet the demands of the most complex business organizations. The responsibility of undertaking these activities falls to the administrative function. Like all other management functions, the management of communication in any organization involves:

- planning
- organizing
- controlling
- monitoring.

The administration function and the management of communication

An effective system of communication is based upon certain key principles:

- accessibility
- reliability
- relevance
- accuracy
- frequency.

If these principles inform the development of communication within the organization, then the users of the system will have *confidence* in its ability to meet the needs of the organization. The first task of the manager with responsibility for addressing the communication needs of the organization is to undertake a *needs analysis*. In simple terms this involves:

- identifying the communication needs of the various departments, teams and individuals;
- identifying the most effective methods in which their needs can be met with due regard to fitness for purpose, costs, uses and any associated security implications;
- establishing systems and procedures which are known and understood by all staff within the organization;
- ensuring that all users are fully briefed on the systems and procedures;
- ensuring that there is technical back-up and relevant supplies of consumables;
- establishing systems which engage the users in evaluating the effectiveness of the system in meeting their needs.

We can look at all these various aspects of managing a communications strategy with reference to a case study. Let us consider a situation in which a business organization is seeking to introduce a new computer network which will give users access to e-mail facilities – in other words, the ability to send messages and to download files and reports so that they are communicated to users over the computer network. How should the business seek to manage the introduction of this new communication system? Table 15.2 (opposite) identifies the stages which could form the basis of an *administration plan*.

This chapter has shown the importance of *information* as a management tool in the decision-making process and has highlighted the importance of *information flows* between the functional areas. Additionally, we have seen why it is important for management decisions and the associated business goals to be communicated

Communication systems

effectively to staff. Finally, we identified the key role played by the administration function in establishing systems and procedures relating to developments and improvements in communication. In the final chapter, we will outline the influence of information technology within the business environment and how it is used to enhance the role of management information and improve business communications.

Table 15.2 Planning the introduction of e-mail

Administration plan	Activity	Benefits
Inform users of e-mail facility	• staff development	• staff are made aware of the uses of e-mail • staff skills are improved
Establish systems and procedures for the use of e-mail	• produce a company manual detailing the procedures for the use of e-mail	• speed • accessibility • frequent • allows for immediate response • saves paper • saves time • multiple user access to information • ability to download reports from other files • improvements in access to management information
Monitoring and evaluation	• establish a user group • analyse data about technical problems • report to relevant individuals and management teams	• two-way communication • consultative management • identify problems • make recommendations • agree action plan, responsibilities and associated timescales

Activity

Draw up a set of simple guidelines and procedures which could be distributed to staff attending a training session following the introduction of e-mail facilities in their company.

Communication in business

> *There now follow some quick questions and revision exercises. They relate specifically to the chapter you have just studied. You are advised to attempt the questions without reference to the text, and then compare your answers and solutions with those on pages 288–90.*

Communication systems

QUESTIONS

1. What is **data**?
2. Explain the term **data processing.**
3. Define the term **management information.**
4. What do the initials **MIS** stand for?
5. List **5** uses of management information.
6. List **4** data requirements of the finance/accounts function.
7. Describe **2** decisions which need to be taken by the business organization relating to business activity.
8. List **6** pieces of data which are derived when a business organization sells one of its products.
9. What is a **marketing strategy**?
10. List the **4** elements of the marketing mix.
11. List the **4** stages of the product life cycle.
12. List **6** advantages of a well-informed workforce.
13. List **5** ways a business can communicate its business goals to its staff.

EXERCISES

1. Examine the role of the administration function in the development of an effective communications system.
2. What is the relationship between the marketing mix and the product life cycle?
3. 'Successful marketing is based on effective communication.' Discuss.

ANSWERS TO QUESTIONS

1. Data is the raw facts and figures which are derived from business activities.
2. Data processing is the means by which raw data is converted into more meaningful information.
3. The information derived from processing raw data which can assist those managers who are engaged in the decision-making process.
4. Management information system
5. - Planning activities
   - Monitoring targets
   - Evaluating performance
   - Coordinating business performance
   - Informing the decision-making process.
6. - Costs
   - Sales
   - Profits
   - Reserves.
7. - What to produce?
   - Where to produce?
8. - Sales revenue
   - Stock levels
   - Delivery dates
   - Type of retail outlet where the product was sold
   - Location of retail outlet
   - Name and address of the consumer.
9. The way in which the business organization will seek to coordinate the whole range of its marketing activities in order to enhance business performance and meet the targets identified within its long-term strategic plan
10. - Product
    - Place
    - Price
    - Promotion.
11. - Introduction
    - Growth
    - Maturity
    - Decline.
12. - Increased productivity
    - Good industrial relations

- Achievement of targets
- Positive impact on staff morale
- Motivated staff
- Better understanding between managers and their staff.

13
- Company newsletters
- Team meetings
- Mission statements
- Staff-development activities
- Publication of an annual review of company activities.

SOLUTIONS TO EXERCISES

1 The administration function plays a crucial role in the business organization by ensuring that systems and procedures are in place which assist the coordination of a complex and diverse range of business activities. One of the most important aspects of the administration function's role is to ensure that an effective communication system is in place across the organization and that the various sections, teams and individuals represented within the organization are aware of the procedures and systems upon which the communications networks are based. Managers who are responsible for the administration function will therefore need to ensure that the communication system meets the needs of users, that the users are aware of the system and procedures, that any training requirements are identified and met, that office supplies and stock meet the requirements of the users, and that there is an effective monitoring and evaluation system which leads to continuous quality improvements in communication across the organization.

2 The marketing mix is based on the principle that an effective marketing strategy concerns 4 key elements:
- product
- place
- price
- promotion.

A successful marketing strategy will need to take account of all of these elements if the business is to meet its targets. The product must meet consumer requirements which have been identified by in-depth market research, and the business must ensure that there are effective distribution channels are in place so that sales can be achieved. Successful sales will also be dependent upon a range of promotional activities and associated pricing strategies including discounts and special offers.

Successful marketing will also be based on an understanding of the product life cycle. This concept identifies the 'life' of a product as being made up of 4 parts or stages:

- introduction
- growth
- maturity
- decline.

The marketing mix needs to take account of the product life cycle since different marketing strategies will be appropriate for different stages in the product's life cycle. For example, at the introduction of a new product the business may decide to offer price discounts in order to gain a market share, whereas in the growth phase, the business will be more concerned with establishing a brand image for the product in order to differentiate it from its competitors.

3 Successful marketing is based on the principle that the business organization is able to meet the needs of existing and potential customers. Communication is central to the marketing function for a number of reasons. Marketing demands that the business is aware of customer requirements. This can be achieved by an effective system of marketing research in which the views and preferences of consumers are ascertained. The results of this research must be analysed and communicated in an appropriate form to those people in the organization who have the responsibility for making decisions. Sales figures and sales trends along with other market information must be constantly up-dated in order to provide managers with management information. At the same time the business must ensure that it is receiving constant feedback from its customers on the quality of its products and the level of customer service provided by its operations. In this way, if the business is seen to be responsive to customer requirements, it can establish consumer loyalty to its products and services. Promotional activities, company literature and a high media profile will all form part of a communications strategy which will serve to promote the marketing of the company and its products.

POINTS TO REMEMBER

- Management information is the information derived from processing raw data which can assist those managers who are engaged in the decision-making process.
- Management information can be used to plan, monitor, evaluate and coordinate business activities and operations.
- Management information is required by all the functional areas within the business.
- Data generated by one of the functional areas is likely to be important to other areas within the organization and, as such, the organization needs to establish systems and procedures which enhance coordination between the functional areas.
- The marketing mix and the product life cycle are both examples of how management information can be used to inform the long-term plans of the business organization.
- The effective communication of business goals to employees will enable them to understand the motives and actions of the business and its management team and the associated requirements for management information.

16

Information technology in the business environment

> **After carefully studying this chapter, you should be able to:**
> 1 *describe the importance of new technology to the main functional areas;*
> 2 *understand the need for IT in the development of business communication;*
> 3 *understand the impact of new technology on internal and external communications.*

> **Extended Syllabus references**
> 2.8 Describe the importance of new technology to the main functional areas
> 6.3 Understand the impact of new technology on internal and external communications:
>   6.3.1 to and from customers
>   6.3.2 between the functional areas
>   6.3.3 between individuals and teams
>   6.3.4 in multisite and international organizations
> 6.7 Understand the need for IT in the development of business communications:
>   6.7.1 electronic mail/intranet
>   6.7.2 Internet
>   6.7.3 teleconferencing

The purpose of this chapter is to consider the role of business information technology in the operation of business functions and to describe the various ways in which such technology can contribute to the level of business activity which is undertaken by the business organization. The focus of the chapter will be on the *applications* of information technology in the business world and will concentrate primarily on how these applications can assist business communication.

Business information systems

Before we consider information technology in any detail it is important to determine the scope and nature of the subject matter as it applies to the study of Business Practice. Our study is concerned with an understanding and appreciation of the *applications* of new technology in the business environment – in other words, how organizations use information technology to meet their business requirements. Many of these applications will be based upon the role of the computer in business but, increasingly, the technology used in the design and production of computers is being combined with telecommunication technologies to develop new types of products, business networks and communication systems.

Conventional applications of new technology which concern the use of computers within the workplace, centre upon 4 main kinds of software package:

- word-processing
- spreadsheet
- database
- graphics.

The main characteristic of all these packages is the amount of data which can be:

- stored
- accessed
- manipulated
- retrieved
- processed.

Table 16.1 (overleaf) provides a summary of the standard features which are incorporated in the main computer software types and which form the basis of most commercially produced business applications.

In essence, the main advantage of new technology and the associated computer applications is that it allows for the efficient and effective processing of data to produce information, which, as we described in the previous chapter, is a key requirement of the business organization and its management team.

In the previous chapter we stressed that information *flows* through the organization and that the activities of each of the functional areas are interrelated. In this section we will now develop this theme by looking at 2 specific aspects of the business organization and its information requirements:

- the importance of new technology to the functional areas;
- the influence of new technology on the development of communication systems.

It is important to note at this stage that the impact and influence of new technology will be felt throughout the business organization and the environment within which it operates, and that technology is constantly changing in the light of the needs of business and society in general. Students of Business Practice must therefore ensure

Communication in business

Table 16.1 Summary of the main software applications

Application	Description	Common features
Word processing	A computer software package which allows the production of high quality business documents	- editing facilities - creates templates from which standard business documents can be prepared - mail-merge - spellcheck - thesaurus - document saving and retrieval facilities
Database	A computer software package which consists of a collection of records filed in such a way that it allows information to be easily retrieved and manipulated in a variety of formats	- retrieval of selected information from individual records - summary documents produced from full range of files held - search facilities
Spreadsheet	A computer software package which stores large amounts of numerical data and is able to perform complex calculations and present them in a variety of visual formats	- allows the input of large amounts of complex numerical data - manipulation of data to perform complex calculations - automatic calculation - present calculations in a variety of visual formats
Graphics	A computer software package which combines text production facilities with artwork, in order to produce documents of a professional standard	- allows the user to experiment with different designs and layouts - typesetting facilities - Desk Top Publishing (DTP) packages
Integrated	A computer software package which allows different packages (WP, database, spreadsheet, DTP) to be used simultaneously	- same data can be used for each of the main applications - data and information can be transferred from one application to another

that they keep their knowledge of the *impact* and *influence* of new technology applications up-to-date if they are to make their own informed judgements of the role of new technology in the world of work.

The importance of new technology to the functional areas

It should now be becoming clear that there is a direct link between business performance and the following elements:

- the amount of data which is generated by the business;
- the ability of the organization to process the data;
- the quality, reliability and accuracy of the information;
- the ability to access the information;
- the skills of the managers and their staff to use the communication systems and processes which allow all the above elements to be coordinated in such a way as to improve business performance.

In this section we will look at the ways in which new technology is used by the functional areas and the implications for the management and internal organization of the business.

We should now be familiar with the roles of the respective functional areas and their information requirements. How can new technology applications improve the quality, speed and flow of this information and, with it, the ability of the functional areas to perform their roles more efficiently and effectively? The best way to show the advantages of new technology within a particular functional area is by comparing manual systems of storing, retrieving and communicating data and information, with computerized systems. Figure 16.1 shows the process involved in meeting a sales order. A closer examination allows us to draw the following conclusions:

- although the process will be coordinated by the sales function, it needs to be communicated to other functional areas;
- the data and resulting information is generated from a paper-based system;
- a number of different documents need to be despatched to the purchaser and to different functional areas within the organization;
- the system is time-consuming and subject to delays and inefficiencies;
- the system does not generate accurate and precise information at any one time since some orders may not have been recorded in the relevant financial records;
- loss of documents can cause serious disruption to the system;
- processing the data within the system would produce valuable management information.

Communication in business

What would be the benefits of computerizing the process outlined in Figure 16.1?

The central feature of a computerized system, in which all computers in the organization are linked together by a *computer network*, is that the process of dealing with customer orders can be *integrated*. In this way, one piece of data entered on to the computer will automatically update the information available to the other functional areas throughout the business organization. Hence, entering details of the sales order onto the computer network will immediately:

- update the customer database;
- amend stock records;
- record the financial details in the appropriate ledgers;
- schedule delivery dates.

Similar examples can be drawn from the activities of the other functional areas.

The *finance function*, quite obviously lends itself to computerization given its reliance on the need for accurate financial and numerical data from which it can produce accurate *management information* in the form of management accounts. The finance function can also use new technology to support *decision-making activities* such as *break-even analysis*.

The *research and development* function will be more concerned with the applications of new technology in the development of more efficient and effective production techniques, and with researching how the benefits of new technology can be incorporated into new product design. For example, we have seen the introduction of *robotics* into automated production processes, and the design of new products based upon new technology, which reduces the cost of after-sales service by increasing the reliability of the product. Additionally, in some instances, products based upon new technology can perform a greater range of complex tasks, which meets the needs of the consumer, resulting in an increase in market demand and the potential for bigger profits.

Computer technology can also improve the efficiency and effectiveness of business activities which support the roles of the functional areas – such activities as stock control, setting and monitoring targets, and planning activities can all benefit from computerization.

These features of the computer network will lead to important benefits for the business organization:

- less paperwork;
- greater efficiency;
- improved monitoring and control of business activities;

> ### Activity
> Compile a short report which highlights the advantages of computerization to the personnel function.

Information technology

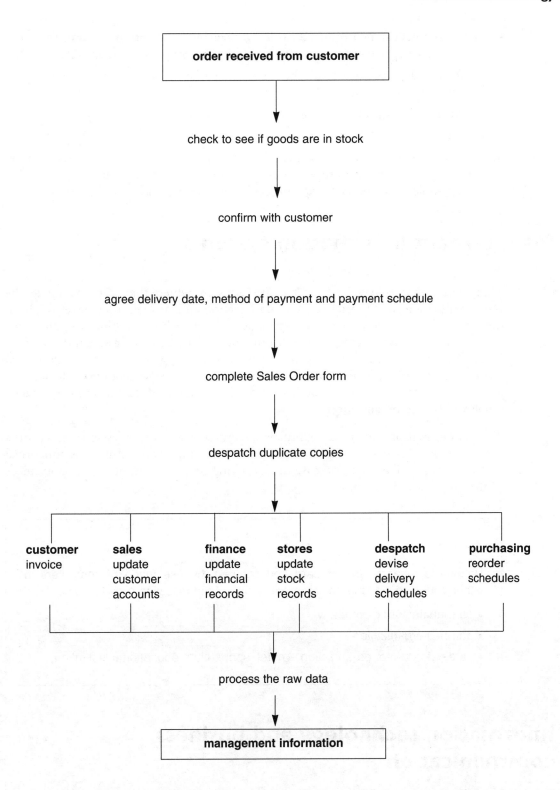

Figure 16.1 Processing a sales order

- update reports can be produced from the available information and transmitted to the relevant departmental managers through the company's e-mail system;
- the finance department will be able to produce management accounts on a regular basis which are accurate, up to date and reliable;
- departmental budgets can be monitored;
- targets can be set and monitored more easily;
- management information is generated automatically – in a paper-based system, management information relies upon the accurate manual recording of data which is then subject to a second-stage process of processing and analysis.

Management information systems

Many organizations have sought to find ways in which they can maximize the opportunities afforded to them by computerization and, as such, they have sought to develop organizational policies and strategies which seek to establish a coordinated system within which management information is generated, accessed and reported. In performing this task these organizations have developed an internal *management information system* (MIS) which is designed to produce management information in an appropriate format which can be accessed by the range of management specialists employed by the organization

The administration function will play a central role in the establishment of a management information system, since specialists employed within this functional area will have professional expertise in identifying the information and support needs of the business and its constituent parts.

Activity

Undertake research to compare and contrast the use made of computers in either your own working environment or one of the following organizations:

- a manufacturing company
- a retail organization
- a service sector organization – hotel, sports club, educational institution.

Information technology and business communication

The development of computer networks and their associated management information systems have led business organizations into thinking about the best way they can communicate management information using a computer network.

Obviously, no matter how good the quality of the information produced by the MIS, if managers cannot gain access to it, the end result will be the same as having no management information at all – the quality of management decisions will be reduced. We have already described how *e-mail facilities* can be a useful communication tool if they are introduced and managed according to the needs of the organization and the skills of its staff to maximize its uses and applications.

Similarly most management information systems now use an internal computer network known as an *intranet*. In order to establish an intranet, computers within an organization must be linked together in order to form a *local area network* (LAN), which enables resources and information to be shared. Then the organization can set about designing systems which provide information to appropriate levels of management within the organization. Each manager will have access, through a computer terminal, to the appropriate level of management information to enable them to perform their management roles and duties. Some information may be sensitive or confidential, so the intranet system may be designed so that information of this nature can only be accessed by senior managers.

In practice, when data is put into the system, the updates will automatically be reflected in the various aspects of management information held within the network. Thus, although managers have access to the information, they cannot alter it unless the data from which it is derived is altered – in other words, individual managers cannot change the information which appears on their computer screens. An intranet system therefore provides management with access to 'real-time' management information which means that decisions can be made on the basis of accurate and reliable information.

The same principles which apply to an intranet – establishing a local area network by linking computers in the same organization together – also apply to much larger *global communication networks*, to which computers can be linked by telecommunication technology in the form of a *modem*. Such technology creates a wide area network (WAN), allowing information to be communicated instantaneously across the globe. The *Internet* is extremely powerful communication technology and, although the benefits of the system have yet to be fully utilized, we shall see that it is beginning to have a dramatic effect on how business organizations operate.

In the context of our current discussion, however, the Internet and other wide area networks can have a dramatic effect upon communication systems in multisite organizations which are located either in one country or in different countries around the world. In earlier chapters we described the importance of the multinational corporations in the global economy. Statistics emphasize the immense size of such organizations:

- in 1995, the giant Japanese company, Mitsubishi, generated sales of $184 billion, which is more than half the size of Russia's GDP;
- in the same year, the sales of the Ford Motor Company exceeded $130 billion, putting it ahead of the GDP of such countries as South Africa, Portugal and Saudi Arabia.

Certainly, such organizations require access to a global communication system in order to transmit important pieces of management information and to meet their managers' communication needs for exchanging information, giving orders, requesting advice, and asking for information.

This aspect of communication *between managers*, either from the same company or from different companies, has also been the subject of a communications revolution. One of the most time-consuming aspects of a manager's role is the time spent arranging and attending meetings. This can sometimes involve travelling time, and an expense account, along with the time of secretaries, assistants and the administrators who provide the back-up support. In many instances, meetings also result in the manager being away from the office, which may lead to crucial decisions having to be delayed until their return. In other words *meetings cost money*.

The purpose of *teleconferencing* is to allow discussions or meetings to take place between individuals who are separated geographically, using computer terminals. The same principle applies to the telephone network: many telephone companies are now able to offer a service which links together a group of people who can talk to each other simultaneously. One of the main telecommunication companies in the UK, British Telecommunications plc, for example, offers a service known as Conference Call. In its publicity material the company is able to state:

'Meetings may be essential, but even a quick project update can take half a day for the people who attend. *Conference Call* lets you talk to three or more people in different locations, without leaving your desk. So if a face-to-face meeting isn't absolutely necessary, you can avoid a journey. With the time you'll save, you can spend more time preparing' (*British Telecommunications plc. Conference Call leaflet No PHME 31463*).

Activity

Undertake research to find the range of services offered by telecommunications companies to the business community which seek to:

- communicate management information
- improve communication systems, networks and procedures.

The impact of new technology on internal and external communications

In this final section of our study of Business Practice we shall attempt to draw some conclusions from the various themes which we have explored throughout this book as they relate to the subject of business communication. In doing so we will consider the impact of new technology in a variety of different settings:

- to and from customers
- between the functional areas
- between individuals and teams
- in multisite and international organizations.

Internal communication

The primary objective of *internal communication* is to provide all those who work within an organization with a common purpose. We have already seen that if good communication is achieved, a number of benefits can be identified for the business and their employees engaged in individual activities or operating within teams. These benefits can be broadly summarized as:

- helping to motivate employees;
- improving teamwork;
- improving morale;
- improving quality.

New technology can play a vital role in maximizing the benefits to be gained in all these areas, but the organization seeking to introduce significant changes in the way it uses such technology to improve communications and implement change, needs to proceed with caution. Any radical change in an organization is likely to cause a degree of uncertainty, controversy and concern amongst its staff. Rationalization, restructuring and reorganization are all useful management strategies which can serve to increase the efficiency and effectiveness of business performance. If such policies are combined with the introduction of new technology and computerization, then the business needs to analyse very carefully how it will manage the situation.

The starting point for those involved in managing the change is to identify clearly the reasons for any concerns which individuals and staff teams may have regarding the impact of new technology. In most business organizations such concerns centre upon:

- fear of job losses
- lack of skills
- existing skills becoming redundant
- access to the new system
- increase in stress levels
- insecurity
- fear of the unknown
- fear of loss of status
- lower staff morale.

The successful management of change in an organization – in our case, change related to the impact of the introduction of information technology and computerization – needs to address all these issues, and the only way this can be done is by *involving people who will be affected by the changes*. In other words, improving communications by the introduction of new technology is best undertaken with reference to the principles of good communication:

Communication in business

- involve people;
- keep staff informed;
- engage in dialogue with staff through two-way communication;
- clearly communicate the need for any changes;
- use existing skills;
- organize relevant team meetings and individual interviews as appropriate;
- be prepared to listen and incorporate new ideas and suggestions to meet overall business objectives;
- information presented to staff should be clear, concise and not open to interpretation.

Table 16.2 summarizes the impact and organizational benefits of introducing a computer network incorporating a management information system based upon the intranet. The table would provide a useful starting point for the business which was seeking to introduce such a system since those managers who are charged with the responsibility of managing the change could use it as a checklist when communicating with staff.

Activity

With reference to Table 16.2, identify 3 other ways in which the introduction of the new computer network might impact upon the functional areas, teams and individuals.

Identify how the introduction of the new computer network might impact upon other aspects of business practice:

- quality control
- motivation of staff
- shareholders
- corporate image
- corporate identity.

One of the most common methods of communication which is used by an organization seeking to implement change is the publication of a business report which acts, in effect, as a *position statement*. Although the house-style of reports may be different between different organizations, the basic principles of report writing can be summarized as follows:

- follow a timetable which involves *planning*, *designing*, *drafting*, and *revising* the report;
- keep the report as short as possible;
- highlight action points;
- identify timescales and responsibilities as appropriate;

Information technology

- keep the reader interested;
- make recommendations which are logically consistent with the main findings in the report.

Table 16.2 The impact and benefits of a new computer network

	Impact	Organizational benefits
Between the functional areas	• improved coordination • shared information • integrated management reports • integrated decision-making	• improved management information • improved planning • monitoring business plans • improved efficiency and effectiveness • speed, accuracy and reliability of the information are improved
Between individuals and teams	• working conditions and practices • monitoring performance of individuals and their contributions to the team • improved access to communications • better able to monitor individual and team targets	• improved access to information • quality of communication improves • impact on corporate image and identity • staff skills improve

> **Activity**
>
> Write a report on behalf of SLK Associates, a business engaged in the design and manufacture of designer clothes, outlining the impact and benefits of introducing a computerized management information system into the business.

External communication

We described in the previous section how the development of multinational corporations within the global market has led to the development of an international communications network which combines the benefits of telecommunications with computer technology. Although the application of this technology has been in existence for some time, it has only been during the last few years that the implications and uses of *Internet* are starting to be understood. So far in our analysis of business communications, we have identified the Internet as an increasingly important aspect of global communication. However, we also need to understand the impact of this system on external communication, particularly with regard to communication with *customers*.

One of the prime objectives of external communication is to *improve customer service*, in order to:

- provide customers with prompt and efficient feedback on their enquiries;
- provide information on company products;
- win new customers;
- establish a loyal customer base;
- improve competitive advantage;
- influence corporate image.

How can new technology, and in particular the Internet, contribute to these business goals? As increasing numbers of people have purchased home computers, so the potential for them to access Internet facilities has increased; they are, in effect, *computerized consumers*. In practice, this means they have access to a range of goods and services which are promoted in the global marketplace, over the Internet, by business organizations throughout the world. It should also be noted that, although we have highlighted the importance of multinational corporations in the global market, the fact remains that the smallest of firms which has access to the relevant technology can also join this market in order to promote itself on an international scale. The effect of such developments, referred to as *e-commerce*, is to:

- increase competition;
- increase the number of consumers;
- increase the range and variety of goods;
- change the way in which consumers seek to purchase and pay for the goods;
- increase the amount of information which is available to consumers which can be used to influence their spending decisions;
- lead to significant price reductions

The range of applications which can be accessed by the Internet is increasing at a dramatic rate. Examples include booking hotels, car rentals and flights, as well as supermarket shopping by computer, with delivery to the home. More importantly, the Internet now incorporates *electronic auction sites,* which are designed to provide the consumer with information on the best available prices for a whole range of products ranging from air tickets to books and clothes. It has been calculated that, based on current trends, by the year 2000 some $200 billion worth of business will be generated from the Internet. The message for business organizations is therefore quite clear:

- they must find creative ways of operating within the global marketplace in order to ensure their long-term survival;
- the necessary changes are likely to result in different organizational structures;
- different ways of working and different employment patterns are likely to emerge;
- organizations will need to find more creative ways of establishing their corporate identity;
- traditional ways of shopping and consumer behaviour patterns are likely to change;
- customer loyalty will be more difficult to establish and maintain.

In essence, over the next decade, the business environment is likely to see enormous changes, and successful business organizations will be those which have the foresight and creative energy to plan, develop and manage change. Such business organizations will need to employ individuals who have a range of skills and the ability to understand and appreciate the changing nature of the business environment.

A study of Business Practice, and an appreciation of the main themes which have been developed in this book, will provide a sound basis for helping those affected to cope with the changes they are likely to experience in their working lives. More importantly, it will enable them to understand more fully the contribution which they can make to the overall success of their organization in a rapidly changing business environment.

There now follow some quick questions and revision exercises. They relate specifically to the chapter you have just studied. You are advised to attempt the questions without reference to the text, and then compare your answers and solutions with those on pages 307–9.

Communication in business

QUESTIONS

1. Describe the main features of a **word-processing** package.
2. Describe the main features of a **spreadsheet** package.
3. Describe the main features of a **database** package.
4. Explain the term **integrated computer software.**
5. List **6** advantages of a computer network to the business organization.
6. What is a **LAN**?
7. What is a **WAN**?
8. What is an **intranet**?
9. List **4** advantages of an intranet.
10. What is the **Internet**?
11. What is meant by the term **global communication**?
12. Describe the main features of an **e-mail system.**
13. What is **teleconferencing**?
14. List **6** areas of concern which may be identified in a period of organizational change.
15. List **6** ways these areas of concern can be reduced.
16. Summarize the basic principles of writing a report.

EXERCISES

1. Describe the impact and benefits of a new computer network on the relations between the functional areas and between individuals and teams.
2. Outline the benefits to the organization of effective internal and external communication.
3. 'Developments in information technology have a direct impact on business communications.' Discuss this statement with reference to an organization with which you are familiar.

While attempting to answer the questions and exercises on this page, you are strongly advised not to read on and to cover the answers on the following page with a sheet of paper.

ANSWERS TO QUESTIONS

1. Allows the production of high-quality business documents through such features as editing, document templates, thesaurus, spell checks and document saving and retrieval facilities.

2. Stores large amounts of numerical data and is able to perform complex calculations. Such packages allow for the presentation of data in a variety of formats including graphical representations. Spreadsheet packages can also be used as 'modelling tools' for business planning purposes.

3. Consists of a collection of files stored in such a way to allow information to be retrieved and manipulated in a variety of formats.

4. A computer software package which allows different functions to be used simultaneously.

5.
   - Greater efficiency
   - Less paperwork
   - Improved quality of management information
   - Monitoring of budgets
   - Monitoring of targets and overall business performance
   - Greater control of business activities.

6. Local Area Network – enables computers to be linked together within an organization in order to share and communicate information.

7. Wide Area Network – enables computers from different organizations to be linked together in order to expand the communication network.

8. A local area network which links computers together in such a way as to allow information to be communicated and accessed by a number of users. Such information can be regularly updated, thus assisting management information requirements. The system will also allow the introduction of e-mail facilities within the organization.

9.
   - Improved communication
   - Access to management information is improved
   - Management information can be updated on a regular basis
   - Saves time.

10. A global communication network based upon computer technology which allows information to be accessed and transmitted across the globe instantaneously, using a computer terminal.

11. A communication system within which computers in different countries are linked together using the Internet and satellite technology.

12. A computer application based on a computer network system which allows the user to send and receive messages and information from other computer terminals within the computer network.

13. Allows discussions or meetings to take place between individuals who are separated geographically, using a number of computer terminals, telephones and

television monitors.

14
- Fear of job losses
- Fear of loss of status
- Insecurity
- Low staff morale
- Skill shortages
- Increase in stress levels.

15
- Involve staff
- Keep staff informed
- Present information in a clear and concise format
- Clearly communicate the need for change
- Organize team meetings
- Be flexible.

16
- Keep the report as short as possible.
- Highlight action points.
- Identify timescales and responsibilities.
- Make recommendations which are logically consistent.

SOLUTIONS TO EXERCISES

1 A business organization must ensure that communication links and information flows between the main functional areas are of a high quality if it is to maximize its business performance. A new computer network will allow both managers and staff in different functional areas to communicate with each other more efficiently and effectively, thus reducing the necessity for paperwork and time-consuming meetings. At the same time, managers can have access to up-to-date management information which will improve the quality of the decision-making process within the business. More importantly, this information will be updated automatically as a result of the business activities in which the business is engaged – orders from customers can be immediately processed and stock figures automatically adjusted along with the relevant financial records. The result is that communication and information flows become more accurate and up-to-date, ensuring that decisions made by management are relevant and effective.

2 Effective internal communication can lead to a number of benefits for the business organization including better access to management information, more effective decision-making, improvements in staff morale, higher productivity, the achievement of targets, better quality products and a higher level of customer service. All these factors will serve to enhance the image of the company amongst its key stakeholders.

External communication is also of vital importance and will be primarily based on the need to improve customer service and expand the market for the company's products and services. Effective external communication should be based upon winning new customers by providing them with information on company products and with prompt and efficient feedback on their enquiries. In this respect, it is important for the business to understand the importance of those retail outlets in which the company's products may be sold, since establishing an efficient distribution network will ensure that the company's products are readily available to the consumer.

3 Most business organizations have come to appreciate that developments in information technology will have a direct influence and impact on their business activities. In general terms there are likely to be common factors which will influence all business organizations with regard to developments in information technology. These can be summarized as:

- communication systems
- computer networks
- computing equipment
- staff training and development
- consumer requirements and expectations
- management information requirements
- administration functions and requirements
- global communications
- new production techniques.

POINTS TO REMEMBER

- Word processing, spreadsheets, databases and graphics packages are all examples of applications of new technology which concern the use of computers in organizations.
- All these applications are able to manipulate large amounts of data which can be processed to produce management information.
- Computer applications are of prime importance to the functional areas since they are required to store, access, manipulate, retrieve and process large amounts of data.
- Computer applications can be integrated in such a way as to incorporate automatic changes and updates over a range of business activities and operations.
- An integrated computer network can provide the basis of a computerized management information system designed to produce reliable, accurate and up-to-date information which contributes to effective decision-making.
- Linking together a computer system via a local area network enables management information to be accessed via an intranet system.
- On a global scale, the Internet allows individual companies to communicate with each other via a global communications network based upon computer technology.
- New technology can have a positive impact on the quality of business communications although some of those directly involved with the introduction of new technology may view the process with concern.
- There is a need to involve the people who will be affected by any major changes in the organization and to communicate clearly with them.

Appendix 1: Examination Questions and Model Answers

INTRODUCTION

This section contains a selection of examination questions and a series of model answers which are drawn from the LCCIEB Business Practice Third Level examination.

Students of this examination are required to attempt 4 questions from a choice of 6. All questions carry equal marks and will relate to a particular theme drawn from the 6 sections of the LCCIEB Third Level syllabus.

The questions will be based upon a short scenario or case study followed by a specific task or a series of related tasks.

Responses to the questions will usually be required in the form of :

- bullet points
- short notes
- factsheets
- diagrams or charts
- essay style
- short reports
- briefing notes.

Appendix 1: Examination Questions

QUESTION 1

You have been asked to write a report on the benefits of establishing an integrated computer system for a small clothes manufacturer.

Task: Draft a set of bullet points which could form the basis of your report. The points should cover the following areas:

1. 5 significant benefits of installing a computer

    (10 marks)

2. 5 areas where costs will be incurred in installing and operating such a system

    (5 marks)

3. your own recommendations on how the company might wish to proceed in the form of a set of action points.

    (10 marks)
    (Total 25 marks)

MODEL ANSWER TO QUESTION 1

1   Benefits of installing a computer

There are a number of benefits which would assist the clothes manufacturer in providing a more efficient and effective way of organizing its operations:

1.1   use of stock-control computer packages would help in stocktaking and stock evaluation.

1.2   personnel records and payroll systems could be computerized.

1.3   helping the company to monitor cash flow and produce a range of financial reports, which will help the company to monitor its performance and set targets for business growth and development (via spreadsheets).

1.4   installation of a computer system would have a positive impact on the company's image with its customers. There is an increasing expectation of customers that business will use new technology.

1.5   database could be established for client records; useful to have this information to mailshot clients on news of new products, services or special offers.

2   Costs of installing such a computer

The company must take into account the full range of costs including:

2.1   hardware

2.2   software

2.3   staff training

2.4 additional insurance costs

2.5 depreciation costs.

3 Recommendations

In drawing up the action plan, the clothes manufacturer should be made aware of the basic factors involved when making significant purchasing decisions. In this instance, due regard should be given to the following points:

- *fitness for purpose* – the computer should bring positive benefits to the company;
- *value for money* – these benefits must be seen in the context of saving time and money;
- *costs* – decisions need to be made regarding the available budget.

It follows from these points that an action plan/checklist can be drawn up:

- decide on budget available;
- undertake a needs analysis;
- draw up a schedule of what the company requires;
- conduct research on available systems (own research or engage a specialist consultant);
- visit other clothes manufacturers who have installed a computer system (useful to devise a checklist of questions to ask during the visit);
- consider purchase options (leasing, hire purchase);
- draw up detailed schedule for installation (time, date, level of disruption to services, staff training);
- install the system;
- begin operations;
- monitor the benefits and check against the needs analysis – are the benefits making a positive impact on the company's operations?

Appendix 1: Examination Questions

QUESTION 2

One of your clients, Select Personnel, wants to set up its own marketing department.

Task: You are asked to prepare a report for the managing directors of Select Personnel outlining the following:

1. 5 main benefits to the business organization of successful marketing

    (10 marks)

2. how the marketing department would work with 3 other departments in the development of a new product.

    (15 marks)
    (Total 25 marks)

MODEL ANSWER TO QUESTION 2

Report prepared for the managing directors of Select Personnel

Brief: To report on the benefits of establishing a marketing department.

1. **Introduction – the benefits to the business of successful marketing**

    1.1 There are a number of important benefits which are gained as a result of successful marketing. In the first instance, however, it is as well to point out the 2 main aspects of marketing which are concerned with the **marketing mix** and the **product life cycle**.

    1.2 The marketing mix – the business needs to understand that marketing is concerned with a management decision-making process related to 4 essential elements: **price, product, promotion and place**. Successful marketing will therefore involve making decisions on all aspects of a product and not simply one component such as price.

    1.3 The product life cycle – each product is likely to have a 'life cycle' involving its **introduction** to the market, the **growth** in sales, its position in the market when it has gained recognition and **maturity** and finally the **decline** phase when sales begin to fall. Marketing helps the business to analyse where a product is placed on its own 'product life cycle' thus ensuring **effective decision-making** regarding its price and related promotional activities.

    1.4 From this provisional analysis we can see that successful marketing is **an aid to management decision-making**.

    1.5 A successful marketing department will bring a number of other benefits to the business organization:

1.5.1 it enables the organization to predict future demand of products within the market

1.5.2 it enhances the company's image with consumers

1.5.3 it assists in the development of business planning and strategic planning

1.5.4 successful marketing can lead to increased business performance, growth, new products and new business opportunities.

2 The marketing department and new product development

2.1 In this section of the report we shall see how the activities of the marketing department have a direct impact on other functional areas within the organization. This will involve considering in the first instance the activities with which the marketing department will be involved in the development of a new product.

2.1.1 Marketing of a new product – activities

- market research
- market demand (analysis of results)
- analyse impact of various pricing strategies
- decide on relevant sales and promotional activities
- implement pilot-testing in specific areas of the market.

2.2 As a result of these activities, the marketing department will have a direct impact on management activities, decisions and information within the other departments.

2.2.1 Finance and accounts

- will engage in costing and pricing analysis based upon the market research information provided by the marketing department;
- will also attempt to ascertain likely profit levels and engage in **break-even analysis**;
- will prepare financial reports to senior management team on the financial impact of the new product development;
- will monitor the marketing budget against budget profile.

2.2.2 Administration

- will need to establish effective communication system between the various departments to ensure that management information is presented in an appropriate format and within agreed timescales;
- will ensure that systems and procedures are established for diary bookings, committee meetings, preparation of agendas and distribution of minutes.

2.2.3 Personnel

- will need to be kept informed of new product development if it will result in additional staff being required;
- may have to engage in manpower planning exercise to ascertain the longer-term human resource needs of the organization;
- will require information on any new skills which may be required by the existing workforce.

3 Conclusion

3.1 All successful business organizations engage in marketing activities.

3.2 A marketing department is a specialist unit employing the skills necessary to coordinate the marketing function.

3.3 Successful marketing has a direct impact on business performance.

3.4 The development of a marketing department will impact on all the other functional areas within the business.

QUESTION 3

A major client is seeking to obtain a prestigious International Certificate of Quality and wishes to use the services of your company to help identify the standards required to gain the certificate.

Task: Devise a set of notes which show the contribution that 3 of the following make to improving the quality of the organization's services:

1. target-setting
2. customer service
3. training and development
4. service standards.

(25 marks)

1 Target-setting

1.1 Target-setting enables the business to quantify and measure improvements in quality.

1.2 Target-setting can be used to reward success if targets are met.

1.3 Target-setting can be used in staff appraisal schemes to monitor the individual's contribution to specific areas of quality within the job role.

1.4 Target-setting enables the business to concentrate on particular aspects of quality which may be causing concern.

1.5 Target-setting can be used in the context of continuous quality improvements; targets should be continuously monitored and sufficiently challenging to make a real difference to improving quality.

2 Customer service

2.1 Customer service includes the whole range of services provided to customers and clients which promote loyalty and enhance the reputation of the organization.

2.2 Customer service can include such elements as advice and guidance on products and the level of after-sales service provided to the customer.

2.3 Improvements in customer service are usually centred upon the perceptions/views of the customers/clients; for example, analysis of completed questionnaires following the purchase of a product or service.

2.4 Improvements in the quality of customer service can lead to direct benefits to the organization in the form of:
- improved sales
- repeat business
- enhanced reputation
- increased market share
- increased profitability.

3 Training and development

3.1 Successful business organizations recognize the importance played by training and development in improving the quality of their business activities.

3.2 Training and development activities can target specific issues relating to quality, eg customer service, telephone training, skill development.

3.3 Staff training activities can have a positive impact on morale, performance and labour retention – all factors which are known to have a direct relationship with quality of services and products.

3.4 Specialized training/briefing sessions can be arranged in order for managers to inform staff of the importance of quality within the company's strategic plan and overall aims and objectives.

3.5 Training in specific job-related skills may result in a reduction in the number of defective products being produced. This has 2 main benefits:

    3.5.1 costs are reduced as less time and resources are required to rectify mistakes;

    3.5.2 reputation of the company improves as the quality of its products improves.

4 Service standards

4.1 Service standards are measures/standards of quality published by operating units, teams and functional areas within the business organization.

4.2 The main aim of service standards is to acknowledge a public commitment to the importance of quality.

4.3 Service standards promote a quality culture within the organization since they acknowledge the fact that a quality service is required by both **external** and **internal** clients.

Appendix I: Examination Questions

    4.4 Service standards promote a team culture and highlight the importance of teamwork in the achievement of quality targets.

    4.5 The introduction of in-house service standards as 'performance indicators' can be assessed and tested by the use of questionnaires completed by other staff/teams within the organization. The results can be published to show the actual performance against the service standards.

QUESTION 4

Athena House is to produce a series of factsheets called 'Services to Business'. The factsheets will cover the services offered by a range of organizations which can provide help and advice to the business community.

Task: Prepare a factsheet which describes how commercial banks and insurance companies can assist the business organization. State the range of services they provide and the benefits to the business organization.

(25 marks)

MODEL ANSWER TO QUESTION 4

Commercial banks

1. **What are the commercial banks?**

    Commercial banks are the high street banks found in most towns and cities. They are used by both private individuals and business organizations and offer a wide range of financial services.

2. **What financial services do the commercial banks provide?**

    Commercial banks exist to provide a wide range of financial services relating to:

    – payments

    – deposits

    – loans

    – advice

    – specialized services.

3. **Some examples of the services provided by the commercial banks**

    3.1 *Payment services* – these services include cheques, credit cards, standing orders and direct debits.

    3.2 *Deposit services* – these services cover such features as current accounts, deposit accounts and specialized savings accounts.

3.3 *Loans* – the 2 main types of loans offered by the commercial banks are bank loans (fixed-term loans with a set rate of interest) and bank overdrafts (short-term loans on current accounts with a variable interest rate).

3.4 *Advice* – commercial banks provide advice to their customers (individuals, small businesses and corporate clients) on a range of financial matters – pensions; savings; investments; long-term financial planning; insurance.

3.5 *Specialized services* – commercial banks promote their own 'financial products' such as investment schemes, savings plans and insurance.

Insurance companies

1 **What are the insurance companies?**

Insurance companies are specialist financial service organizations which are involved in risk management, risk assessment and risk transfer.

2 **What financial services do insurance companies provide?**

2.1 Insurance companies offer a wide range of insurance policies which are purchased by private individuals and business organizations.

2.2 In addition, insurance companies provide advice to their customers on the ways in which they may seek to reduce levels of risk. For example, they might advise their business clients on matters relating to security of stock and fire hazards.

2.3 Insurance companies also issue policies which seek to promote financial security. Such policies may include pensions, life assurance and health insurances. These can be used by the business to offer 'fringe benefits' to their employees which may reduce labour turnover and attract high quality staff.

3 **Some examples of the services provided by the insurance companies**

3.1 *Compensation policies* – these policies involve paying a sum of money (the insurance premium) to the insurance company in order for personal/business risks to be transferred to them; examples of such policies include motor insurance, property insurances.

3.2 *Benefit policies* – these policies result in the policyholder receiving some form of financial benefit usually as a result of long-term savings and investments; examples include pensions and endowment policies.

3.3 *Protection policies* – these policies are usually related to life insurance policies which pay out a sum of money in the event of the policyholder's death.

3.4 *Liability policies* – these protect the policyholder in the event that their actions cause injury or damage to a third party; examples include public liability, employer liability, product liability.

4 **What are the benefits to the business organization of these financial institutions?**

4.1 *Sources of finance* – as institutional investors, the insurance companies purchase shares in public limited companies; commercial banks provide loans and overdrafts to finance new business developments.

4.2 *Sources of advice* – insurance companies can provide assistance and advice to the business on matters relating to risk control, including how to minimize losses associated with such risks as fire and burglary; commercial banks provide advice to small firms on matters relating to finance, cash flow, marketing and the design and production of business plans, which will enable the business to put forward a well-argued case for a business loan.

4.3 *New businesses* – the existence of insurance is of direct benefit to new firms, since their owners are willing to engage in business risks on the basis that a number of the insurable risks can be transferred to the insurance companies; the lending operations of the commercial banks encourage the growth of new businesses.

4.4 *Business activity* – business activity is based upon the production of goods and services in response to changes in the level of market demand. Insurance companies and banks offer a range of services which can directly affect the level of demand in the economy and with it the level of business activity undertaken by business organizations.

QUESTION 5

'Enterprise 2000', an organization which seeks to promote the development of small firms, has given a grant to Athena House to participate in a publicity campaign aimed at those people who are seeking help in starting up their own business.

Athena House has decided to use the grant to produce a factsheet on 'Business Finance'.

Task: Produce a set of notes which highlights the following points:

1 the importance of budgeting and the reasons for keeping financial records
(10 marks)

2 the main financial records kept by the business organization and the information contained within them.
(15 marks)
(Total 25 marks)

MODEL ANSWER TO QUESTION 5

1 **The importance of budgeting and the reasons for keeping financial records**

   1.1 **Budgeting**

   1.1.1 Budgeting is an important business function since it is part of business planning.

   1.1.2 Budgeting enables businesses to set financial targets and monitor business activity.

   1.1.3 Budgeting provides managers with important management information which they can use to control resources and inform resource-allocation decisions within the business.

   1.1.4 An effective budgeting process can promote efficiency savings thereby saving money which can be used for other expenditure plans.

   1.1.5 Budgeting is an aid to decision-making since managers can appraise alternative courses of action.

   1.2 **Reasons for keeping financial records**

   1.2.1 Business performance can only be monitored from accurate records.

   1.2.2 Financial records allow the company to set and monitor targets and highlight any issues of concern regarding profit levels, creditors and debtors.

   1.2.3 Financial records allow the business to monitor its internal activities. Each department/functional area will be allocated a budget, and records need to be kept to ensure that budget holders do not overspend.

   1.2.4 In large organizations, financial records are a source of information for existing shareholders and potential investors.

   1.2.5 In small organizations, financial records are important reference documents which can be presented to banks when applying for business loans.

2 **Financial records kept by the business organization**

   2.1 There are a number of financial records produced by the business organization.

   The main ones are listed below:
   - balance sheet
   - trading account
   - profit and loss account
   - ledgers
   - cash flow forecasts.

2.1.1 *Balance sheet* – records what a business owns and what it owes at one point in time; will contain information relating to its assets and liabilities; also contains information relating to the owner's capital (for sole traders) and shareholders' funds (for PLCs).

2.1.2 *Trading account* – provides information of the gross profit (or loss) made by the business as a result of its trading activities; this information is arrived at by calculating the sales revenue and then subtracting the cost of those sales.

2.1.3 *Profit and loss account* – this is an extension of the trading account and identifies other income earned by the business along with other expenses that it has paid out including its tax liabilities; in addition it shows how the resulting net profits are distributed and/or retained.

2.1.4 *Ledgers* – these financial records assist in the compilation of both the profit and loss account and the balance sheet; they are specialized financial records which record sales, purchases and cash transactions.

2.1.5 *Cash-flow forecasts* – these are not 'official' financial records but are forecasts used as an aid to management decision-making; cash-flow forecasts identify the likely income and expenditure commitments of the company over a set period of time; a useful indicator of potential difficulties which the company may face over the period of the business plan.

QUESTION 6

'The Workplace of the Future' is the theme of a government-sponsored conference which will be held at the local university's business school. You will be joining a team of staff from Athena House who will be presenting a series of seminars on business communication.

Task: Produce a set of notes which will be used in one of the seminars to identify how business communications are influenced by new technology. The notes should highlight the following areas:

1 how management information can be used by managers to monitor business performance

(10 marks)

2 how new technology can improve the management information provided by any 3 of the main functional areas.

(15 marks)
(Total 25 marks)

Appendix 1: Examination Questions

MODEL ANSWER TO QUESTION 6

1 Management information and monitoring business performance

1.1 Management information includes a range of information which allows managers to make decisions, set targets and monitor trends in business activity.

1.2 Business organizations need access to management information not only to make decisions but also to monitor business performance against targets established within the strategic plan.

1.3 Management information is usually derived from a series of data which arise from business activity. As such, buying, selling, planning and organizing will result in changes in costs, outputs, revenue and profits. This data needs to be processed, ie put in some meaningful form in order to produce **information**.

1.4 Examples of management information include:
   - trends in sales over time
   - management accounts
   - market research (including market segmentation, analysis of the level of competition)
   - the results of break-even analysis.

1.5 Monitoring business performance is important since it allows managers to ascertain if there are any potential difficulties or issues which they need to take into account.

1.6 The monitoring function is an important management activity linked to the planning process. Part of this process will involve establishing targets and determining the levels of responsibility of managers in monitoring the targets.

1.7 Management information and the monitoring of business performance are likely to result in liaison and consultation between the functional areas within the business. For this reason it is important that internal communications are of a high standard and that management information is up to date, relevant and accurate.

2 Information technology and management information

2.1 Information technology and its applications have greatly improved the quality of management information which can be made available and accessed by managers.

2.2 The use of computers and associated software packages, such as spreadsheets, databases and word processing packages, allow for data to be manipulated and integrated in order to produce management reports which are up to date and accurate.

2.3 Other applications of information technology allow managers themselves to access information 'on-line'. Computer networks can download information through a company's own intranet system, and e-mail facilities allow managers to communicate with each other in an efficient and effective manner.

2.4 Information technology is relevant to all functional areas in terms of planning, monitoring and controlling the quality of management information generated by business activity:

2.4.1 *finance* – engaged in budgetary control and planning: accurate records produce relevant management information in the form of **management accounts.**

2.4.2 *sales and marketing* – engaged in research and promotional activities: need to record data and analyse results of market research; computer packages can be used to predict likely sales and profit levels; database of customers can be used to promote sales activities.

2.4.3 *personnel* – management decision-making concerns devising a human resource plan and an associated strategy for its implementation: use of information technology can predict and analyse changes in staffing levels based on age, gender, labour retention.

2.4.4 *administration* – an important role in establishing effective and efficient communication systems within the organizations; responsible for ensuring that records and reports are issued in appropriate house-style; can advise managers on appropriate IT systems to improve communications (eg e-mail) and take a leading role in identifying relevant skills required by managers to access management information.

QUESTION 7

You receive a letter from a college inviting you to give a talk to a group of students who are about to start work experience placements in local businesses. The theme of your talk will be 'Influences on Business'.

Task: Write a set of notes entitled 'Influences on Business' using 3 of the following headings:

1. the role of the consumer
2. the role of the government
3. the international marketplace
4. the importance of new technology
5. shareholders.

(25 marks)

MODEL ANSWER TO QUESTION 7

Influences on business

1. **The role of the consumer**

    1.1 The consumer has a direct influence on the business organization through spending patterns in a competitive market.

    1.2 In a competitive market there are a number of buyers and sellers. The sellers (business organizations) compete against each other to sell their goods to the consumer. Consumers demand goods, ie. they purchase goods and services from the business organizations.

    1.3 In a competitive market, the consumer will be attracted by lower prices. Equally the demand for particular products can be influenced by advertising which seeks to change consumer preferences and tastes for certain products.

    1.4 Consumer demand can also be influenced by market segmentation in that certain sections of the market can be targeted by the business organization – in effect, the market can be divided up on the basis of age, gender, amount of disposable income.

    1.5 There will be a direct relationship between the level of consumer demand and sales revenue. Sales revenue can assist cash flow and have an impact on profit levels.

    1.6 Consumers are also influenced by non-price factors such as the level of customer service, quality and how far they can identify with the corporate image projected by the business organization.

    1.7 The successful business organization will therefore develop business strategies which seek to:

    1.7.1 monitor price levels;

    1.7.2 improve customer service;

    1.7.3 strive to improve quality;

    1.7.4 promote a positive corporate image.

2. **The role of government**

    2.1 Most governments will incorporate a range of policy aims and objectives which are likely to include:

    2.1.1 the control of inflation

    2.1.2 the promotion of economic growth

    2.1.3 the promotion of international trade

    2.1.4 creating conditions in which employment opportunities can be generated.

Appendix I: Examination Questions

2.2 Government policies will be introduced which seek to achieve these economic aims and objectives. These policies can be broadly classified as:

    2.2.1 *fiscal policies* – concerned with changes in taxation and government expenditure.

    2.2.2 *monetary policies* – concerned with changes in the rate of interest and its impact on the money supply.

2.3 Both fiscal and monetary policies can have a direct influence on business organizations:

    2.3.1 fiscal policies will involve the government establishing spending priorities – on health, housing, education, infrastructure;

    2.3.2 monetary policies, which incorporate changes in rates of interest, will influence the level of business investment and the volume of consumer expenditure.

2.4 In some instances government policies will concentrate on specific aspects such as:

    2.4.1 training schemes

    2.4.2 imposition of tariffs (taxes) and quotas (physical limits) on imports

    2.4.3 establishment of a minimum wage and associated conditions of service.

3 The international marketplace

3.1 The international marketplace contains buyers and sellers located in countries throughout the world. This so-called global market exerts an influence on business organizations in the way they operate and are organized.

3.2 The international marketplace contains millions of consumers who provide the business organization with the opportunity to produce more goods and services. This increase in output can lead to opportunities for the business to benefit from internal economies of scale, leading to lower unit costs of production.

3.3 The international market also increases competition; the existence of large numbers of consumers exerts a downward influence on the general level of prices.

3.4 The international marketplace encourages international specialization whereby countries concentrate on the production of certain goods and services and then exchange them with their trading partners.

3.5 International trade can be distinguished from domestic trade on the basis of:

    3.5.1 customs

    3.5.2 language

    3.5.3 size of market

    3.5.4 currencies.

3.6 Many countries have sought to maximize the advantages inherent in the international marketplace by establishing trading blocs or free-trade areas. Examples include the European Union and ASEAN. Such organizations seek to maximize the benefits of international trade for the constituent member states.

3.7 The international marketplace has resulted in the establishment of multinational corporations (MNCs) who have subsidiaries located in countries throughout the world.

4 Influence of new technology

4.1 The influence of new technology on the business environment can be classified in 3 main areas:

    4.1.1 the importance of new technology to the functional areas

    4.1.2 the influence of new technology on the development of communication systems

    4.1.3 the role of new technology in generating management information.

4.2 In the context of the business environment, new technology is seen to exert an influence in terms of a number of software applications including:

    4.2.1 word-processing

    4.2.2 spreadsheets

    4.2.3 database

    4.2.4 graphics.

4.3 The main characteristic of all these packages is the amount of data which can be:

    4.3.1 stored

    4.3.2 accessed

    4.3.3 manipulated

    4.3.4 retrieved

    4.3.5 processed.

4.4 With regard to the functional areas, there are a number of advantages which can be identified as a result of the introduction of new technology/software applications:

    4.4.1 *finance and accounts* – lends itself to computerization given the need to produce up-to-date and accurate management accounts and financial records;

    4.4.2 *personnel* – needs access to up-to-date personnel records; payroll systems;

    4.4.3 *research and development* – can introduce automated production lines and robotics;

    4.4.4 *marketing* – can analyse the results of market research.

4.5 Communication systems can also be developed incorporating new technology. Such systems can include:

- 4.5.1 computer networks established within the firm (local area networks) or across a geographical area (wide area networks);
- 4.5.2 global communication networks can be accessed over the Internet;
- 4.5.3 teleconferencing allows discussions or meetings to take place between individuals who are separated geographically, using a number of terminals;
- 4.5.4 communications between the functional areas can also be improved by the introduction of a computer network which incorporates e-mail facilities, which reduces the need for paperwork and provides access to immediate information flows.

4.6 The successful business organization will need to have access to high-quality management information if it is to be able to engage in effective decision-making activities. New technology allows the business to develop a Management Information System (MIS). Such a system processes raw data in order to produce information which can assist those managers who are engaged in the decision-making process. As a management tool, an MIS system based upon new technology can be used by the business to:

- 4.6.1 plan its activities;
- 4.6.2 monitor its targets;
- 4.6.3 evaluate its performance;
- 4.6.4 inform decisions regarding its future development;
- 4.6.5 coordinate the main business functions.

5 Influences of shareholders

5.1 Limited companies are owned by shareholders who enjoy limited liability. This is a legal concept which protects the personal possessions of shareholders in the event of business failure. In such cases the shareholders will lose only the amount they have invested in the business.

5.2 Shareholders purchase shares for a number of reasons:

- 5.2.1 to receive a share of company profits;
- 5.2.2 in the hope that the value of their shares will increase over time;
- 5.2.3 to influence company policy.

5.3 Company policy may be influenced by those shareholders who have voting rights (the ordinary shareholders). The shareholders elect the board of directors who, in turn, are responsible for the long-term development of the company and the associated business policies and strategies.

5.4 Shareholders can form themselves into unofficial 'shareholder interest groups'. Such groups may seek to influence company policy on a range of issues such as:

5.4.1 pay and remuneration of senior directors

5.4.2 environmental policies

5.4.2 the trading activities of the company.

5.5 The most influential shareholders are the institutional investors, since they are likely to own the largest proportion of the ordinary shares. Examples of such shareholders include banks, insurance companies and pension funds.

5.6 Shareholders can also influence the business by the pattern of their behaviour – selling the shares will result in a fall in their value, whereas an increase in demand for shares will have the opposite effect.

In any event the value of a company's shares will determine its market capitalization, ie. the overall 'worth' of the company.

QUESTION 8

One of your clients is thinking about introducing an induction programme for new staff and an appraisal scheme for existing staff.

Task: Write a set of briefing notes for the managing director of the company outlining the benefits of introducing induction and staff appraisal identifying clearly how both contribute to the process of manpower planning.

(25 marks)

MODEL ANSWER TO QUESTION 8

Briefing notes prepared for managing director

1 **Benefits of introducing an induction programme**

1.1 Staff induction is a structured staff development/training activity especially geared towards new employees.

1.2 Induction programmes will usually contain the following aspects:

1.2.1 introduction to colleagues/department/senior staff

1.2.2 overview of personnel practices and procedures

1.2.3 tour of company premises

1.2.4 overview of company products and services including the company's mission statement

1.2.5 health and safety issues

1.2.6 opportunities for staff training and development

1.2.7 introduction to the job and key tasks.

1.3 The benefits of a good induction programme can be summarized as:

    1.3.1 promotes a good image of the company;

    1.3.2 improves the motivation of staff;

    1.3.3 improves job satisfaction;

    1.3.4 part of a good communications strategy;

    1.3.5 makes staff understand the corporate identity of the organization.

2 Benefits of introducing a staff appraisal scheme

2.1 Staff appraisal is a process of reviewing an individual's performance at work.

2.2 Can be used to set individual targets, identify staff training needs, or both.

2.3 Targets can either be quantitative or qualitative; performance against these targets may be subject to grading/measurement; appraisal may also be linked to remuneration.

2.4 Staff appraisal is usually undertaken by the line manager on an annual basis with an interim review to assess progress.

2.5 The benefits of staff appraisal can be summarized as follows:

    2.5.1 can identify the strengths and weaknesses of the individual member of staff;

    2.5.2 can be used to identify training needs;

    2.5.3 can motivate staff by recognizing their achievements;

    2.5.4 can be used to monitor the efficiency and effectiveness of the organization's recruitment, selection and training policies;

    2.5.5 may lead to improvements in quality and, in turn, a positive culture for the organization.

3 Contribution of staff appraisal and induction to manpower planning

3.1 Manpower planning is the process of making sure the business has enough of the right staff to provide the required labour inputs into the production process.

3.2 Involves short, medium and long term planning in line with organizational aims and objectives.

3.3 Helps to identify future training needs.

3.4 Manpower planning may also involve reductions in staffing on the basis of:

    3.4.1 redundancies

    3.4.2 early retirements

    3.4.3 reorganization/restructuring.

3.5 Manpower planning will be undertaken by the personnel or human resources function, and both induction and staff appraisal will be 2 important aspects which inform the manpower planning strategy of the business.

QUESTION 9

Athena House, the local Chamber of Commerce and the local college have worked together to produce a quarterly journal called 'In Focus'. The subject matter for the next issue will be 'Administration Systems'.

Task: Write a factsheet which explains the importance of the administration function to the business organization. The factsheet should clearly identify:

1 the role of the administration function

(5 marks)

2 the main staff engaged in administration and how they contribute to the effectiveness of business performance

(10 marks)

3 the contribution made by the administration function to effective communications in the business organization.

(10 marks)
(Total 25 marks)

MODEL ANSWER TO QUESTION 9

1 The role of the administration function

1.1 The administration function is a management role which is concerned with planning, organizing, controlling, monitoring and implementing systems and procedures.

1.2 Such systems and procedures are necessary for the constituent parts and functions of the organization to operate efficiently.

1.3 It is important that these systems and procedures are effectively communicated to managers and their staff and checked against targets and plans.

2 The main staff engaged in the administration function

2.1 Four categories of staff can be identified within the administration function:

2.1.1 *administration managers* – may control a large department; responsible for making sure that the systems work effectively; usually a 'systems' expert concerned with the cost control of such systems and having a full overview of company operations.

2.1.2 *personal assistants to managers* – ensure that efficient and effective secretarial and administrative support is provided to individual managers; may include such services as diary schedules, arranging

Appendix 1: Examination Questions

        meetings, research activities, progress-chasing, arranging business trips and monitoring action points stemming from minutes of meetings.

   2.1.3 *supervisory staff, such as office managers* – ensure that key sections within the organization are meeting the needs of the main functional areas; may be engaged in providing specialist services such as reception, general office or post room.

   2.1.4 *clerical staff* – provide the day-to-day services for the rest of the organization; will include staff such as office juniors, filing clerks, administration officers, secretaries, data input staff and telephonists.

3 The contribution of the administration function to effective communications in the business

  3.1 All organizations need good, clear lines of communication.

  3.2 The specialist staff employed within the administration function have responsibility for establishing communication systems and are required to:

      3.2.1 identify the communication needs of the various departments;

      3.2.2 determine the most effective methods by which these needs can be met;

      3.2.3 establish systems and procedures which are known and understood by all staff within the organization;

      3.2.4 ensure that there is technical back-up and adequate supplies of consumables;

      3.2.5 establish systems which engage the users in evaluating the effectiveness of the system in meeting their needs.

  3.3 In this process, consultation with staff will be vital in order to assess their communication needs; for managers, this will involve identifying the most efficient and effective way of generating management information.

  3.4 The communication system which is produced as a result of this exercise will be based on the principles of:

      3.4.1 accessibility

      3.4.2 reliability

      3.4.3 relevance

      3.4.4 accuracy

      3.4.5 frequency.

QUESTION 10

The consultants employed by Athena House are aware that many firms do not appreciate the importance of management information. You are part of a planning team which has been given the responsibility of producing some material which will be distributed to company clients.

Appendix 1: Examination Questions

Task: 1 write an explanation of 'management information' which can be used in presentations, seminars and Athena House literature

(5 marks)

      2 identify 4 examples of management information and their importance to the business organization.

20 marks)
(Total 25 marks)

MODEL ANSWER TO QUESTION 10

1   Management information

1.1 Management information can be broadly defined as the information derived from processing raw data which can assist those managers who are engaged in the decision-making process. Management information is therefore a management tool which is used by the business to:

    1.1.1 plan its activities;

    1.1.2 monitor its targets;

    1.1.3 evaluate its performance;

    1.1.4 inform decisions regarding its future development;

    1.1.5 coordinate the main business functions.

In this respect management information is usually related to trends in business performance which can be used to inform the planning process.

2   Examples of management information and their importance to the business organization

2.1 Management accounts are usually prepared monthly and distributed to key budget holders within the organization. They are important to the business because they:

    2.1.1 identify potential overspends on cost-centre budgets;

    2.1.2 monitor actual income/expenditure levels against budget profile;

    2.1.3 identify areas which are under-performing;

    2.1.4 provide the basis for identifying any remedial action which may be required in order to overcome potential overspends.

2.2 Sales figures can also provide useful management information:

    2.2.1 analyse sales figures over time to identify trends;

    2.2.2 identify comparative sales figures of different product lines;

    2.2.3 monitor sales figures against targets;

    2.2.4 disaggregate sales figures on the basis of geographical region, different retail outlets;

    2.2.5 monitor the efficiency and effectiveness of the sales force.

2.3 Personnel data comprises a range of information relating to the organization's workforce. Management information in this area can focus upon:

2.3.1 manpower planning;

2.3.2 identifying potential difficulties in implementing future business plans;

2.3.3 identifying possible difficulties in future employment and recruitment opportunities.

2.4 Management information relating to the marketing activities of the business can identify important aspects which will inform future business planning. These will include:

2.4.1 market research

2.4.2 results of pilot testing

2.4.3 market share

2.4.4 number of competitors

2.4.5 level of disposable income

2.4.6 market segmentation

2.4.7 results of break-even analysis

2.4.8 opportunities for development, diversification and targeting.

QUESTION 11

A delegation of overseas businessmen and women are scheduled to visit your company in the near future. They are keen to gain an insight into 'corporate image' and the factors that influence corporate image.

Task: Write a set of notes which can be distributed to the visiting delegation outlining:

1 what is meant by the term 'corporate image'

(5 marks)

2 the way in which the business organization can influence its corporate image.

(20 marks)
(Total 25 marks)

MODEL ANSWER TO QUESTION 11

1 Corporate image

1.1 Corporate image is the way in which a company seeks to present itself to its own employees and the outside world.

1.2 The term is closely linked to the idea that business organizations can develop a unique business culture based upon shared beliefs, habits, patterns of behaviour and traditions developed by people within the organization.

1.3 In a competitive market, corporate image can provide the business with a competitive advantage even if its prices are higher than its competitors. In other words, corporate image is increasingly being used as a 'marketing tool' which is used to 'sell' the business rather than the product it produces.

2 How the business can influence its corporate image

2.1 The business can seek to develop its corporate image by focusing on both its internal organization, systems and procedures and by concentrating on its external relations with its shareholders, customers, clients and suppliers.

2.2 Internal factors which can influence a company's corporate image might include the following:

2.2.1 *company policies* – equal opportunities, recruitment policies, staff training opportunities, working conditions and single-status arrangements;

2.2.2 *relations with staff* – pay, consultation, profit-sharing schemes, medical facilities, social facilities and fringe benefits;

2.2.3 *relations between management and unions/staff associations* – fair and open procedures to handle grievances, bargaining and negotiating in good faith, mutual respect, participative and consultative management styles.

2.3 External factors which may influence corporate image may include:

2.3.1 *relationship with shareholders* – fair return on their investment, keeping shareholders informed, responding to shareholders' views;

2.3.2 *relationships with customers and clients* – good customer service, quality products, value for money, product safety;

2.3.3 *relationships with suppliers* – open and fair dealings, payment for goods within agreed terms, provide information about proposals and plans which might affect them;

2.3.4 *relations with local community* – respect for environmental factors, set an example as a good employer, create and maintain employment opportunities, participate in local community initiatives and charitable works;

2.3.5 *the national and international dimension* – donations to political parties, relationship with suppliers in developing countries, promotion of 'good causes', research into new products, help and assistance to low-wage countries.

Appendix 1: Examination Questions

QUESTION 12

The local newspaper is organizing a 'Business Forum' which will be based on 'Starting Your Own Business'. You have been asked to represent your company at one of the seminars about business planning.

Task: 1 devise a factsheet which identifies the purpose of a Business Plan

(10 marks)

      2 write a set of notes for the delegates describing the information contained within a business plan.

(15 marks)
(Total 25 marks)

MODEL ANSWER TO QUESTION 12

1 The purpose of a business plan

1.1 One way the business can seek to reduce the level of risk inherent in its operations is to engage in a process of business planning.

1.2 The purpose of business planning is to undertake an in-depth and systematic analysis of the goals and objectives of the business and identify the ways in which it will achieve them. In this respect, planning gives structure and direction to the business and enables the owner(s) to check and monitor progress.

1.3 The process of business planning will involve:

    1.3.1 *asking questions* – what resources are available?

    1.3.2 *making choices* – identifying potential markets.

    1.3.3 *obtaining information* – what is the level of competition?

    1.3.4 *managing resources* – how many staff does the business need to employ?

    1.3.5 *monitoring and evaluating* – monitor targets and business performance.

1.4 Successful business planning will enable the business to:

    1.4.1 seek sources of finance;

    1.4.2 obtain the finance;

    1.4.3 monitor progress;

    1.4.4 estimate costs;

    1.4.5 confirm that there is the potential for profitable business activity to be undertaken.

2 Information contained in a business plan

2.1 A useful function of the business plan is to present it to a bank or another source of finance in order to obtain financial resources in the form of a loan.

Appendix 1: Examination Questions

2.2 The main components of a business plan are as follows:

2.2.1 *background information* – name and address of the business; product or service being offered; competitive edge; legal status.

2.2.2 *business objectives* – mission statement; quality indicators; targets; timescales.

2.2.3 *market research and marketing plan* – is there a market for the product? number of consumers; distribution network; after-sales service; identifying suppliers.

2.2.4 *resource implications* – labour and raw materials; capital equipment and premises costs; production plan; production process.

2.2.5 *financial targets* – projected budgets; cash-flow forecast; estimated profits; sales and turnover.

Appendix 2: Advice for students taking LCCIEB examinations

Before the examination

1 Make sure you are familiar with the Extended Syllabus and with the format of the examination paper.

2 It is useful to read the report of the Chief Examiner which is produced following the marking of scripts submitted in each examination series. The Chief Examiner's Report will both highlight general comments on the examination paper as a whole and contain comments and advice on each of the questions in the examination paper.

3 Candidates will also find it useful to read the Model Answers which are published after each examination series.

4 An understanding of Business Practice will be enhanced if candidates are aware of current issues which impact on the business environment and business organizations. It may be useful to create a portfolio of examples which are extracted from the press and business journals. The portfolio could be divided up into the 6 sections of the Extended Syllabus and used for revision purposes when attempting past examination questions.

5 Draw up a systematic revision programme which incorporates the following:

   plan — draw up a revision timetable.

   organize — take specific themes within the course eg quality, management, functional areas, staff appraisal, and identify if you can make any connections with other aspects of your study of Business Practice.

   monitor — keep a check on your revision timetable.

   evaluate — self-assessment questions to test your knowledge.

6 You should be able to use specialist terms with confidence – examples include:

   - appraisal
   - target-setting
   - rationalization
   - functional areas
   - budgetary control
   - performance indicators
   - management accounting
   - quality assurance.

Appendix 2: Advice for students

7 The best way of approaching the use of such specialist terms is to be able to *define* them and provide a range of *appropriate examples*.

Examination technique – some useful tips

The following list is by no means exhaustive, but many candidates fail to remember some elementary rules when sitting the examination. In some instances this can lead to failure in the final examination even though the candidate may have sufficient knowledge of the subject matter to obtain a pass mark.

- Read the examination instructions before attempting to answer any questions.
- Read through the examination questions – *twice*.
- Circle those questions you feel confident about attempting. Do not worry at this stage if you can only attempt one or 2 of the questions. You will find that once you start writing the answers to these questions, your thoughts will begin to flow more freely.
- A preliminary list of main points should be drawn up for each question. This may not be a formal 'plan' of the answer but will be a useful reference.
- Do not concentrate on one or 2 words in the question – make sure you fully understand what the question is asking.
- Time should be allocated efficiently *for* each question (with reference to the allocation of marks), and *across* the examination paper as a whole. In other words do not spend half the examination answering just one question.
- Remember that diagrams and charts can enhance answers and that points can be numbered.

The examination

The examination will consist of a series of situations, scenarios or small case studies. You will be asked to display your knowledge and understanding of the subject matter along with your ability to apply this understanding to the case in point.

Responses will be required in the form of:

- bullet points
- short notes
- short reports
- briefing notes
- factsheets.

In those cases where the question demands a response in the form of a short report, you should provide a report title followed by any findings you wish to highlight in the main body of the report. The report should conclude with 2 or 3 recommendations.

Appendix 2: Advice for students

It is appropriate for the answers to be written in numbered points with the answer being divided into sections as needed. Candidates should refer to the Business Practice model answers which are provided in this book for further details of the approach they should adopt when attempting the examination paper.

Candidates are strongly advised to leave sufficient time to read through their work once they have completed the required number of tasks.

Index

absenteeism 197–8, 212
acceptance houses 69
accounting function 106, 110, 164–77; information technology 296–8, *see also* finance
activities: business finance 64–70, 75; concept 13–19; decision-making 18–19, 23, 146–8, 272–3, 276–82; definition 15, 23; entrepreneurs 15; group roles 126–42; overview 5–24; roles 126–42; SWOT/PEST analysis 149–50
administration function 106, 112, 275, 283–5, 298
administrative plans 155–6, 284–5
advertising 27, 43, 111, 114, 222–3, 226, 279–80
advice, examination 339–41
after-sales service 190, 278
AGMs *see* annual general meetings
amalgamation 47–50
annual general meetings (AGMs) 127–8
answers, examination questions 311–37, 339–41
applications 292–5, 304
appraisal schemes 107, 206–9, 215, 240, 283
Articles of Association 11, 132
assets 14, 165–6, 170–1, 177, 193, *see also* capital
Association of British Chambers of Commerce 71
Association of British Insurers 72
Association of British Travel Agents 72
auction sites 304
audits 110
autocratic management 229–30
automation 108–9, 296
average costs *see* unit costs

bad debts 62, 165
balance of payments 86–8, 89–95
balance sheets 110, 170–1
Bank of England 92–3
banks 64–70, 72, 75, 92–5; business plans 153–5; cheques 164–6; merchant banks 69–71; overdrafts 66, 68, 165–6; reconciliations 165; statements 164–6, *see also* commercial banks
beliefs 222–30, 237
benefits, information technology 262–3, 302–3
bills of exchange 69
boards: concept 10, 131–2; election 127–8; roles 131–2, 139–40; strategic plans 155, *see also* directors
bookkeeping 165, *see also* accounting
break-even analysis 173–6, 296
budgetary control 91–2, 171–2, 298
building societies 67
business information systems 293–5, *see also* information...
business insurance 59–63, 69, 75, 95
business plans 153–5, 159–60, *see also* planning

cafédirect 222
capital 14–15, 40–1, 104–6, 108–9, 177; assets 14, 165–6, 170–1, 177, 193; economic growth 79; investment 79, 93, 165–6, 192, *see also* finance
cash flow 177
central banks 92
centralized purchasing 109–10
Certificate of Incorporation 11
chair of the board 131
Chambers of Commerce 71–2
Chancellor of the Exchequer 91
change management 134, 301–3, 305
channels, communication 255–6
cheques 164–6
chief executives 131
clients 135–6, 235–7, 252–4, 300–5, *see also* customers

Index

commercial banks 64–9; business environment 68–9; profits 65; services 65–9, 71, 95
commitment, human resources 205, 209–12, 282–3
communications 112, 253–310; administration function 283–5; beliefs 222–3; channels 255–6; concept 252–5, 271–2, 284, 302; costs 261–3; global networks 299–300, 304–5; house-style 260–1; human resources 133–5, 198, 210–12, 253–70, 282–3, 300–3; importance 252–4, 282, 302; information technology 261–3, 298–305, 309; internal/external aspects 260, 300–5; international organizations 120–1, 123–4, 299–300, 304–5; management 264–5, 284–5, 300, 302; methods 257–60; objectives 282–3; oral method 258–9; performance 271–91; poorness symptoms 255–6; promotional activities 111, 222, 226, 279–80; purchasing considerations 262–3; reports 259, 261–2, 298, 302–3; routes 256–7; strategy 260–1; systems 254–60; types 255–60, 264–5; visual method 259–60; written method 259, 261–2, 298, 302–3, see also information...
company secretaries 132
competition 26–32, 37–8, 50, 95, 277–8, 280–1; banking 66–7; e-commerce 304; financial services sector 70–1; government objectives 119–20, 123; imperfect competition 32, 38; monopolies 32–3, 38, 50, 119–20; perfect competition 28–32, 37
competitive advantage 113, 187–90, 224
computer systems see information technology
conferencing 300
confidence 79, 129, 284
consultative management 229–30
consumers 26–38, 68, 135–6; confidence 79; corporate identity 224–6, 254; power 95, 111, see also customers
contract of employment 205–6
contracted-out functions 118, 192
control 108–12, 228; administration function 112, 283–5; budgetary control 171–2, 298; information benefits 276–82; quality control 109, 237; stock control 109, see also monitoring
coordination 112, 113–18, 136, 156–7, 228, 273–5, 303
Corporate Abuse (Wright) 228–9
corporate governance 130–31
corporate hospitality 111, 114
corporate identity 224–6, 254, 305
corporate image 224–6, 232, 254, 279
corporation tax 168–9
cost of living 80
costs: break-even analysis 173–6, 296; communications 261–3; efficiency/effectiveness 191–3; elements 168–9, 173; information technology 262–3; new products 58; opportunity costs 15, 18–19, 23, 109, 147; production 18, 30–2, 44–6, 112–13; risk 58–9; types 173
credit insurance 62
credit notes 164–6
culture 221–34; human resources 225, 227–30; influences 225–6; management 225–30; single status culture 225; target setting 188–9, 197, 230, 239; TQM 237–8, 240; types 227–30
cumulative preference shares 128
current accounts 66
current assets 170
customer services 135–6, 189–91, 202, 226, 236–7, 246, 304
customers 277–8, 300–5; concept 135–6, 235–7, 252–4; loyalty 236–7, 246, 305; satisfaction surveys 241–2, see also consumers
cyclical unemployment 84, 93, 98

data 273–8, 293–8
database packages 293–5
decentralized purchasing 109–10
decision-making: finance function

Index

163–71, 179–80, 275, 296; growth 46–50; importance 18–19, 23, 110, 146–8, 272–3; information importance 272–84; styles 229–30
deed of partnership 9
demand 26–32
departmental structures 113–18, 135–6, 157
deposits 65–6
depreciation 177
depressions 84
development: human resources 107–8, 133–5, 192, 194–6; new products 111–14; R&D 106, 112–13, 192, 241, 275, 296
direct costs *see* variable costs
direct taxation 91, 93–5, 168–9
directors: concept 10, 131–2; types 131–2, *see also* boards
diseconomies of scale 45–6
distribution 43, 128–9, 131, 279
diversification 41, 50
dividends 127–9
downsizing 192
duties 205–6

e-commerce 304
e-mail 120–1, 284–5, 298, 299
economic depressions 84
economic growth 78–9, 85, 89–95, 97–9
economies of scale 42–6, 50, 51–2, 55, 116–17, 124
education: government 85; LCCI 71–2
effective communication systems 254–5, 282–3
effectiveness 191–4, 205
efficiency 17, 44–5, 191–4
electronic auction sites 304
employees *see* human resources
employment, government objectives 83–5, 89–95, 98
empowerment 211–12, 215
entrepreneurs 15
environment 5–24, 63, 64–70, 72, 75; business finance 64–70; changes 134, 301–3, 305; corporate image 224–6, 232, 254; 279; culture 224–6; decision-making importance 18–19, 23; definition 15; government 77–100; information technology 292–310; marketplace 25–38; opportunity costs 15, 18–19, 23; risk 19, 23, 43, 58–63; size of firms 39–56; specialization 15, 16, 17–18, 23, 40, 44, 51; trading cycle 15–16, 18, 23, 104–6
equal opportunities 108, 222–3
equilibrium price 29–30, 37
equipment 14, 165–6
Euro 85, 87
European Union 85, 87
evaluation, planning 146–8, 152
examination questions 311–37, 339–41
exchange rate 87–8
executive directors 132
expenses 168–9, *see also* costs
exports 68, 69–71, 85–8, 90–5
external clients 135, 235–7, 252–4, 304–5
external customers 135, 235–7, 252–4, 304–5
external economies of scale 51–2, 55

factoring 166
fair trade 222
Fayol, Henri 228, 232
feedback 258–9
fidelity guarantee insurance 62
finance 64, 106, 110, 162–81, 275; concept 162–3, 166–7, 179–80; decision-making 163–71, 179–80, 275, 296; growth 46–7; influence 57–76, 179–80; information technology 296–8; limited companies 10–11; needs 163; partnerships 8–9; performance indicators 41, 88, 192–4; planning 151, 153–4; public corporations 12–13; sole traders 7–8; sources 165–7; terms used 177, *see also* banks; capital
financial accounting 110, 164–71
financial economies of scale 43
financial institutions 130–1
financial insurance 62
financial services 57–76
firms: growth 46–50; size 39–56;

Index

small firms 51–2, 54–5, 75, 118, 147–8, 152, 304, *see also* organizations
fiscal policy 90–2, 93–5, 98
fitness for purpose, business equipment 262–3
fixed assets 166, 170
fixed costs 173–6
food scares 27–8
foreign currency 87–8
formal communication 255–6
functions 5–24, 103–25, 131–4, 156–7, 180, 190, 273–84, 295–8, 301–3

geographic specialization 51
global communications 299–300, 304–5
global economy 85–8, 119–21, 123–4
goals 107, 150, 282–3, *see also* objectives; targets
goods *see* products
government: Chambers of Commerce 71; competition policy 119–20, 123; economic growth 78–9, 85, 89–95, 97–9; employment 83–5, 89–95, 98; international organizations 119–20, 123–4; international trade 85–8, 89–95, 119–20, 123–4; involvement 6–7, 12–13, 93–5; objectives 77–100, 119–20, 123, 129–30; policies 89, 90–5, 97–8, 119–20, 123, 129–30; prices 80–3, 89–95; role 77–100
grapevine 256
graphics packages 293–5
gross profits 168–9
growth: firms 46–50; government objectives 78–9, 85, 89–95, 97–9
guarantees 62, 278

health services 95
Hertzberg 197, 228, 233
hire purchase (HP) 166
horizontal communication 256–7
horizontal integration 49–50
house-style, communications 260–1
HP *see* hire purchase
human resources 104–8, 132, 133–5, 194–9, 204–17; absenteeism 197–8, 212; appraisal schemes 107, 206–9, 215, 240, 283; change 134, 301–3, 305; commitment 205, 209–12, 282–3; communications 133–5, 198, 210–12, 253–70, 282–3, 300–3; concept 133–5, 139, 205–6; contract of employment 205–6; culture 225, 227–30; duties 205–6; effectiveness 205; empowerment 211–12, 215; equal opportunities 108, 222–3; information technology 300–5; job satisfaction 197–8, 210, 282–3; legal responsibilities 108, 132, 205–6; MBO 239; motivation 133–4, 147, 194–8, 225, 227–30, 282–3; multiskilling 195–6; organization charts 114–18, 261; performance 194–9, 205–13, 282–3; quality systems 211, 237–40; responsibilities 108, 132, 205–6; rights 134, 205–6; specialization 17–18, 40, 117, 133; suggestion schemes 210–11; target setting 187–8, 206–9, 230, 239; teams 133, 188–9, 209–12, 215–16, 237–40, 283, 303; training/development 107–8, 133–5, 192, 194–6, 206–9; turnover 194–7, 212; wages 81, 133–5, 225, 228; worker directors 132, *see also* people

IMF *see* International Monetary Fund
imperfect competition 32, 38
imports 68, 69–71, 85–8, 90–5
indirect costs *see* fixed costs
indirect taxation 91
industrial relations 108
inflation 80–2, 89–95, 97–8
informal communication 256
information: control/monitoring means 276–82; financial information 163, 169–76; flow 275–6, 293–8; functional areas 273–84, 295–8, 301–3; importance 110, 112, 120–1, 146–8, 163, 272–84; planning 146–8, 152, 153–4; requirements 272–3, 274–5, 284, *see also* communications
information technology 150,

Index

292–310; communications 261–3, 298–305, 309; computerization 296–8, 300–5, 309; concept 292–5, 296–8, 300–5, 309; e-commerce 304; e-mail 120–1, 284–5, 298, 299; functional areas 295–8, 301–3; global communications 299–300, 304–5; impact 300–5, 309; Internet 120–1, 284–5, 298, 299–300, 304–5; intranet 299, 302–3; networks 296, 299–300, 302–5; purchasing considerations 262–3; software 293–5, 307; strategic plans 112
infrastructure 51, 98
innovation 52, 209–10
input *see* resources
Institute of Bankers 72
institutional investors *see* financial institutions
insurable interest, concept 60
insurance 59–63, 69, 75, 95, 130–1
integrated software 294, 296
integration 49–50, 55
interest rates 65, 92–3, 98
internal clients 136, 235–7, 252–4, 300–3
internal customers 136, 235–7, 252–4, 300–3
internal diseconomies of scale 45–6
internal economies of scale 42–6, 50, 55, 116–17, 124
internal growth 46–7
international business organizations 41, 50–2, 119–21, 123–4, 299–300, 304–5
International Monetary Fund (IMF) 87
international trade: Chambers of Commerce 71–2; government objectives 85–8, 89–95, 119–20, 123
Internet 120–1, 284–5, 298, 299–300, 304–5
intranet 299, 302–3
investment 165–6; economic growth 79, 93; efficiency 192, *see also* capital
invisible trade 86
invoices 164–6

job satisfaction 197–8, 210, 282–3
joint-stock banks *see* commercial banks
joint-stock companies *see* limited companies
land and buildings 167

LANs *see* local area networks
lateral integration 50
LCCI *see* London Chamber of Commerce and Industry
leasing 166
ledgers 165
legal considerations 132; human resources 108, 132, 205–6; international organizations 119
liabilities 62–3, 170–1
liability insurance 62–3
life cycle, product 50, 280–2
life insurance 63
limited companies 41–2, 64–5, 68, 70, 127–32; concept 10–12; finance 10–11; limited liability 10–11; types 11
limited liability: limited companies 10–11; partnerships 9
listed companies 11, 41–2
loans 65–6, 68, 92–3
local area networks (LANs) 299–300
London Chamber of Commerce and Industry (LCCI) 71–2
long-term finance 167
loyalty, customers 236–7, 246, 305

McGregor 197, 228, 233
machinery 14, 165–6
management 145–81; accounting 110, 171–6; by objectives (MBO) 239; change 134, 301–3, 305; communications 264–5, 284–5, 300, 302; culture 225–30; functions 133–4, 180; information importance 272–84; information technology 273, 298, 301–3; levels 155–6; meetings 300; styles 229–30, 264–5; teleconferencing 300; theory 227–8, 232–3
management information systems (MIS) 273, 298, 302–3
managing directors 131–2
market price, concept 29, 36–7
market-driven activities 16
marketing 105–6, 111, 123, 153–4, 275; economies of scale 43, 50, 55; mix 278–80; strategy 277–82
marketing research 111, 123, 153–4, 277–8
marketplace 25–38
Maslow 197, 228

mass unemployment 84
material facts 60, 74
Mayo 228, 233
MBO *see* management by objectives
medium-term finance 166
meetings 300
Memorandum of Association 11, 132
merchant banks 69–71
mergers 48
messages, concept 254–5
MIS *see* management information systems
mission statements 149, 222–3, 261, 283
MNCs *see* multi-national corporations
model answers, examination questions 311–37, 339–41
modems 299–300
monetary policy 92–5, 98
money 64, *see also* finance
monitoring 189; administration function 112, 283–5; budgetary control 171–2, 298; growth 46; information benefits 276–82; planning 146–8, 152; quality 237–42, *see also* control
monopolies 32–3, 38, 50, 119–20
mortgages 167
motivation 133–5, 147, 194–8, 225, 227–30, 282–3
multi-national corporations (MNCs) 41, 50–2, 119–21, 123–4, 299–300, 304–5
multiskilling, human resources 195–6

national income 78–9, 82, 89–95, 99
nationalized industry *see* public corporations
needs 284–5; information technology 262–3; Maslow 197, 228; motivation 197
net profits 168–9
networks 71–2, 296, 299–300, 302–5
new products 58, 111–14
non-executive directors 132
non-verbal communication 258

objectives 77–100, 107, 119–20, 123, 150–5; communications 282–3; MBO 239, *see also* targets
one-way communication 258, 265
operational management 155–6, 274
opportunity costs 15, 18–19, 23, 109, 147

oral communications 258–9
order processing 295–7
ordinary shares 127–8
organizational skills 15, 105–6, 228
organizations 49–50, 55, 81; beliefs 222–30; charts 114–18, 261; client relationships 136, 235–6, 252–4, 304–5; confidence 79, 129, 284; coordination 112, 113–18, 136, 156–7, 273–5, 303; corporate identity/image 224–6, 232, 254, 279, 305; decision-making importance 18–19, 23, 110, 146–8, 272–3, 296; economies of scale 42–6, 50, 51–2, 55, 116–17, 124; functional areas 103–25, 131–4, 136, 156–7, 190, 273–84, 295–8, 301–3; group roles 126–42; growth 46–50; internals 103–25; MNCs 41, 50–2, 119–21, 123–4, 299–300, 304–5; networks 71–2, 296, 299–300, 302–5; opportunity costs 15, 18–19, 23, 109, 147; overview 5–24; physical features 41–2; purposes 6, 13–15, 104–6, 130–1; risk 19, 23, 43, 58–63, 74–6, 147; size 39–56; small firms 51–2, 54–5, 75, 118, 147–8, 152, 304; specialization 15, 16, 17–18, 23, 40, 44, 51, 113–18; stakeholder concept 19, 126–36, 139, 221, 236, 252–4; success criteria 15, 28, 112–13, 135–6, 186–7, 191–217, 283, 300–5; teams 133, 188–9, 209–12, 215–16, 237–40, 283, 303; TQM 237–8, 240; trading cycle 15–16, 18, 23, 104–6, 124; types 6–13, 41, 50–2, 119–21; values 222–30, *see also* culture; firms; information...
output: break-even analysis 173–6, 296; costs 44–5; efficiency/effectiveness 193; overview 104–6; TQM 237–8, 240
overdrafts 66, 68, 165–6
overheads *see* fixed costs

parent companies 120–1
participative management 229–30
partnerships: concept 8–10; finance 8–9; limited liability 9; size restrictions 8–9
pension funds 130–1
people 14–15, 81, 104–8, 132–5; economic growth 79; employment

347

Index

83–5; insurance 62–3, *see also* human resources
per capita national income 82–3, 99
perfect competition 28–32, 37
performance 17, 262–3; communication systems 271–91; human resources 194–9, 205–13, 282–3; improvement 191–213; indicators 41, 80–4, 88–95, 98–9, 192–4, 206–9; overview 186–7; teams 209–12, 212, 215–16, 237–40, *see also* quality
personnel 104–8, 133–5, 194–6, 274, *see also* human resources
PEST (political, economic, social, technological) concept 149–50
petty cash 165
place, marketing mix 278–80
planning 107–12, 145–61, 228; administrative plans 155–6, 284–5; components 153–5, 159–60; concept 146–8, 159; e-mail 284–5; framework 148–52; growth 46; purposes 146–8, 159; schedules 112; types 152–6
plant 14, 165–6
points to remember: communications 270, 291, 310; culture 234; environment 24; finance 76, 181; government 100; group roles 141–2; human resources 217; information technology 310; internal organization 125; marketplace 38; performance 203, 217; planning 161; quality 247; size of firms 56
policies: government 89, 90–5, 97–8, 119–20, 123, 129–30; shareholders' influence 130–1
position statements 302–3
poverty 85
preference shares 128
preferred trading partners 85, 236–7
prices 224; demand and supply 26–32, 36–8; exchange rates 88; government objectives 80–3, 89–95; inflation 80–2, 89–95, 97–8; marketing mix 279; shares 48, 129–30
pricing strategies 172–6, 279–80
private limited companies 11
private sector 6–12; concept 6–7, 95; limited companies 10–12; partnerships 8–10; sole traders 7–8
privatizations 7, 13, 93–5

production 17, 42–6, 193, 283; costs 18, 30–2, 44–6, 112–13; function 105–6, 108–9, 274
productive factors 40–1, 44–5, 61, 104–6, 108–9, 124; communications 261–3; efficiency/effectiveness 191–4; national income 78–9, 82, 89–95, 99, *see also* resources
products 13–19, 26–31, 42–6; life cycle 50, 280–2; marketing mix 278–80; new-products 58, 111–14; visible trade 86
profit and loss accounts 110, 167–70
profits 16, 29–38, 41, 46–7, 76; commercial banks 65; concept 167–70; distribution 128–9, 131; gross calculation 168–9; margins 193; net calculation 168–9; sales 105–6, 111; shares 127–30
promotional activities 111, 222, 226, 279–80
property insurance 61
proposal forms, insurance 59–60
public corporations: concept 12–13; finance 12–13
public limited companies 11, 41–2, 68, 70, 127–32
public sector 6–7, 12–13
public utilities 12–13
purchase orders 164–6
purchasing 16, 26–38, 109–10, 164–6, 262–3, 275; economies of scale 43, 50

quality 14, 186–8, 205, 210–11, 235–47; assurance 237; circles 211, 240; control 109, 237; guidelines 151; monitoring 237–42, *see also* performance
quality of life 82–3, 95
questionnaires 241–2

R&D *see* research and development
rate of interest 65, 92–3, 98
rationalization 47, 191–2, 301
raw data 273–8, 295–8
raw materials 14–15, 40–1, 79, 104–10
real income 81
real wages 81
regional unemployment 84, 98
Registrar of Joint Stock Companies 10–11

Index

regulatory bodies 95, 119
reports 259, 261–2, 298, 302–3
research and development (R&D) function 106, 112–13, 192, 241, 275, 296
reserves 87
resources 13–19, 23, 40–1, 44–5, 61, 104–10; budgetary control 171–2, 298; economic growth 79; planning 146–8, 151, 153–4, *see also* human resources
responsibilities 108, 132, 205–6
restructuring 47
retail price index (RPI) 80
return on net assets employed 193
rights 134, 205–6
risk 19, 23, 43, 58–63; concept 58–9, 76, 147; costs 58–9; insurance 59–63, 69, 74–5, 95; shares 127–8
risk-bearing economies of scale 43
robotics 296
routes, communication 256–7
RPI *see* retail price index

sales 189–91, 277–8; after-sales service 190, 278; function 105–6, 111, 275; information technology 295–7; order processing 295–7; product life cycle 50, 280–2; revenue 173–6; turnover 41, 173–6; volume 41, *see also* selling
satisfaction surveys, customers 241–2
savings: accounts 66; inflation effects 81
seasonal unemployment 84
security, business equipment 262–3
selling 16, 26–38, 41–3, 189–91, *see also* sales
services 13–19, 26–31; Chambers of Commerce 71–2; commercial banks 65–9, 71, 95; customers 135–6, 189–91, 202, 226, 236–7, 246, 304; financial services 57–76; health services 95; invisible trade 86; merchant banks 69–71; sole traders 8
shareholders 41, 127–31, 168–9, 170–1; concept 10; influence 130–1, 139; restrictions 11
shares 127–31; dealing services 68; dividends 127–9; government policies 129–30; issues 70; prices 48, 129–30; profits 127–30; risk 127–8; rumours 129; speculation 130; takeovers 48, 129; types 127–8
short-term finance 166
single status culture 225
size, firms 39–56
skills 71–2, 79, 85, 105–6, 194–6
small firms 51–2, 54–5, 75, 118, 147–8, 152, 304
SMART (specific, measurable, achievable, realistic, time-constrained) concept 208
software 293–5, 307
sole traders: concept 7–8; finance 7–8
specialization: concept 15, 16, 17–18, 23, 133; departmental structures 113–18; economies of scale 43–4, 51, 116–17, 124; merchant banks 69–70
speculation 130
sponsorship 111, 114, 222, 226
spreadsheet packages 293–5, 307
Springett, Pauline 229
stakeholder concept 19, 126–36, 139, 221, 236, 252–4
standard of living 81–3, 89–95, 98–9
standards 14, 237–42
statements of account 164–6
stock control 109
stock markets 11
strategic management 155–6
strategic plans 112, 147–8, 152, 155
strategies: communications 260–1; marketing 277–82; pricing 172–6, 279–80
structural unemployment 84, 98
subrogation 60
subsidiary companies 120–1
success criteria, organizations 15, 28, 112–13, 135–6, 186–7, 191–217, 283, 300–5
suggestion schemes 210–11
supply 28–32
survey standards 239
surveys 239, 241–2
SWOT (strengths, weaknesses, opportunities, threats), concept 149–50

takeovers 48, 129
targets: MBO 239; setting 150–4, 187–9, 202, 206–9, 230, 239, 298; SMART principles 208, *see also* objectives

Index

taxation 90–5, 98, 168–9
Taylor, Frederick 197, 228, 232
teams 133, 188–9, 209–12, 215–16, 237–40, 282–3, 303
technical economies of scale 43, 50
teleconferencing 300
timescales, target achievement 151, 189
tips, examination 339–41
total quality management (TQM) 237–8, 240
TQM *see* total quality management
trade credit 166
trading accounts 168
trading cycle, concept 15–16, 18, 23, 104–6, 124
training: Chambers of Commerce 71–2; economic growth 79, 85, 94–5; human resources 107–8, 133–5, 192, 194–6, 206–9
transferable skills 196
transitional unemployment 84
turnover 41, 173–6, 194–7, 212
two-way communications 258, 264–5, 302

unemployment: government objectives 83–5, 89–95, 98; types 84–5
unit costs 44–6, 55, 112–13, 193
unlimited liability 7–9; partnerships 9; sole traders 7–8
utmost good faith 60

values 222–30, 237
variable costs 173–6
variance analysis 172
vertical communication 256–7
vertical integration 49
visible trade 86
visual communications 259–60

wages 81, 133–5, 225, 228
wide area networks (WANs) 299–300, 302–3
word-processing packages 293–5, 307
worker directors 132
working capital 166
Wright, Lesley 228–9
written communications 259, 261–2, 298, 302–3